HORIZON
Writings of the Canadian Prairie

HORIZON
Writings of the Canadian Prairie

Edited by
Ken Mitchell

Toronto
Oxford University Press
1977

FOR MY MOTHER AND FATHER

I wish to express my thanks to Laurence Ricou of the University of Lethbridge, Susan Woods of the University of British Columbia, Dick Harrison of the University of Alberta, and William Toye and Richard Teleky of the Oxford University Press, all of whom made helpful contributions to this book. I am also grateful to my research assistant, Winona Kent, and to the University of Regina for a research grant.

K. M.

ISBN 19-540262-6

1 2 3 4—0 9 8 7

Printed in Canada by
Web Offset Publications Limited

Contents

Acknowledgements

DOUGLAS BARBOUR. 'Houses' reprinted from *A Poem as Long as the Highway*, 1971, by permission of Quarry Press and the author. GEORGE BOWERING. 'The Oil' from *Rocky Mountain Foot* and 'Grandfather' from *Touch: Selected Poems* are both reprinted by permission of The Canadian Publishers, McClelland and Stewart Limited, Toronto. ELIZABETH BREWSTER. 'The Future of Poetry in Canada' reprinted from *Sunrise North*, © 1972, by permission of Clarke, Irwin & Company Limited. BARRY BROADFOOT. All extracts from *The Pioneer Years, 1895-1914* reprinted by permission of Doubleday & Company, Inc. EUGENE CLOUTIER. Both extracts reprinted from *No Passport* by permission of the Oxford University Press (Canadian Branch). RALPH CONNOR. 'The Pilot's Measure' reprinted from *The Sky Pilot* by permission of The Canadian Publishers, McClelland and Stewart Limited, Toronto. GABRIEL DUMONT. 'The Battle of Duck Lake' reprinted from the *Canadian Historical Review*, 1949, by permission of G. F. G. Stanley, the translator. PIERRE FALCON. 'The Battle of Seven Oaks' is reprinted by permission of James Reaney, the translator. GARY GEDDES. 'Snakeroot' from *Snakeroot* reprinted by permission of the author and Talonbooks. JAMES GRAY. 'Landladies and a Want-ad Husband' reprinted from *The Winter Years* by permission of The Macmillan Company of Canada Limited. FREDERICK PHILIP GROVE. 'The Sale' from *Tales from the Margin*, edited by Desmond Pacey, reprinted by permission of McGraw-Hill Ryerson Limited. MAARA HAAS. 'Manitoba Drought' reprinted by permission of the author. PAUL HIEBERT. Extract reprinted from *Sarah Binks* by permission of the Oxford University Press (Canadian Branch). MARY HIEMSTRA. Extract reprinted from *Gully Farm* by permission of The Canadian Publishers, McClelland and Stewart Limited, Toronto. GARY HYLAND. 'Neesh' reprinted by permission of the author. HENRY KREISEL. 'The Prairie: A State of Mind' reprinted by permission of the author. ROBERT KROETSCH. 'Elegy for Wong Toy', 'The Stone Hammer Poem', and 'F. P. Grove: The Finding' reprinted from *The Stone-Hammer Poems*, Oolichan Books, by permission of the author. Extract from 'A Conversation with Margaret Laurence' reprinted from *Creation*, New Press, by permission of the author. MARGARET LAURENCE. 'The Loons' reprinted from *A Bird in the House* by permission of The Canadian Publishers, McClelland and Stewart Limited, Toronto. DOROTHY LIVESAY. 'Day and Night' from *Collected Poems: The Two Seasons* reprinted by permission of McGraw-Hill Ryerson Limited. JACK LUDWIG. 'Requiem for Bibul' reprinted by permission of the author. NELLIE McCLUNG. 'The Play' reprinted from *Purple Springs* by permission of the Estate of Nellie McClung. BARRY McKINNON. 'I Wanted to Say Something' reprinted from *I Wanted to Say Something* by permission of the author. ELI MANDEL. 'There Is No One Here Except Us Comedians' reprinted from *Crusoe: Poems Selected and New* by permission of the author. ANNE MARRIOTT. 'The Wind Our Enemy' reprinted from *Sandstone and Other Poems* by permission of the author. SID MARTY. 'The Prairie' reprinted from *Tumbleweed Harvest* by permission of the author. FREDELLE BRUSER MAYNARD. 'Satisfaction Guaranteed—the 1928 Eaton's Catalogue' from *Raisins and Almonds*, © 1972 by Fredelle Bruser Maynard, reprinted by permission of Doubleday & Company, Inc. CLAUDE MELANÇON. 'Creation of Man' from *Indian Legends of Canada*, translated by David Ellis, reprinted by permission of Gage Publishing. W. O. MITCHELL. 'Saint Sammy' reprinted by permission of the author. ROBERT MOON. 'Regina Riot' reprinted from *This Is Saskatchewan*, © 1953, by permission of the author. JOHN NEWLOVE. 'Doukhobor' from *The Cave* and 'The Pride' from *Black Night Window* reprinted by permission of The Canadian Publishers, McClelland and Stewart Limited, Toronto. R. E. RASHLEY. 'Night Journey and Departure' is reprinted by permission of Mrs Laura Rashley. GWEN PHARIS RINGWOOD. 'Still Stands the House' reprinted by permission of Samuel French (Canada) Ltd. SINCLAIR ROSS. 'A Field of Wheat' reprinted from *The Lamp at Noon and Other Stories* by permission of The Canadian Publishers, McClelland and Stewart Limited, Toronto. GABRIELLE ROY. 'The Move' reprinted from *The Road Past Altamont* by permission of The Canadian Publishers, McClelland

and Stewart Limited, Toronto. GEORGE RYGA. Extract reprinted from *Hungry Hills* by permission of the author. STEPHEN SCOBIE. 'Streak Mosaic' reprinted by permission of the author. ROBERT STEAD. Chapter 13 reprinted from *Grain* by permission of the Estate of Robert Stead. WALLACE STEGNER. 'The Question Mark in the Circle' from *Wolf Willow*, © 1955, 1962 by Wallace Stegner, reprinted by permission of The Viking Press. ANDREW SUKNASKI. 'Lanterns' reprinted from *Leaving* by permission of the author and Repository Press. 'Philip Well' reprinted from *Wood Mountain Poems* by permission of The Macmillan Company of Canada Limited. MERNA SUMMERS. 'Willow Song' reprinted from *The Skating Party* by permission of Oberon Press. ANNE SZUMIGALSKI. 'Nettles' from *Woman Reading in Bath*, © 1974 by Anne Szumigalski, reprinted by permission of Doubleday & Company, Inc. LORNA UHER. 'I Am A Lake' and 'Immigrant' reprinted by permission of the author. ED UPWARD. 'Self-refracting' reprinted by permission of the author. W. D. VALGARDSON. 'Hunting' reprinted from *God Is Not a Fish Inspector* by permission of Oberon Press. MIRIAM WADDINGTON. 'The Nineteen Thirties Are Over' and 'Ukrainian Church' reprinted from *Driving Home* by permission of the Oxford University Press (Canadian Branch). RUDY WIEBE. 'Where Is the Voice Coming From?' reprinted from *Where Is the Voice Coming From?* by permission of The Canadian Publishers, McClelland and Stewart Limited, Toronto. J. F. C. WRIGHT. Extract reprinted from *Slava Bohu* by permission of Holt, Rinehart and Winston. DALE ZIEROTH. 'Father' from *Clearing: Poems From a Journey*, 1973, reprinted by permission of House of Anansi Press.

Picture Credits

FACING PAGE 1 Fred Huffman. 8 'Assiniboin Hunting Buffalo' by Paul Kane. Courtesy the National Gallery of Canada. 14 Public Archives of Canada. 16 Fort Garry about 1870 by G. Kemp. Manitoba Archives. 21 Gabriel Dumont at Fort Assiniboine, May 1885. Glenbow-Alberta Institute. 24 Saskatchewan Archives. 26 Riel addressing the jury in the courthouse, Regina, July 1885. Photograph by O. B. Buell. Public Archives of Canada. 40 Almighty Voice, c. 1892-4. Glenbow-Alberta Institute. 43 Saskatchewan Government. 48 Saskatchewan Archives. 50 Glenbow-Alberta Institute. 55 Glenbow-Alberta Institute. 56 Manitoba Archives. 64 Alberta Government. 71 Provincial Archives of Alberta, H. Pollard Collection. 74 Drawing by Doug Panton. 76 Public Archives of Canada. 92 Manitoba Archives. 99 Provincial Archives of Alberta, E. Brown Collection. 100 Saskatchewan Archives. 107 'The Blizzard' by William Kurelek, from *A Prairie Boy's Winter*, courtesy Tundra Books. 111 Glenbow-Alberta Institute. 124 Public Archives of Canada. 134 Provincial Archives of Alberta, E. Brown Collection. 150 Provincial Archives of Alberta, H. Pollard Collection. 199 Roger Boulton. 202 Glenbow-Alberta Institute. 214 Chris Lund. Courtesy NFB Photothèque. 227 Patrick Pettit. Courtesy *The Regina Leader-Post*. 237 Saskatchewan Archives. 260 Audio Visual Department, the University of Regina.

Preface

Out of the Prairie West and the emotions evoked by its infinity of earth and sky, by its solitude and separateness and harsh climate, has come a body of writing that is different in theme, subject, and tone from that of the rest of Canada.

If the environment has had a powerful influence on the people who live there, creating a particular attitude to life, so has the history of the region made an imprint on the Prairie state of mind. The southern areas of Alberta and Saskatchewan and of southwestern Manitoba—gently rolling plains, occasionally cut by river canyons—was once the home of large herds of buffalo and nomadic Indian bands. It was first opened up by French-Canadian explorers and fur traders from Quebec, many of whom took Indian wives. After the fall of New France in 1759 the French-Canadian connection with the Northwest remained in the Métis—people of mixed blood. They became an influential, though defiant, population with quite different interests from those of the English-speaking settlers who formed the Red River Settlement in 1812. Later in the century the Métis leader, Louis Riel, performed acts of resistance that led to the creation of the province of Manitoba in 1870.

The formation of the North West Mounted Police in 1873 ensured a more peaceful settlement of the western frontier than occurred in the United States. By the time the Canadian Pacific Railway was opened in 1885, making the West accessible, many new settlements had been created. The federal government's immigration policy in the 1890s, when a flood of new settlers gave the Prairies ethnic diversity, led to the creation of Alberta and Saskatchewan in 1905 and to a western boom that receded before the First World War. The Depression of the 1930s was greatly exacerbated on the Prairies by natural disasters and by the collapse of the wheat economy. It intensified a mood of disillusionment, a sense of inequality with the rest of the country. The tradition of revolt that had been begun with Louis Riel continued in the form of movements that had far-reaching consequences. These included the women's suffrage movement which, under such feminists as Nellie McClung, demanded equal voting rights for women (Manitoba was the first province to grant women the vote in 1916); the growth of the United Farmers parties in Alberta and Manitoba; and the formation in 1932 of the CCF (Co-operative Commonwealth Federation), whose Regina Manifesto of 1933 outlined a platform of social planning, public ownership, and welfare measures to replace the capitalist system.

All these strands of the Prairie experience appear in this anthology. The central image of Prairie writing, however, found in early descriptive accounts and continuing through to the present, is the land itself—a symbol of hope, fulfilment, or despair for those who came to conquer it and make it fruitful; an imaginative landscape for the creative writer who responds to it with emotion and memory.

'It all begins in innocence' (Barry McKinnon), when settlers perceived the world 'as it had taken shape and form from the hands of the Creator' (W. F. Butler). In time they 'came to conceive the land as enemy and fought/back with god and muscle and stupidity' (Barry McKinnon). A stubborn, bull-headed lot who were tested by disaster, they had a love-hate relationship with the land. Their tightly disciplined responses to nature's trials were braced by rigid spiritual convictions, which imposed restraints that could burst with sudden violence.

It was of course the children of these settlers who first interpreted Prairie life. Though one of Stephen Scobie's characters asked 'What would I want to go away for?', many have succumbed to 'the *idea* of leaving', which Adele Wiseman, referring to Manitoba, has called 'a Provincial Obsession'. It is not possible, however, for writers to disown the influence of the Prairie experience, which is built of extremes and set against infinity. Their work is permeated with a characteristic defiance of life's trials and challenges. Many of them are attracted to Indian culture at least partly because the heroic stance, testing, and pride in the face of defeat are very much part of their vision, part of the Prairie character.

After the land was settled, these characteristics faced their greatest test in the Depression, when western pride—George Monro Grant called it 'western bumptiousness'—expressed itself in creative political action. It is not surprising that the Depression became almost as crucial an image of the Prairie experience as the land itself.

The conquest of the land; survival; human endurance and frailty; nostalgia for the secure family circle that was a bulwark against lonely, bleak surroundings; the beauties that unfolded when nature turned benign—these things all feed the idea of the Prairie. It lives in people's minds even after they have left; or in an object, such as Robert Kroetsch's Indian stone hammer

smelling a little of cut
grass or maybe even of
ripening wheat or of
buffalo blood hot
in the drying sun.

For the creative writer the Prairie has become a symbolic place in the geography of the imagination, one that continues to evoke love and allegiance, as it inspires works of literature:

Sometimes I write
my poems for that

stone hammer.

KEN MITCHELL
Regina, Sask.

THE CREATION OF MAN

(A Piegan myth)

Claude Mélançon

Long ago, the Spirits above sent the Great Water to flood the world below where men and women used to live. Afterwards Napiwa, the Old Man, created our floating island from a grain of sand in the following manner. When the time came to look for this grain of sand, Napiwa was floating on a raft with Nanoss, the Old Woman, and all the animals. He sent the otter down first. She dived at sunrise and when she surfaced at sunset she was dead. The Old Man examined her paws but didn't find anything, so he told the beaver it was his turn to dive. Two days later, the beaver surfaced lifeless, his paws empty. The loon was next. He stayed under water for three days before he died and he brought back nothing. Napiwa then asked the muskrat to go, and he stayed under for four days. When he floated back up to the surface he, too, was dead. However, one of his front paws was closed. Napiwa opened it, removed the grain of sand hidden inside, and from it made our island.

When he thought our island was big enough, Napiwa sent a young wolf to find out where it ended, but the wolf died of old age before he got there. Nevertheless, the Old Man was satisfied and set out on a journey with the Old Woman.

The two of them were walking beside a river with banks of clay when the Old Woman said to the Old Man,

'Your island is big and beautiful, but something's missing. How about filling it up with some people?'

'That's fine by me,' said the Old Man, 'but I'll have the first word.'

'All right,' said the Old Woman. 'And I'll have the last word.'

'I'll get started then,' announced Napiwa. 'Men will be made of wood and they'll grow like trees.'

'No!' said Nanoss. 'They'll be made of flesh and will reproduce their kind like animals.'

'Let it be so,' said the Old Man. 'But they'll have square faces, with the mouth running up and down and the eyes above, one on top of the other, and an ear on either side of the nose.'

'I don't like that design,' said Nanoss. 'Men will have round faces, with the mouth horizontal, and an eye on either side of the nose. Their ears will be placed on each side of the head. Otherwise, they won't be able to hear their enemies coming without getting a noseful of dirt.'

'Let it be so,' said the Old Man. 'But they'll have four arms and four legs, and ten fingers on each hand.'

'That's far too many,' said Nanoss. 'They won't work any better if they have four arms rather than two, and four legs won't let them walk any more quickly. They'll have two arms, two legs, and four fingers and a thumb on each hand.'

'Let it be so,' said Napiwa. 'But men won't have to eat or wear clothes. They and their wives will spend all their time together playing with their children.'

'No! No!' said Nanoss. 'Men will become bored doing nothing, and their wives will get tired of having them around all the time. Men will hunt all day and won't return to the teepee until sunset. While they're gone, women will gather wood and nuts, pick fruit, and dig up roots. They will also dry meat and tan hides. While they work, they'll think of their men and be glad to see them come home.'

'Let it be so,' said the Old Man. 'But men and women will not die. They will live forever and never part.'

'No,' said Nanoss. 'It's better that they die. Otherwise your island will have too many people, and there won't be enough food for everybody.'

'I don't think it should be so,' replied the Old Man.

'But we agreed,' insisted the Old Woman.

'No, I tell you,' replied the Old Man.

'And I'm telling you "Yes,"' shouted the Old Woman.

'All right! All right!' said Napiwa. 'We'll settle this another way. I'm going to throw this chip of wood into the water. If it floats, men will remain dead for four days and then come back to life.'

He threw the chip of wood into the water, and it floated.

'There, you see,' said Napiwa.

'No,' replied Nanoss, 'we're not going to settle it like that. I'm going to throw a stone into the water. If it floats, men will remain dead for four days and then continue to live. If it sinks, they'll be dead forever.'

She threw the stone in, and it sank immediately.

'There we are,' said Nanoss. 'Now men will feel a little sympathy for one another.'

'Let it be so,' said the Old Man.

Several moons later, Nanoss gave birth to a little girl whom she loved very much. But when the child was old enough to help her mother with the chores, she died. Nanoss regretted having wanted men to remain dead forever. She went to find the Old Man and said to him,

'Can't we go over that problem we disagreed about last time?'

'No,' said the Old Man. 'That problem's settled. What's done is done.'

Translated by DAVID ELLIS

THE CREES

William Francis Butler

1872

The Crees are perhaps the only tribe of prairie Indians who have as yet suffered no injustice at the hands of the white man. The land is still theirs, the hunting-grounds remain almost undisturbed; but their days are numbered, and already the echo of the approaching wave of Western immigration is sounding through the solitudes of the Cree country.

It is the same story from the Atlantic to the Pacific. First the white man was the welcome guest, the honoured visitor; then the greedy hunter, the death-dealing vender of fire-water and poison; then the settler and exterminator—every where it has been the same story.

This wild man who first welcomed the new-comer is the only perfect socialist or communist in the world. He holds all things in common with his tribe—the land, the bison, the river, and the moose. He is starving, and the rest of the tribe want food. Well, he kills a moose, and to the last bit the coveted food is shared by all. That war-party has taken one hundred horses in the last raid into Blackfoot or Peagin territory; well, the whole tribe are free to help themselves to the best and fleetest steeds before the captors will touch one out of the band. There is but a scrap of beaver, a thin rabbit, or a bit of sturgeon in the lodge; a stranger comes, and he is hungry; give him his share and let him be first served and best attended to. If one child starves in an Indian camp you may know that in every lodge scarcity is universal and that every stomach is hungry. Poor, poor fellow! his virtues are all his own; crimes he may have, and plenty, but his noble traits spring from no book-learning, from no schoolcraft, from the preaching of no pulpit; they come from the instinct of good which the Great Spirit has taught him; they are the whisperings from that lost world whose glorious shores beyond the Mountains of the Setting Sun are the long dream of his life. The most curious anomaly among the race of man, the red man of America, is passing away beneath our eyes into the infinite solitude. The possession of the same noble qualities which we affect to reverence among our nations makes us kill him. If he would be as the African or the Asiatic it would be all right for him; if he would be our slave he might live, but as he won't be that, won't toil and delve and hew for us, and will persist in hunting, fishing, and roaming over the beautiful prairie land which the Great Spirit gave him; in a word, since he will be free—we kill him. Why do I call this wild child the great anomaly of the human race? I will tell you. Alone amongst savage tribes he has learnt the lesson which the great mother Nature teaches to her sons through the voices of the night, the forest, and the solitude. This river, this mountain, this measureless meadow speak to him in a language of their own. Dwelling with them, he learns their varied tongues, and his speech becomes the echo of the beauty that lies spread around him. Every name for lake or river, for mountain or meadow, has its peculiar significance, and to tell the Indian title of such things is generally to tell the nature of them also. Ossian never spoke with the voice of the mist-shrouded mountain or the wave-beat shores of the isles more thoroughly than does this chief of the Blackfeet or the Sioux speak the voices of the things of earth and air amidst which his wild life is cast.

BY ENGLISH YET NOT SEEN

Henry Kelsey

1690

In 1690 Henry Kelsey became the first white man to see the Prairies when he journeyed west from York Factory, a Hudson's Bay Company post on the Hayes River. He wrote this poem as an introduction to his journals, which recount the two-year trip and his adventures with Indians.

In sixteen hundred and ninety'th year
I set forth as plainly may appear
Through God's assistance for to understand
The natives language and to seek their land
And for my masters' inteerst I did soon
Sett from ye house ye twelfth of June
Then up ye River I with heavy heart
Did take my way and from all English part
To live amongst ye natives of this place
If God permits me for one, two years space
The inland country of good report hath been
By Indians, but by English yet not seen
Therefore I on my journey did not stay
But making all ye haste I could upon our way
Gott on ye borders of ye Stone Indians country
I took possession of ye tenth instant July
And for my masters I speaking for ym all
This Neck of land I Deering's Point did call
Distant from hence by Judgment at ye best
From ye house six hundred miles southwest

Through rivers wch run strong with falls
Thirty Three 'Carriages' (Portages) five lakes in all
The Ground begins for to be dry, with wood
Poplo and Birch with Ash that's very good
For the natives of that place wch knows
No use of better than their wooden Bows
According to the use and custom of this place
In September I brought those natives to a peace
But I had no sooner from these natives turned my back
Some of the home Indians came upon their track
And for old grudges and their minds to fill
Came up with them, six tents of wch they kill'd
This ill news kept secrett was from me
For none of those home Indians did I see
Until that they their murder all had done
And the Chief Acter was he yts called ye Sun
So far I have spoken concerning of the spoil
And now will give account of that same country's soil
Which hither part is very thick with wood
Affords small nuts with cherryes very good
Thus it continues till you leave the woods behind
And then you have beast of several kind
The one is a Black a Buffillo great
Another is an Outgrown Bear wch is good meat
His skin to gett, I have used all ye ways I can
He is man's food and he makes food of men
His hide they would not me it preserve
But said it was a god and they should starve
This plain affords nothing but Beasts and grass
And over it in three day's time we past
Getting unto ye woods on the other side

THE PRAIRIE OCEAN

No ocean of water in the world can vie with its gorgeous sunsets; no solitude can equal the loneliness of a night-shadowed prairie: one feels the stillness, and hears the silence, the wail of the prowling wolf makes the voice of solitude audible, the stars look down through infinite silence upon a silence almost as intense. . . . One saw here the world as it had taken shape and form from the hands of the Creator. Nor did the scene look less beautiful because nature alone tilled the earth, and the unaided sun brought forth the flowers.

WILLIAM FRANCIS BUTLER, 1872

THE BATTLE OF SEVEN OAKS

Pierre Falcon

1816

On 19 June 1816, in a skirmish at 'Frog Plain' near the Red River Settlement (in present-day Winnipeg), Cuthbert Grant and a band of Métis (bois-brûlés) killed Robert Semple, the governor of Assiniboia, and twenty Hudson's Bay Company settlers. Falcon was present at the battle.

Would you like to hear me sing
Of a true and recent thing?
It was June nineteen, the band of Bois-Brûlés
  Arrived that day,
  Oh the brave warriors they!

We took three foreigners prisoners when
We came to the place called Frog, Frog Plain.
They were men who'd come from Orkney,
  Who'd come, you see,
  To rob our country.

Well we were just about to unhorse
When we heard two of us give, give voice.
Two of our men cried, 'Hey! Look back, look
  back!
    The Anglo-Sack
    Coming for to attack.'

Right away smartly we veered about
Galloping at them with a shout!
You know we did trap all, all those Grenadiers!
  They could not move
  Those horseless cavaliers.

Now we like honourable men did act,
Sent an ambassador—yes, in fact!
'Monsieur Governor! Would you like to stay?
  A moment spare—
  There's something we'd like to say.'

Governor, Governor, full of ire.
'Soldiers!' he cries, 'Fire! Fire!'
So they fire the first and their muskets roar!
  They almost kill
  Our ambassador!

Governor thought himself a king.
He wished an iron rod to swing.
Like a lofty lord he tries to act.
  Bad luck, old chap!
  A bit too hard you whacked!

When we went galloping, galloping by
Governor thought that he would try
For to chase and frighten us Bois-Brûlés.
  Catastrophe!
  Dead on the ground he lay.

Dead on the ground lots of grenadiers too.
Plenty of grenadiers, a whole slew.
We've almost stamped out his whole army.
  Of so many
  Five or four left there be.

You should have seen those Englishmen—
Bois-Brûlés chasing them, chasing them.
From bluff to bluff they stumbled that day
  While the Bois-Brûlés
  Shouted 'Hurray!'

Tell, oh tell me who made up this song?
Why it's our own poet, Pierre Falcon.
Yes, it was written this song of praise
  For the victory
  We won this day.
Yes, it was written, this song of praise—
  Come sing the glory
  Of the Bois-Brûlés.

Translated by JAMES REANEY

BUFFALO HUNT

Paul Kane

1846

For the next two or three days we fell in with only a single buffalo, or small herds of them; but as we proceeded they became more frequent. At last our scouts brought in word of an immense herd of buffalo bulls about two miles in advance of us. They are known in the distance from the cows, by their feeding singly, and being scattered wider over the plain, whereas the cows keep together for the protection of the calves, which are always kept in the centre of the herd. A half-breed, of the name of Hallett, who was exceedingly attentive to me, woke me in the morning, to accompany him in advance of the party, that I might have the opportunity of examining the buffalo whilst feeding, before the commencement of the hunt. Six hours' hard riding brought us within a quarter of a mile of the nearest of the herd. The main body stretched over the plains as far as the eye could reach. Fortunately the wind blew in our faces: had it blown towards the buffaloes, they would have scented us miles off. I wished to have attacked them at once, but my companion would not allow me until the rest of the party came up, as it was contrary to the law of the tribe. We, therefore, sheltered ourselves from the observation of the herd behind a mound, relieving our horses of their saddles to cool them. In about an hour the hunters came up to us, numbering about one hundred and thirty, and immediate preparations were made for the chase. Every man loaded his gun, looked to his priming, and examined the efficiency of his saddle-girths.

The elder men strongly cautioned the less experienced not to shoot each other; a caution by no means unnecessary, as such accidents frequently occur. Each hunter then filled his mouth with balls, which he drops into the gun without wadding; by this means loading much quicker and being enabled to do so whilst his horse is at full speed. It is true, that the gun is more liable to burst, but that they do not seem to mind. Nor does the gun carry so far, or so true; but that is of less consequence, as they always fire quite close to the animal.

Everything being adjusted, we all walked our horses towards the herd. By the time we had gone about two hundred yards, the herd perceived us, and started off in the opposite direction at the top of their speed. We now put our horses to the full gallop, and in twenty minutes were in their midst. There could not have been less than four or five thousand in our immediate vicinity, all bulls, not a single cow amongst them.

The scene now became one of intense excitement; the huge bulls thundering over the plain in headlong confusion, whilst the fearless hunters rode recklessly in their midst, keeping up an incessant fire at but a few yards' distance from their victims. Upon the fall of each buffalo, the successful hunter merely threw some article of his apparel—often carried by him solely for that purpose—to denote his own prey, and then rushed on to another. These marks are scarcely ever disputed, but should a doubt arise as to the ownership, the carcase is equally divided among the claimants.

The chase continued only about one hour, and extended over an area of from five to six square miles, where might be seen the dead and dying buffaloes, to the number of five hundred. In the meantime my horse, which had started at a good run, was suddenly confronted by a large bull that made his appearance from behind a knoll, within a few yards of him, and being thus taken by surprise, he sprung to one side, and getting his foot into one of the innumerable badger holes, with which the plains abound, he fell at once, and I was thrown over his head with such violence, that I was completely stunned, but soon recovered my recollection. Some of the men caught my horse, and I was speedily remounted, and soon saw reason to congratulate myself on my good fortune, for I found a man who had been thrown in a similar way, lying a short distance from me quite senseless, in which state he was carried back to the camp.

I again joined in the pursuit; and coming up with a large bull, I had the satisfaction of bringing him down at the first fire. Excited by my success, I threw down my cap and galloping on, soon put a bullet through another enormous animal. He did not, however, fall, but stopped and faced me, pawing the earth, bellowing and glaring savagely at me. The blood was streaming profusely from his mouth, and I thought he would soon drop. The position in which he stood was so fine that I could not resist the desire of making a sketch. I accordingly dismounted, and had just commenced, when he suddenly made a dash at me. I had hardly time to spring on my horse and get away from him, leaving my gun and everything else behind.

When he came up to where I had been standing, he turned over the articles I had dropped, pawing fiercely as he tossed them about, and then retreated towards the herd. I immediately recovered my gun, and having reloaded, again pursued him, and soon planted another shot in him; and this time he remained on his legs long enough for me to make a sketch. This done I returned with it to the camp, carrying the tongues of the animals I had killed, according to custom, as trophies of my success as a hunter.

I have often witnessed an Indian buffalo hunt since, but never one on so large a scale. In returning to the camp, I fell in with one of the hunters coolly driving a wounded buffalo before him. In answer to my inquiry why he did not shoot him, he said he would not do so until he got him close to the lodges, as it would save the trouble of bringing a cart for the meat. He had already driven him seven miles, and afterwards killed him within two hundred yards of the tents. That evening, while the hunters were still absent, a buffalo, bewildered by the hunt, got amongst the tents, and at last got into one, after having terrified all the women and children, who precipitately took to flight. When the men returned they found him there still, and being unable to dislodge him, they shot him down from the opening in the top.

Hundreds of thousands of skeletons dot the short scant grass; and when fire had laid barer still the level surface, the bleached ribs and skulls of long-killed bison whiten far and near the dark-burnt prairie. There is something unspeakably melancholy in the aspect of this portion of the North-west. From one of the westward jutting spurs of the Touchwood Hills the eye sees far away over an immense plain; the sun goes down, and as he sinks upon the earth the straight line of the horizon becomes visible for a moment across his blood-red disc, but so distant, so far away, that it seems dreamlike in its immensity. There is not a sound in the air or on the earth; on every side lie spread the relics of the great fight waged by man against the brute creation. All is silent and deserted—the Indian and the buffalo gone, the settler not yet come.

WILLIAM FRANCIS BUTLER, 1872

FORT ELLICE

Henry Youle Hind

1859

Fort Ellice was at one period a post of considerable importance, being the depot of supplies for the Swan River District, now removed to Fort Pelly. The buildings are of wood, surrounded by a high picket enclosure. Mr McKay, one of the sub-officers, was in charge at the time of our arrival. Some twenty years ago, before the small pox and constant wars had reduced the Plain Crees to one-sixth or eighth of their former numbers, this post was often the scene of exciting Indian display. Mr McKay remembers the time when the entire tribe who now hunt on the Qu'Appelle and South Branch would approach the Fort to receive their supplies, to the number of eight hundred warriors, splendidly mounted, and singing their war songs. Twenty years ago the tribe numbered 4000, in five hundred tents, at the present day they do not exceed 120 tents, which represent a population of 960 or 1000 souls. Formerly Fort Ellice used to be visited by the Crees alone, now it numbers many Ojibways among the Indians trading with it. The Ojibways or Saulteaux have been driven from the woods by the scarcity of game, the large animals, such as moose, deer and bear having greatly diminished in numbers. Many of the wood Indians now keep horses and hunt on the Plains.

On the 11th July, a number of hunters attached to Fort Ellice came in with provisions, such as pemican and dried buffalo meat, which they had prepared in the prairies a few days before, about thirty miles from the Post, where the buffalo were numerous. Fort Ellice, the Qu'Appelle Post, and the establishment on the Touchwood Hills being situated on the borders of the great Buffalo Plains, are provision trading posts. They obtain from the Plain Crees, the Assiniboines and the Ojibways, pemican and dried meat to supply the brigades and boats in their expeditions to York Factory on Hudson Bay, and throughout the northern interior. Pemican is made by pounding or chopping buffalo meat into small pieces and then mixing it with an equal quantity of fat. It is packed in bags made of the hide of the animal, in quantities of about ninety pounds each. Dried meat is the flesh of the buffalo cut into long and broad thin pieces about two feet by fifteen inches, it is smoked over a slow fire for a few minutes and then packed into a bale of about 60 pounds. We had many opportunities of seeing the Cree women on the Qu'Appelle, cut, prepare and pack dried meat.

At Fort Ellice, the thunder storms were as violent as on the Souris, not a day passed without lightning, thunder, and generally violent rain of half an hour's duration. The grasshoppers at this Post had destroyed the crops last year, and, at the time of our visit, the young brood were well advanced, their wings being about one third of an inch long. Full grown insects from the south were flying overhead or alighting in clouds around us, so that all hopes of obtaining a crop from the garden or potatoe fields were abandoned for this year. Provisions were very scarce at the Post, and had it not been for the fortunate arrival of the hunters with some pemican and dried meat, we should have been compelled to hunt or kill the ox.

* * *

At 4 p.m. on the 12th July, we left Fort Ellice and travelled due west through a pretty country near the banks of the Qu'Appelle or Calling River. We passed one quagmire, and, after breakfast on the following day, arrived at the Cross Woods; they consist of aspen, with a splendid undergrowth. The pasturage is excellent, and the road good. Observed today the grasshoppers descending from a great height perpendicularly, like hail—a sign of approaching rain. On the 12th, we passed through a fair rolling country, the soil consisting of sandy loam with much vegetable matter in the valleys. Aspen groves are numerous, and many little lakes, margined with reeds afford quiet breeding places for duck. The road is good in summer, but wet and soft in the spring.

The grasshoppers, yesterday, were excellent prognosticators, a violent thunder storm in the afternoon commenced in the east, (all preceeding storms had come from the west) and was accompanied by exceedingly heavy rain and a very boisterous wind. The storm continued for several hours. At 9 in the evening, the air was calm and the heavens clear and bright; at 10, the storm returned from the west, and a more terrific and sublime exhibition of elemental warfare none of us had ever before witnessed. Three times the lightning struck the earth so close to us that there was no perceptible interval between the flash and the shock. It was distinctly heard to *hiss* through the air, and, instead of penetrating the ground at once, it seemed to leap from bush to bush for a distance of 60 or 70 yards. So close did one flash approach us that when we had recovered from the shock and our eyes had regained their powers, several of us met each other, groping from cart to cart, to see if any of the party had been struck. It is remarkable that although the wind was blowing violently before and after the two flashes just described occurred, yet, between them, an interval of about three quarters of a minute, there was a dead calm, and a calm of short duration succeeded each flash in our immediate vicinity.

'LET US HIE TO THE WEST . . .'

Anonymous

1879

Let us hie to the West—to the far distant West!
The mountains beyond it lie covered with gold!
On east of those mountains there millions can rest,
Where railroads in motion they'll shortly behold.

Away to the West, the far distant West!
Away to the lands that are verdant and green!
Saskatchewan Valley has lands of the best
Where rivers run slowly the valleys between!

WESTERN BUMPTIOUSNESS

Our hopes were founded not only on what we saw, but on the descriptions of the settlers and on their brave and cheery tone. They ignored rather than anticipated difficulties. They had a pride in the new land they had made their own, and faith in its future. Everywhere, in conversation with them, we found combined with this confidence, the rising of that national sentiment, that pride in their country, which is both a result and a safe-guard of national dignity and independence, as distinguished from a petty provincialism. This Great West will, in the future, probably manifest this spirit more than even the Eastern Provinces, and so be the very backbone of the Dominion; just as the prairie States of the neighbouring republic are the most strongly imbued with patriotic sentiments. The sight, the possession of these boundless seas of rich land stirs in one that feeling of—shall we call it bumptiousness—that Western men have been accused of displaying. It is easy to ridicule and caricature the self-sufficiency, but the fact is, a man out West feels like a young giant, who cannot help indulging a little tall talk, and in displays of his big limbs.

GEORGE MONRO GRANT, 1872

A RAILWAY?

If there were a prospect of the western prairies being soon occupied by a producing population, it might in that case be remunerative to have a line of railway constructed entirely within the British territory that would have for its object the connection of Canada with our new colonies on the Pacific coast; but this would justly rank as a great national enterprise, in value much beyond the more western extension of our Canadian provinces. JAMES HECTOR, 1861

SONG OF THE NORTH-WEST

D.R.

1879

I've heard, and I may state—
   I think it suits our case,—
This world would be a gloomy one
   If hope were not its base.
It shows itself quite plain 'round here,
   And clings close as a leech.
To see our faces brighten up
   Just make this little speech:
      Wait for the railroad,
      Wait for the railroad!
      Wait for the railroad!
      And we'll all take a ride!

LAYING THE TRACKS

James H. E. Secretan

1880s

The line was now covered with graders, and contractors' camps were strung out for hundreds of miles. Track-laying swiftly followed, and though in those days they had no track-laying machines, the rapidity with which it was done was astonishing. Donald Grant, a seven-foot giant, was in charge of this work with a gang of about 125 men. Winnipeg was the base of supplies, and construction trains ran on a regular schedule. Each train contained material for exactly one mile of tracks, so many cars of rails and fastenings, ties, telegraph poles, and bridge material when required. It all worked like clockwork. These trains, loaded in the Winnipeg yards, came up to the front regularly on time, were rapidly unloaded. The empty train backed out and the ties were pitched on the prairie and loaded on the wagons which were waiting for them at the end of the track. They were then distributed by hand, rails were handed along by the men with the iron car, followed by the spiking gang; and in less time than you could possibly imagine, another mile of the great railway was completed. While all this was taking place on the plains, work was also proceeding in the mountains. A tote road was built through the Kicking Horse Pass to bring in supplies, and contracts were let for the heavy rock excavation and tunnels. Along the bleak North Shore of Lake Superior, the heaviest kind of work was also being rushed to completion.

I was often amused during the track-laying on the plains at the sight of the Indians who would arrive apparently from nowhere, simply appearing. Squatted on their haunches in double rows, they would take in the proceedings, only occasionally emitting a grunt of half-concealed surprise and admiration as the 'fire-wagons,' as they called the engines, slowly pushed the steel rails to the front. I often wondered what thoughts penetrated the dusky domes of the savage warriors as they saw those two little bands of steel slowly but surely creeping westward across their old hunting grounds. They would sit for hours patiently watching the wonders of the paleface, and then when evening came they would fade away in the dusk and go home to relate to their families that they had seen thousands of white men springing up like blades of grass on the prairie.

AN ENCOUNTER WITH RIEL

William Francis Butler

1870

Louis Riel's acts of resistance in the Red River Rebellion included the occupation of Fort Garry in November 1869, the declaration of a Provisional Government, and the taking of prisoners. Colonel William F. Butler, who was about to join Colonel Garnet Wolseley's Red River Expedition coming from the east, visited Riel at Fort Garry in July 1870.

Passing from the village along the walls of the fort, I crossed the Assineboine River and saw the 'International' lying at her moorings below the floating bridge. The captain had been liberated, and waved his hand with a cheer as I crossed the bridge. The gate of the fort stood open, a sentry was leaning lazily against the wall, a portion of which leant in turn against nothing. The whole exterior of the place looked old and dirty. The muzzles of one or two guns protruding through the embrasures in the flanking bastions failed even to convey the idea of fort or fortress to the mind of the beholder.

Returning from the east or St Boniface side of the Red River, I was conducted by my companion into the fort. His private residence was situated within the walls, and to it we proceeded. Upon entering the gate

I took in at a glance the surroundings—ranged in a semi-circle with their muzzles all pointing towards the entrance, stood some six or eight field-pieces; on each side and in front were bare looking, white-washed buildings. The ground and the houses looked equally dirty, and the whole aspect of the place was desolate and ruinous.

A few ragged-looking dusky men with rusty firelocks, and still more rusty bayonets, stood lounging about. We drove through without stopping and drew up at the door of my companion's house, which was situated at the rear of the buildings I have spoken of. From the two flag-staffs flew two flags, one the Union Jack in shreds and tatters, the other a well-kept bit of bunting having the fleur-de-lis and a shamrock on a white field. Once in the house, my companion asked me if I would see Mr Riel.

'To call on him, certainly not,' was my reply.

'But if he calls on you?'

'Then I will see him,' replied I.

The gentleman who had spoken thus soon left the room. There stood in the centre of the apartment a small billiard table, I took up a cue and commenced a game with the only other occupant of the room—the same individual who had on the previous evening acted as messenger to the Indian Settlement. We had played some half a dozen strokes when the door opened, and my friend returned. Following him closely came a short stout man with a large head, a sallow, puffy face, a sharp, restless, intelligent eye, a square-cut massive forehead overhung by a mass of long and thickly clustering hair, and marked with well-cut eyebrows—altogether, a remarkable-looking face, all the more so, perhaps, because it was to be seen in a land where such things are rare sights.

This was M. Louis Riel, the head and front of the Red River Rebellion—the President, the little Napoleon, the Ogre, or whatever else he may be called. He was dressed in a curious mixture of clothing—a black frock-coat, vest, and trousers; but the effect of this somewhat clerical costume was not a little marred by a pair of Indian mocassins, which nowhere look more out of place than on a carpeted floor.

M. Riel advanced to me, and we shook hands with all that *empressement* so characteristic of hand-shaking on the American Continent. Then there came a pause. My companion had laid his cue down. I still retained mine in my hands, and, more as a means of bridging the awkward gulf of silence which followed the introduction, I asked him to continue the game—another stroke or two, and the mocassined President began to move nervously about the window recess. To relieve his burthened feelings, I inquired if he ever indulged in billiards; a rather laconic 'Never,' was his reply.

'Quite a loss,' I answered, making an absurd stroke across the table; 'a capital game.'

I had scarcely uttered this profound sentiment when I beheld the

President moving hastily towards the door, muttering as he went, 'I see I am intruding here.' There was hardly time to say, 'Not at all,' when he vanished.

But my companion was too quick for him; going out into the hall, he brought him back once more into the room, called away my billiard opponent, and left me alone with the chosen of the people of the new nation.

Motioning M. Riel to be seated, I took a chair myself, and the conversation began.

Speaking with difficulty, and dwelling long upon his words, Riel regretted that I should have shown such distrust of him and his party as to prefer the Lower Fort and the English Settlement to the Upper Fort and the society of the French. I answered, that if such distrust existed it was justified by the rumours spread by his sympathizers on the American frontier, who represented him as making active preparations to resist the approaching Expedition.

'Nothing,' he said, 'was more false than these statements. I only wish to retain power until I can resign it to a proper Government. I have done every thing for the sake of peace, and to prevent bloodshed amongst the people of this land. But they will find,' he added passionately, 'they will find, if they try, these people here, to put me out—they will find they cannot do it. I will keep what is mine until the proper Government arrives;' as he spoke he got up from his chair and began to pace nervously about the room.

I mentioned having met Bishop Taché in St Paul and the letter which I had received from him. He read it attentively and commenced to speak about the Expedition.

'Had I come from it?'

'No; I was going to it.'

He seemed surprised.

'By the road to the Lake of the Woods?'

'No; by the Winnipeg River,' I replied.

'Where was the Expedition?'

I could not answer this question; but I concluded it could not be very far from the Lake of the Woods.

'Was it a large force?'

I told him exactly, setting the limits as low as possible, not to deter him from fighting if such was his intention. The question uppermost in his mind was one of which he did not speak, and he deserves the credit of his silence. Amnesty or no amnesty was at that moment a matter of very grave import to the French half-breeds, and to none so much as to their leader. Yet he never asked if that pardon was an event on which he could calculate. He did not even allude to it at all.

At one time, when speaking of the efforts he had made for the advantage of his country, he grew very excited, walking hastily up and down the room with theatrical attitudes and declamation, which he evidently fancied had the effect of imposing on his listener; but, alas! for the vanity of man, it only made him appear ridiculous; the mocassins sadly marred the exhibition of presidential power.

An Indian speaking with the solemn gravity of his race looks right manful enough, as with moose-clad leg his mocassined feet rest on prairie grass or frozen snow-drift; but this picture of the black-coated Metis playing the part of Europe's great soldier in the garb of a priest and the shoes of a savage, looked simply absurd. At length M. Riel appeared to think he had enough of the interview, for stopping in front of me he said,—

'Had I been your enemy you would have known it before. I heard you would not visit me, and, although I felt humiliated, I came to see you to show you my pacific inclinations.'

Then darting quickly from the room he left me. An hour later I left the dirty ill-kept fort. The place was then full of half-breeds armed and unarmed. They said nothing and did nothing, but simply stared as I drove by. I had seen the inside of Fort Garry and its president, not at my solicitation but at his own; and now before me lay the solitudes of the foaming Winnipeg and the pathless waters of great inland seas.

THE BATTLE OF DUCK LAKE

Gabriel Dumont

1885

The initial skirmish of the North West Rebellion, the Battle of Duck Lake, took place after Superintendent Crozier of Fort Carlton—on the North Saskatchewan River—refused to surrender his fort to Riel's forces. On the way to Duck Lake for provisions, a detachment of Crozier's men was intercepted by Gabriel Dumont, Riel's adjutant-general, and a band of armed Métis.

On March 25th, 1885, being at St Antoine de Padoue, which is half a mile from Batoche, when the mounted police appeared on the other side of the river, I asked Riel to give me 30 men so that we could go to Duck Lake and ransack our opponents' storehouses. When I got there, Mitchell had fled. I got Magnus Burnstein, his clerk, to give me the keys to his warehouse, and helped myself to the contents.

I then left with ten men to reconnoitre the road to Carlton, taking care to send scouts in advance.

After midnight, my scouts, Baptiste Oueliet and Baptiste Arcand, saw two men on horseback go by, Ross and Astley. My brother Edouard,

Philippe Gariépy, Baptiste Deschamps, an Indian and I pursued them. Although my men were armed, I gave orders that they were not to harm anyone who did not resist.

We caught up to them at Duck Lake, and I swooped down upon them. I took aim at them saying in Indian: 'Don't try to escape, or I'll kill you'. Ross said to me 'I'm a surveyor.' I knocked him down off his horse. Seeing his revolver, I grabbed it from him, telling him 'You're no surveyor, you're a liar.'

Astley escaped, and as my men wanted to kill him, I ordered them not to do anything to him. However, he fell off his horse and they seized him. We took them both disarmed to Duck Lake, and kept them prisoners. I told them that if they behaved, they would be well treated.

We took possession of their horses.

This man Ross whom I had taken into custody in this manner was a sheriff. He must have been very frightened because, in his testimony, he said we numbered fifty when there were only 5 of us. He also claimed in the same testimony that his companion had kept him from shooting, he certainly didn't have time to do so, because I jumped on him too fast.

We were going out to stable our horses when someone shouted: 'Here come the police', but it was only three scouts whom my brother Edouard, Patrice Fleury, my brother-in-law James Short, and I chased and who escaped. Patrice Fleury said he saw Mackay among those scouts.

My companions had a lead over me in the chase after the fugitives, and I realized that they had fallen into an ambush of some forty mounted policemen who were taking aim at them. I galloped my charger towards my comrades shouting at them to get off their horses. I myself dismounted, because I heard a sergeant swear he was going to kill me. I immediately aimed at him yelling 'It is I who will kill you.' Then he emptied his rifle, putting it across his knees. I promptly pounced on him and knocked him over with the barrel of my rifle. When I lifted my gun up again a shot went off by accident. Then Thomas Mackay rushed at me saying 'Be careful Gabriel.' I answered him, 'You'd better be careful yourself, or I'll blow your brains out.' And I flung myself upon him. He turned his horse which had its back feet sunk in snow, and it reared up. I gave Mackay a push in the back with my rifle. He spurred his horse and it gave a leap forward and got away. Meanwhile, Mackay kept telling me, 'Watch out Gabriel' and I kept repeating too, 'You'd better be careful yourself, or I'll slaughter you' and I followed him with my gun.

My brother had jumped into one of the police vehicles to capture the two men in it. But they whipped their horses and made him tumble out. The cart passed over him.

There were about twenty double-yoked sleighs, and there were two men in each. Mackay commanded the retreat. I shouted at him, 'What did you come here for?' He replied that he had come to talk to us. 'But don't run away like this,' I answered him. 'we were told that you would

come with men, Where are they? You're only one blockhead.'

When I saw they were going to run away, I stopped my men from running after them. They weren't numerous enough to check them, there were only three of them.

We went back to Duck Lake, and we had scarcely let our horses out to eat, when we heard someone shout again, 'Here come the police.' We immediately jumped on horseback, and without delay I had my men occupy a hillock which commanded the plain, and from where the enemy would have been able to level their guns on us.

We were only a few men on horseback and a few men on foot, waiting for the police who had been reinforced by eighty men commanded by Crozier, who had rejoined Mackay's forty runaways. They had a cannon with them.

I sent in pursuit of their scouts several men to whom I gave orders not to shoot, because Riel had asked us not to be the first to fire.

I gave orders to my horsemen, who numbered 25, to go down into a hollow, where we were under shelter from the cannon.

Crozier, accompanied by an English half-breed, approached one of our Indians who was unarmed and, it seems, gave him his hand. The Indian then tried to grab the gun out of the hands of the English Métis who was, I believe, John Dougall Mackay. This English Métis fired, and I think it was this rifle shot which killed my brother Isidore and made him fall from his horse, stone dead.

What makes me think that it was this shot which killed my brother is that this Métis had an interest in killing him, seeing that my brother was the only one armed.

As soon as the shot was fired, the police and the volunteers commanded by Crozier, fired a round, and the Indian who was with my brother, was killed.

All this happened without any parley taking place between the two sides.

Charles Nolin, who at first had been full of boasting, had come with us to the fight, against his will. At the first shot, he fled, taking his sister-in-law's cart, going off in the direction of Prince Albert where he gave himself up.

As soon as the shooting started, we fired as much as we could. I myself fired a dozen shots with my Winchester carbine, and I was reloading it to begin again, when the English alarmed by the number of their dead, began to withdraw. It was time they did, for their cannon which until then had kept my infantry men from descending the slope, was silenced because the gunner, in loading it, put in the shot before the powder. My infantrymen then began to surround them.

This first encounter had lasted half an hour.

In their flight they had to go through a clearing, so I lay in wait for them saying to my men, 'Courage, I'm going to make the red coats jump in their carts with some rifle shots.' And then I laughed, not because I took any pleasure in killing, but to give courage to my men.

Since I was eager to knock off some of the red coats, I never thought to keep under cover, and a shot came and gashed the top of my head, where a deep scar can still be seen; I fell down on the ground, and my horse, which was also wounded, went right over me as it tried to get away. We were then 60 yards from the enemy. I wanted to get up, but the blow had been so violent, I couldn't. When Joseph Delorme saw me fall again, he cried out that I was killed. I said to him, 'Courage, as long as you haven't lost your head you're not dead'. I then told Bte Vandal to take my cartridges and my rifle which was famous and which had a range of 800 yards.

All during the battle, this Delorme was at my side fighting like a lion. But before the fight, he had said to me: 'I have never been under fire, if I am afraid, don't spare me but keep me keyed up.'

While we were fighting, Riel was on horseback, exposed to the gunfire, and with no weapon but the crucifix which he held in his hand.

Seeing me fall, my brother Edouard rushed forward to drag me down into the ravine, but I told him to go first to our men who seemed to be discouraged by my fall. He rallied them; they began to shout with joy and started shooting again. It was then my cousin Auguste Laframboise whom I had, only a few minutes before, been urging not to expose himself so much, fell close to my side. A bullet had struck his arm and passed through his body. I crawled and dragged myself over to him, saying to myself: 'I am always going to say a little prayer for him', but wishing to make the sign of the cross with my left hand, since my right side was paralysed, I fell over on my side and, laughing I said, 'Cousin, I shall have to owe it to you.'

I should have liked to say for him the prayer which I made up when we had been blessed by the priest at Belton, in Montana, 'Lord, strengthen my courage, my faith and my honour that I may profit all my life from the blessing I have received in Thy holy name.'

This is an invocation which I have always said after my prayers, morning and night. This blessing we had received on leaving Montana had impressed Riel so much that he often asked me if I remembered it.

When Riel saw Laframboise fall, he said to me, 'Uncle, I am going to have our men on foot advance.' I told him that would be like sending them into the lion's den, and that he would do better to maintain the morale of those still on the battle field.

The enemy was then beginning to retire, and my brother, who had taken command after my fall, shouted to our men to follow and destroy them. Riel then asked, in the name of God, not to kill any more, saying that there had already been too much bloodshed.

However, there was a captain whom the police called Morton, a good shot, who was behind a tree and had killed two of our men; he was hit in the back while trying to get away. As he was screaming and suffering horribly, Guillaume Mackay thought he did him a service by shooting him in the head.

The retreating men left behind nine dead and one man wounded in the leg. Since this last man wanted to continue shooting, Philippe Gariépy threw himself on him, wrenched his gun and bayonet from him and tried to hit him with his weapon. One of our men restrained Gariépy, and urged him to have pity on the miserable creature who was taken to Duck Lake.

In the haste of their flight, Clarke forgot to take along his wild cat fur cap.

The vanquished left behind 4 or 5 carts and 8 uninjured horses, as well as several dead ones. In their carts we found some stove tops behind which they had hidden while firing.

They did, however, remove the bodies of the dead mounted policemen, who could easily be recognized by their red uniforms, but they left on the ground the bodies of nine volunteers. I think they lost 16 men including captain Moore, who had a leg broken and amputated.

After the enemy had fled, my companions tied me on my horse, and we went to Duck Lake, where my wound, which was a deep one, was dressed.

Translated by G. F. G. STANLEY

MIDDLETON'S MARCHING SONG

Anonymous

1885

After the battle at Duck Lake, government troops commanded by General Frederick Middleton were sent to the area.

Riel sits in his chamber o' state
With his stolen silver forks
    and his stolen silver plate,
And all his things spread out in style
    so great:—
He'll not breakfast alone this morning!

O hey Riel, are you waking yet?
Or are yer drums a-beating yet?
If ye're not waking we'll not wait:
For we'll take the fort this morning!

THE TESTIMONY OF LOUIS RIEL

1885

PRISONER: Your Honors, gentlemen of the jury: It would be easy for me to-day to play insanity, because the circumstances are such as to excite any man, and under the natural excitement of what is taking place to-day (I cannot speak English very well, but am trying to do so, because most of those here speak English), under the excitement which my trial causes me would justify me not to appear as usual, but with my mind out of its ordinary condition. I hope with the help of God I will maintain calmness and decorum as suits this honorable court, this honorable jury.

You have seen by the papers in the hands of the Crown that I am naturally inclined to think of God at the beginning of my actions. I wish if you—I do it you won't take it as a mark of insanity, that you won't take it as part of a play of insanity. Oh, my God, help me through Thy grace and the divine influence of Jesus Christ: Oh, my God, bless me, bless this honorable court, bless this honorable jury, bless my good lawyers who have come 700 leagues to try to save my life, bless also the lawyers for the Crown, because they have done, I am sure, what they thought their duty. They have shown me fairness which at first I did not expect from them. Oh, my God, bless all those who are around me through the grace and influence of Jesus Christ our Saviour, change that curiosity into sympathy with me. The day of my birth I was helpless and my mother took care of me although she was not able to do it alone, there was some one to help her to take care of me and I lived. To-day, although a man I am as helpless before this court, in the Dominion of Canada and in this world, as I was helpless on the knees of my mother the day of my birth.

The North-West is also my mother, it is my mother country and although my mother country is sick and confined in a certain way, there are some from Lower Canada who came to help her to take care of me during her sickness and I am sure that my mother country will not kill me more than my mother did forty years ago when I came into the world, because a mother is always a mother, and even if I have my faults if she can see I am true she will be full of love for me.

When I came into the North-West in July, the first of July 1884, I found the Indians suffering. I found the half-breeds eating the rotten pork of the Hudson Bay Company and getting sick and weak every day. Although a half-breed, and having no pretension to help the whites, I also paid attention to them. I saw they were deprived of responsible government, I saw that they were deprived of their public liberties. I remembered that half-breed meant white and Indian, and while I paid attention to the suffering Indians and the half-breeds I remembered that the

greatest part of my heart and blood was white and I have directed my attention to help the Indians, to help the half-breeds and to help the whites to the best of my ability. We have made petitions, I have made petitions with others to the Canadian Government asking to relieve the condition of this country. We have taken time; we have tried to unite all classes, even if I may speak, all parties. Those who have been in close communication with me know I have suffered, that I have waited for months to bring some of the people of the Saskatchewan to an understanding of certain important points in our petition to the Canadian Government and I have done my duty. I believe I have done my duty. It has been said in this box that I have been egotistic. Perhaps I am egotistic. A man cannot be individuality without paying attention to himself. He cannot generalize himself, though he may be general. I have done all I could to make good petitions with others, and we have sent them to the Canadian Government, and when the Canadian Government did answer, through the Under Secretary of State, to the secretary of the joint committee of the Saskatchewan, then I began to speak of myself, not before; so my particular interests passed after the public interests. A good deal has been said about the settlement and division of lands a good deal has been said about that. I do not think my dignity to-day here would allow me to mention the foreign policy, but if I was to explain to you or if I had been allowed to make the questions to witnesses, those questions would have appeared in an altogether different light before the court and jury. I do not say that my lawyers did not put the right questions. The observations I had the honor to make to the court the day before yesterday were good, they were absent of the situation, they did not know all the small circumstances as I did. I could mention a point, but that point was leading to so many that I could not have been all the time suggesting. By it I don't wish it understood that I do not appreciate the good works of my lawyers, but if I were to go into all the details of what has taken place, I think I could safely show you that what Captain Young said that I am aiming all the time at practical results was true, and I could have proved it. During my life I have aimed at practical results. I have writings, and after my death I hope that my spirit will bring practical results . . .

It is true, gentlemen, I believed for years I had a mission, and when I speak of a mission you will understand me not as trying to play the role of insane before the grand jury so as to have a verdict of acquittal upon that ground. I believe that I have a mission, I believe I had a mission at this very time. What encourages me to speak to you with more confidence in all the imperfections of my English way of speaking, it is that I have yet and still that mission, and with the help of God, who is in this box with me, and He is on the side of my lawyers, even with the honorable court, the Crown and the Jury, to help me, and to prove by the extraordinary help that there is a Providence to-day in my trial, as there was a Providence in the battles of the Saskatchewan . . .

I say that I have been blessed by God, and I hope that you will not take that as a presumptuous assertion. It has been a great success for me to come through all the dangers I have in that fifteen years. If I have not succeeded in wearing a fine coat myself I have at the same time the great consolation of seeing that God has maintained my view; that He has maintained my health sufficiently to go through the world, and that he has kept me from bullets, when bullets marked my hat. I am blessed by God. It is this trial that is going to show that I am going to be blessed by man during my existence, the benedictions are a guarantee that I was not wrong when by circumstances I was taken away from adopted land to my native land. When I see British people sitting in the court to try me, remembering that the English people are proud of that word 'fair-play', I am confident that I will be blessed by God and by man also.

Not only Bishop Bourget spoke to me in that way, but Father Jean Baptiste Bruno, the priest of Worcester, who was my director of conscience, said to me: 'Riel, God has put an object into your hands, the cause of the triumph of religion in the world, take care, you will succeed when most believe you have lost.' I have got those words in my heart, those words of J. B. Bruno and the late Archbishop Bourget. But last year, while I was yet in Montana, and while I was passing before the Catholic church, the priest, the Reverend Father Frederick Ebeville, curate of the church of the Immaculate Conception, at Benton, said to me: 'I am glad to see you; is your family here?' I said: 'Yes.' He said: 'Go and bring them to the altar, I want to bless you before you go away.' And with Gabriel Dumont and my family we all went on our knees at the altar, the priest put on his surplice and he took holy water and was going to bless us, I said: 'Will you allow me to pronounce a prayer while you bless me?' He said: 'Yes I want to know what it is.' I told him the prayer. It is speaking to God: 'My Father, bless me according to views of Thy Providence which are bountiful and without measure.' He said to me: 'You can say that prayer while I bless you.' Well, he blessed me and I pronounced that prayer for myself, for my wife, for my children, and for Gabriel Dumont.

When the glorious General Middleton fired on us during three days, and on our families, and when shells went and bullets went as thick as mosquitoes in the hot days of summer, when I saw my children, my wife, myself and Gabriel Dumont were escaping, I said that nothing but the blessing without measure of Father Frederick Ebeville could save me, and that can save me to-day from these charges. The benediction promised to me surrounded me all the time in the Saskatchewan, and since it seems to me that I have seen it. Captain Deane, Corporal Prickert, and the corporal of the guard who have been appointed over me have been so gentle while the papers were raging against me shows that nothing but the benediction of God could give me the favor I have had in remaining so respected among these men. To-day when I saw the glorious General Middleton bearing testimony that he thought I was not insane, and when Captain Young proved that I am not insane, I felt that God was blessing me, and blotting away from my name the blot resting upon my reputation on account of having been in the lunatic asylum of my good friend Dr Roy. I have been in an asylum, but I thank the lawyers for the Crown who destroyed the testimony of my good friend Dr Roy, because I have always believed that I was put in the asylum without reason. To-day my pretension is guaranteed, and that is a blessing too in that way. I have also been in the lunatic asylum at Longue Pointe, and I wonder that my friend Dr Lachapelle, who took care of me charitably, and Dr Howard are not here. I was there perhaps under my own name.

Even if I was going to be sentenced by you, gentlemen of the jury, I have this satisfaction if I die—that if I die I will not be reputed by all men as insane, as a lunatic. . . .

My condition is helpless, so helpless that my good lawyers, and they have done it by conviction (Mr Fitzpatrick in his beautiful speech has proved he believed I was insane) my condition seems to be so helpless that they have recourse to try and prove insanity to try and save me in that way. If I am insane, of course I don't know it, it is a property of insanity to be unable to know it. But what is the kind of mission that I have? Practical results. It is said that I had myself acknowledged as a prophet by the half-breeds. The half-breeds have some intelligence. Captain Young who has been so polite and gentle during the time I was under his care, said that what was done at Batoche, from a military point of view was nice, that the line of defence was nice, that showed some intelligence.

It is not to be supposed that the half-breeds acknowledged me as a prophet if they had not seen that I could see something into the future. If

I am blessed without measure I can see something into the future, we all see into the future more of less. As what kind of a prophet would I come, would it be a prophet would all the time have a stick in his hand, and threatening, a prophet of evil? If the half-breeds had acknowledged me as a prophet, if on the other side priests come and say that I am polite, if there are general officers, good men, come into this box and prove that I am polite, prove that I am decent in my manner, in combining all together you have a decent prophet. An insane man cannot withhold his insanity, if I am insane my heart will tell what is in me.

Last night while I was taking exercise the spirit who guides and assists me and consoles me, told me that to-morrow somebody will come *t'aider*, five English and one French word *t'aider*, that is to help you. I am consoled by that. While I was recurring to my God, to our God, I said, but woe to me if you do not help me, and these words came to me in the morning, in the morning, someone will come *t'aider*, that is to-day. I said that to my two guards and you can go for the two guards. I told them that if the spirit that directs me is the spirit of truth it is to-day that I expect help. This morning the good doctor who has care of me came to me and said you will speak to-day before the court. I thought I would not be allowed to speak; those works were given to me to tell me that I would have liberty to speak. There was one French word in it, it meant I believe that there was to be some French influence in it, but the most part English. It is true that my good lawyers from the Province of Quebec have given me good advice. . . .

I am glad that the Crown have proved that I am the leader of the half-breeds in the North-West. I will perhaps be one day acknowledged as more than a leader of the half-breeds, and if I am I will have an opportunity of being acknowledged as a leader of good in this great country. . . .

British civilization which rules to-day the world, and the British constitution has defined such government as this is which rules the North-West Territories as irresponsible government, which plainly means that there is no responsibility, and by all the science which has been shown here yesterday you are compelled to admit if there is no responsibility, it is insane.

Good sense combined with scientific theories lead to the same conclusion. By the testimony laid before you during my trial witnesses on both sides made it certain that petition after petition had been sent to the Federal Government, and so irresponsible is that Government to the North-West that in the course of several years besides doing nothing to satisfy the people of this great land, it has even hardly been able to answer once or to give a single response. That fact would indicate an absolute lack of responsibility, and therefore insanity complicated with paralysis.

The Ministers of an insane and irresponsible Government and its little one—the North-West Council—made up their minds to answer my petitions by surrounding me slyly and by attempting to jump on me suddenly and upon my people in the Saskatchewan. Happily when they appeared and showed their teeth to devour, I was ready: that is what is called my crime of high treason, and to which they hold me to-day. Oh, my good jurors, in the name of Jesus Christ, the only one who can save and help me, they have tried to tear me to pieces.

If you take the plea of the defence that I am not responsible for my acts, acquit me completely since I have been quarrelling with an insane and irresponsible Government. If you pronounce in favor of the Crown, which contends that I am responsible, acquit me all the same. You are perfectly justified in declaring that having my reason and sound mind, I have acted reasonably and in self-defence, while the Government, my accuser, being irresponsible, and consequently insane, cannot but have acted wrong, and if high treason there is it must be on its side and not on my part.

HIS HONOR: Are you done?

PRISONER: Not yet, if you have the kindness to permit me your attention for a while.

HIS HONOR: Well, proceed.

PRISONER: For fifteen years I have been neglecting myself. Even one of the most hard witnesses on me said that with all my vanity, I never was particular to my clothing; yes, because I never had much to buy any clothing. The Rev. Father André has often had the kindness to feed my family with a sack of flour, and Father Fourmand. My wife and children are without means, while I am working more than any representative in the North-West. Although I am simply a guest of this country—a guest of the half-breeds of the Saskatchewan—although as a simple guest, I worked to better the condition of the people of the Saskatchewan at the risk of my life, to better the condition of the people of the Saskatchewan at the risk of my life, to better the condition of the people of the North-West, I have never had any pay. It has always been my hope to have a fair living one day. It will be for you to pronounce—if you say I was right, you can conscientiously acquit me, as I hope through the help of God you will. You will console those who have been fifteen years around me only partaking in my sufferings. What you will do in justice to me, in justice to my family, in justice to my friends, in justice to the North-West, will be rendered a hundred times to you in this world, and to use a sacred expression, life everlasting in the other.

I thank your Honor for the favor you have granted me in speaking; I thank you for the attention you have given me, gentlemen of the jury, and I thank those who have had the kindness to encourage my imperfect way of speaking the English language by your good attention. I put my speech under the protection of my God, my Saviour, He is the only one who can make it effective. It is possible it should become effective, as it is proposed to good men, to good people, and to good ladies also.

ROUGH BEN

(An Incident of the North-West Rebellion)

Kate B. Simpson

'Starved to death,' sound kind o' hard, eh?
But its true's I'm holdin' this 'ere knife,
An' thet woman dumped in the grave to-day
Jes' *starved to death,* sir, 'pon me life.

Ye wonder how in a land o' plenty,
Where even Injuns wallop around
With their belts a-loosened of overfeedin',
Fur a poor white critter grub ain't found.

Well; y'see ther's starvin' deeper'n eatin',
An' thet ther' woman we slid to-day
Ain't died o' want of bannock and bacon;
No! but a durned sight crueller way.

S'posin' ye sit on the fence rail, mister,
Fur I ain't agoin' to plow nor sow.
See them there oxen—'G'long, ye beggars!'—
(The flies is eatin' their heads off) 'Whoa!'

Wal', some three years ago'r—no matter—
When this yer' place w'ant much to see,
Me and Bill Martin and Bo'lin's brother
Cum' an' squatted, jest whar' we be.

An' by'm'bye other folks, hearin'
Land in the great Nor'-West had riz,
Cum' pourin' in top o' one another,
Each squatter claimin' a patch as his.

An' among the lot thet came tom-foolin'
Was an English chap as had no right
To 'speriment with a Nor'-West winter:
The fool bro't his sister an' took up a site.

Wal', he pitched his tent ('twas a waggon cover),
An' thar' they lived all summer thro',
An' managed some way by winter cummin'
To knock up a shack,—jest them thar' two.

They didn't mix with the folk'ses gen'l,
  But kep' in like, an' read fine books;
An' after a spell the lad got ailin',
  With worrit an' fretted an' pinched like looks.

An' soon he stopped goin' out to water
  The cattle (two head o' steer he'd brought),
I see'd the gal a-tryin' to lead 'em,
  An' I up an offers to guide the lot.

She wasn't proud with me, sir, never,
  Her little hand 'ud lay in my own
Like a grasshapper's wing on an acre of fallow;
  An' her eyes? my God! they'd melt a stone.

Wal', he pinched, an' coughed, an' nigher'n nigher,
  What *she*, cryin', called 'Death's Angel' cum,
An' off he went like a snuff o' candle,
  A-takin' a homestead beyond the sun.

We plowed him in—when the sun was settin'—
  On'y us na'bours around, you see;
An' we left him covered, an' her a-cryin'
  Sumthin' about 'Come back to me!'

An' the cattle died—I'm blest if they didn't,
  Contrairy like—an' the claim he owned,
An' plow'd an' sow'd 'th his two gent's handles,
  W'ant worth a durn when the Injuns cum.

I found her sittin' and kinder cryin'
  By the hill as whar we had rolled him in;
Lookin' so peaked an' white an' ghost-like
  I felt like wishin' she wus with him.

Wal'! the cattle wus dead, the ground w'ant ready,
  An' the Injuns threat'nin' every day,
To hand our wigs to the belts as held 'em
  Chock full o' *rot-gut*, spite o' Hundson's Bay.

All at onc't I see'd her trouble,
  'Twas want o' wimmin to cuddle her in,
An' the nearest petticoat, too, by thunder!
  Thirty miles off—an' *she lived by sin.*

An' sooner'n *that,* I'd—wal', I'd give her
  The best I owned, sir, my land an' life:
It was shelter, you see, an' Injuns comin'
  Jest frightened her into a-bein' *my* wife.

Oh! ye may star' and handle yer shooter,
  But, afore high God, she was dear to me;
I toted her back to my old log cabin,
  An' worshipp'd the groun' she walked—an' she?

Wal', she *tried* to smile an' call me 'Benny',
  When all my life I'd been called 'Rough Ben',
An' I carted her roun' like you'd a luckpenny;
  An' th' Injuns? oh, Gov'ment settled them.

Ye mind the troops cum marchin' up here,
  An' the garrison we wus all shut in,
An' among the red-coats thet came paradin'
  Was as handsom' a chap as ever I seen.

An' while we popped at the redskins' top-knots,
  Them soldier fellows as saved our lives
Cum marchin' into the wood-pile barracks,
  An' what did I see with my own two eyes,

But my little girl as I took under cover
  Grow red an' white and fall like a star,
When out from the file that peart-faced stranger
  Shot like an arrow to whar' she war?

Uncle, sez I, or cousin, mebbe,
  As went to school whar' she got them books?
But when *he kissed my gal* I 'tumbled',
  And shook like the leaves that shadder the brooks.

An' then an' thar' I larned her story
  (Too late! for now she was straight my wife),
For the parson sed 'twas for ever an' ever,
  An' her nor me couldn't alter our life.

Wal', that evenin' I left them airly
  (I'm a'goin' to lead a duck, I sed),
But I know'd that wench's heart was breakin',
  An' I gave her a chance to skip 'th the lad.

But she didn't—I found her thar',
  Mendin' an' bakin' the usual way;
But a look in her eyes ther' was like unto
  A threat'nin' rain on a summer day.

He'd gone an' left her to me as took her
  Jest fur to give her shelter and care
(I know'd 'f the brother 'd lived, she'd never
  A-looked at me, mor'n them oxen thar.)

Somehow she kinder wilted, an' never
  Ask'd no question, but sort o' still;
With thet look o' hunger a-eaten' her heart out—
  Thet's the kind o' starvin' is sure to kill.

I fetch'd the best of eatin' an' drinkin'
  As wus to be bo't in them times out here;
But the days went slidin' into winter,
  An' mister, with snow-fly an empty cheer.

She slid away from me sort o' quiet,
  W' never a moan, but 'Benny, good-night!'
An' me an' the neighbors, as allus loved her,
  Tuck'd her beside him, jest out o' sight.

An' the soldier-lover thet left her starvin',
  I'd like to put a ball through his hide.
What? honor! another's!! *You loved her!!!*
  My God! *You're the chap for who she died!*

Gimme your hand, and here above her,
  Altho' she *wus* mine by a parson's swar',
I hain't no right to that gal's ashes,—
  She died for you, an' you left her thar'.

Me and me oxen's movin' westward,
  You and the gal's best left alone;
She'll rest contenteder; good-bye, I'm goin';
  The claim is your'n, go claim your own.

WHERE IS THE VOICE COMING FROM?

Rudy Wiebe

Almighty Voice (1874-97), a Cree Indian, was arrested in 1895 for slaughtering a cow on a reserve near Duck Lake, N.W.T. He escaped, shot and killed a North West Mounted Police officer who was pursuing him, and became a hero to the Crees before he was finally killed by the police.

The problem is to make the story.

One difficulty of this making may have been excellently stated by Teilhard de Chardin: 'We are continually inclined to isolate ourselves from the things and events which surround us . . . as though we were spectators, not elements, in what goes on.' Arnold Toynbee does venture, 'For all that we know, Reality is the undifferentiated unity of the mystical experience,' but that need not here be considered. This story ended long ago; it is one of finite acts, of orders, of elemental feelings and reactions, of obvious legal restrictions and requirements.

Presumably all the parts of the story are themselves available. A difficulty is that they are, as always, available only in bits and pieces. Though the acts themselves seem quite clear, some written reports of the acts contradict each other. As if these acts were, at one time, too well known; as if the original nodule of each particular fact had from somewhere received non-factual accretions; or even more, as if, since the basic facts were so clear perhaps there were a larger number of facts than any one reporter, or several, or even any reporter had ever attempted to record. About facts that are still simply told by this mouth to that ear, of course, even less can be expected.

An affair seventy-five years old should acquire some of the shiny transparency of an old man's skin. It should.

Sometimes it would seem that it would be enough—perhaps more than enough—to hear the names only. The grandfather One Arrow; the mother Spotted Calf; the father Sounding Sky; the wife (wives rather, but only one of them seems to have a name, though their fathers are Napaise, Kapahoo, Old Dust, The Rump)—the one wife named, of all things, Pale Face; the cousin Going-Up-To-Sky; the brother-in-law (again, of all things) Dublin. The names of the police sound very much alike; they all begin with Constable or Corporal or Sergeant, but here and there an Inspector, then a Superintendent and eventually all the resonance of an Assistant Commissioner echoes down. More. Herself: Victoria, by the Grace of God etc., etc., QUEEN, defender of the Faith, etc., etc.; and witness 'Our Right Trusty and Right Well-beloved Cousin and Councillor the Right Honorable Sir John Campbell Hamilton-Gordon, Earl of Aberdeen; Viscount Formartine, Baron Haddo, Methlic, Tarves and Kellie, in the Peerage of Scotland; Viscount Gordon of Aberdeen, County of Aberdeen, in the Peerage of the United Kingdom; Baronet of Nova Scotia, Knight Grand Cross of Our Most Distinguished Order of Saint Michael and Saint George, etc., Governor General of Canada'. And of course himself: in the award proclamation named 'Jean-Baptiste' but otherwise known only as Almighty Voice.

But hearing cannot be enough; not even hearing all the thunder of A Proclamation: 'Now Hear Ye that a reward of FIVE HUNDRED DOLLARS will be paid to any person or persons who will give such information as will lead . . . (etc., etc.) this Twentieth day of April, in the year of Our Lord one thousand eight hundred and ninety-six, and the Fifty-ninth year of Our Reign . . . ' etc. and etc.

Such hearing cannot be enough. The first item to be seen is the piece of white bone. It is almost triangular, slightly convex—concave actually as it is positioned at this moment with its corners slightly raised—graduating from perhaps a strong eighth to a weak quarter of an inch in thickness, its scattered pore structure varying between larger and smaller on its perhaps polished, certainly shiny surface. Precision is difficult since the glass showcase is at least thirteen inches deep and therefore an eye cannot be brought as close as the minute inspection of such a small, though certainly quite adequate, sample of skull would normally require. Also, because of the position it cannot be determined whether the several hairs, well over a foot long, are still in some manner attached or not.

The seven-pounder cannon can be seen standing almost shyly between the showcase and the interior wall. Officially it is known as a gun, not a cannon, and clearly its bore is not large enough to admit a large man's fist. Even if it can be believed that this gun was used in the 1885 Rebellion and that on the evening of Saturday, May 29, 1897 (while the nine-pounder, now unidentified, was in the process of arriving with the police on the special train from Regina), seven shells (all that were available in Prince Albert at that time) from it were sent shrieking into the poplar bluffs as night fell, clearly such shelling could not and would not disembowel the whole earth. Its carriage is now nicely lacquered, the perhaps oak spokes of its petite wheels (little higher than a knee) have been recently scrapped, puttied and varnished; the brilliant burnish of its brass breeching testifies with what meticulous care charmen and women have used nationally-advertised cleaners and restorers.

Though it can also be seen, even a careless glance reveals that the same concern has not been expended on the one (of two) .44 calibre 1866 model Winchesters apparently found at the last in the pit with Almighty Voice. It also is preserved in a glass case; the number 1536735 is still, though barely, distinguishable on the brass cartridge section just below the brass saddle ring. However, perhaps because the case was imperfectly sealed at one time (though sealed enough not to warrant disturbance now), or because of simple neglect, the rifle is obviously spotted here and there with blotches of rust and the brass itself reveals discolorations almost like mildew. The rifle bore, the three long strands of hair themselves, actually bristle with clots of dust. It may be that this museum cannot afford to be as concerned as the other; conversely, the disfiguration may be something inherent in the items themselves.

The small building which was the police guardroom at Duck Lake, Saskatchewan Territory, in 1895 may also be seen. It had subsequently been moved from its original place and used to house small animals, chickens perhaps, or pigs—such as a woman might be expected to have under her responsibility. It is, of course, now perfectly empty, and clean so that the public may enter with no more discomfort than a bend under the doorway and a heavy encounter with disinfectant. The door-jamb has obviously been replaced; the bar network at one window is, however, said to be original; smooth still, very smooth. The logs inside have been smeared again and again with whitewash, perhaps paint, to an insistent point of identity-defying characterlessness. Within the small rectangular box of these logs not a sound can be heard from the streets of the, probably dead, town.

Hey Injun you'll get hung for stealing that steer
Hey Injun for killing that government cow you'll get three
weeks on the woodpile Hey Injun

The place named Kinistino seems to have disappeared from the map but the Minnechinass Hills have not. Whether they have ever been on a map is doubtful but they will, of course, not disappear from the landscape as long as the grass grows and the rivers run. Contrary to general report and belief, the Canadian prairies are rarely, if ever, flat and the Minnechinass (spelled five different ways and translated sometimes as 'The Outside Hill', sometimes as 'Beautiful Bare Hills') are dissimilar from any other of the numberless hills that everywhere block out the prairie horizon. They are bare; poplars lie tattered along their tops, almost black against the straw-pale grass and sharp green against the grey soil of the plowing laid in half-mile rectangular blocks upon their western slopes. Poles holding various wires stick out of the fields, back down the bend of the valley; what was once a farmhouse is weathering into the cultivated earth. The poplar bluff where Almighty Voice made his stand has, of course, disappeared.

The policemen he shot and killed (not the ones he wounded, of course) are easily located. Six miles east, thirty-nine miles north in Prince Alberta, the English Cemetery. Sergeant Colin Campbell Colebrook, North West Mounted Police Registration Number 605, lies presumably under a gravestone there. His name is seventeenth in a very long 'list of non-commissioned officers and men who have died in the service since the inception of the force.' The date is October 29, 1895, and the cause of death is anonymous: 'Shot by escaping Indian prisoner near Prince Albert.' At the foot of this grave are two others: Constable John R. Kerr,

No. 3040, and Corporal C. H. S. Hockin, No. 3106. Their cause of death on May 28, 1897 is even more anonymous, but the place is relatively precise: 'Shot by Indians at Min-etch-inass Hills, Prince Albert District.'

The gravestone, if he has one, of the fourth man Almighty Voice killed is more difficult to locate. Mr Ernest Grundy, postmaster at Duck Lake in 1897, apparently shut his window the afternoon of Friday, May 28, armed himself, rode east twenty miles, participated in the second charge into the bluff at about 6:30 p.m., and on the third sweep of that charge was shot dead at the edge of the pit. It would seem that he thereby contributed substantially not only to the Indians' bullet supply, but his clothing warmed them as well.

The burial place of Dublin and Going-Up-To-Sky is unknown, as is the grave of Almighty Voice. It is said that a Métis named Henry Smith lifted the latter's body from the pit in the bluff and gave it to Spotted Calf. The place of burial is not, of course, of ultimate significance. A gravestone is always less evidence than a triangular piece of skull, provided it is large enough.

Whatever further evidence there is to be gathered may rest on pictures. There are, presumably, almost numberless pictures of the policemen in the case, but the only one with direct bearing is one of Sergeant Colebrook who apparently insisted on advancing to complete an arrest after being warned three times that if he took another step he would be shot. The picture must have been taken before he joined the force; it reveals him a large-eared young man, hair brush-cut and ascot tie, his eyelids slightly drooping, almost hooded under thick brows. Unfortunately a picture of Constable R. C. Dickson, into whose charge Almighty Voice was apparently committed in that guardroom and who after Colebrook's death was convicted of negligence, sentenced to two months hard labour and discharged, does not seem to be available.

There are no pictures to be found of either Dublin (killed early by rifle fire) or Going-Up-To-Sky (killed in the pit), the two teenage boys who gave their ultimate fealty to Almighty Voice. There is, however, one said to be of Almighty Voice, Junior. He may have been born to Pale Face during the year, two hundred and twenty-one days that his father was a fugitive. In the picture he is kneeling before what could be a tent, he wears stripped denim overalls and displays twin babies whose sex cannot be determined from the double-laced dark bonnets they wear. In the supposed picture of Spotted Calf and Sounding Sky, Sounding Sky stands slightly before his wife; he wears a white shirt and a stripped blanket folded over his left shoulder in such a manner that the arm in which he cradles a long rifle cannot be seen. His head is thrown back; the rim of his hat appears as a black half-moon above eyes that are pressed shut in, as it were, profound concentration; above a mouth clenched thin in a downward curve. Spotted Calf wears a long dress, a sweater which could also be a man's dress coat, and a large fringed and embroidered shawl which would appear distinctly Dukhobour in origin if the scroll patterns on it were more irregular. Her head is small and turned slightly towards her husband so as to reveal her right ear. There is what can only be called a quizzical expression on her crumpled face; it may be she does not understand what is happening and that she would have asked a question, perhaps of her husband, perhaps of the photographers, perhaps even of anyone, anywhere in the world if such questioning were possible for an Indian lady.

There is one final picture. That is one of Almighty Voice himself. At least it is purported to be of Almighty Voice himself. In the Royal Canadian Mounted Police Museum on the Barracks Grounds just off Dewdney Avenue in Regina, Saskatchewan, it lies in the same showcase, as a matter of fact immediately beside, that triangular piece of skull. Both are unequivocally labelled, and it must be assumed that a police force with a world-wide reputation would not label *such* evidence incorrectly. But here emerges an ultimate problem in making the story.

There are two official descriptions of Almighty Voice. The first reads: 'Height about five feet, ten inches, slight build, rather good looking, a sharp hooked nose with a remarkably flat point. Has a bullet scar on the left side of his face about 1½ inches long running from near corner of mouth towards ear. The scar cannot be noticed when his face is painted but otherwise is plain. Skin fair for an Indian.' The second description is on the Award Proclamation: 'About twenty-two years old, five feet ten inches in height, weight about eleven stone, slightly erect, neat small feet and hands; complexion inclined to be fair, wavey dark hair to shoulders, large dark eyes, broad forehead, sharp features and parrot nose with flat tip, scar on left cheek running from mouth towards ear, feminine appearance.'

So run the descriptions that were, presumably, to identify a well-known fugitive in so precise a manner than an informant could collect five hundred dollars—a considerable sum when a police constable earned between one and two dollars a day. The nexus of the problems appears when these supposed official descriptions are compared to the supposed official picture. The man in the picture is standing on a small rug. The fingers of his left hand touch a curved Victorian settee, behind him a photographer's backdrop of scrolled patterns merges to vaguely paradisiacal trees and perhaps a sky. The moccasins he wears make it impossible to deduce whether his feet are 'neat small'. He may be five feet, ten inches tall, may weigh eleven stone, he certainly is 'rather good looking' and, though it is a frontal view, it may that the point of his long and flaring nose could be 'remarkably flat'. The photograph is slightly over-illuminated and so the unpainted complexion could be 'inclined to be fair'; however, nothing can be seen of a scar, the hair is not wavy and shoulder-length but hangs almost to the waist in two thick straight braids worked through with beads, fur, ribbons and cords. The right hand that

holds the corner of the blanket-like coat in position is large and, even in the high illumination, heavily veined. The neck is concealed under coiled beads and the forehead seems more low than 'broad'.

Perhaps, somehow, these picture details could be reconciled with the official description if the face as a whole were not so devastating.

On a cloth-backed sheet two feet by two and one-half feet in size, under the Great Seal of the Lion and the Unicorn, dignified by the names of the Deputy of the Minister of Justice, the Secretary of State, the Queen herself and all the heaped detail of her 'Right Trusty and Right Well Beloved Cousin', this description concludes: 'feminine appearance'. But the pictures: any face of history, any believed face that the world acknowledges as *man*—Socrates, Jesus, Attila, Genghis Khan, Mahatma Gandhi, Joseph Stalin—no believed face is more *man* than this face. The mouth, the nose, the clenched brows, the eyes—the eyes are large, yes, and dark, but even in this watered-down reproduction of unending reproductions of that original, a steady look into those eyes cannot be endured. It is a face like an axe.

It is now evident that the de Chardin statement quoted at the beginning has relevance only as it proves itself inadequate to explain what has happened. At the same time, the inadequacy of Aristotle's much more famous statement becomes evident: 'The true difference [between the historian and the poet] is that one relates what *has* happened, the other what *may* happen.' These statements cannot explain the storyteller's activity since, despite the most rigid application of impersonal investigation, the elements of the story have now run me aground. If ever I could, I can no longer pretend to objective, omnipotent disinterestedness. I am no longer *spectator* of what *has* happened or what *may* happen: I am become *element* in what is happening at this very moment.

For it is, of course, I myself who cannot endure the shadows on that paper which are those eyes. It is I who stand beside this broken veranda post where two corner shingles have been torn away, where barbed wire tangles the dead weeds on the edge of this field. The bluff that sheltered Almighty Voice and his two friends has not disappeared from the slope of the Minnechinass, no more than the sound of Constable Dickson's voice in that guardhouse is silent. The sound of his speaking is there even if it has never been recorded in an official report:

hey injun you'll get
hung
for stealing that steer
hey injun for killing that government
cow you'll get three
weeks on the woodpile hey injun

The unknown contradictory words about an unprovable act that move a boy to defiance, an implacable Cree warrior long after the three-hundred-and-fifty-year war is ended, a war already lost the day the Cree watch Cartier hoist his gun ashore at Hochelaga and they begin the long retreat west; these words of incomprehension, of threatened incomprehensible law are there to be heard just as the unmoving tableau of the three-day siege is there to be seen on the slopes of the Minnechinass. Sounding

Sky is somewhere not there, under arrest, but Spotted Calf stands on a shoulder of the Hills a little to the left, her arms upraised to the setting sun. Her mouth is open. A horse rears, riderless, above the scrub willow at the edge of the bluff, smoke puffs, screams tangle in rifle barrage, there are wounds, somewhere. The bluff is so green this spring, it will not burn and the ragged line of seven police and two civilians is staggering through, faces twisted in rage, terror, and rifles sputter. Nothing moves. There is no sound of frogs in the night; twenty-seven policeman and five civilians stand in cordon at thirty-yard intervals and a body also lies in the shelter of a gully. Only a voice rises from the bluff:

We have fought well
You have died like braves
I have worked hard and am hungry
Give me food

but nothing moves. The bluff lies, a bright green island on the grassy slope surrounded by men hunched forward rigid over their long rifles, men clumped out of rifle-range, thirty-five men dressed as for fall hunting on a sharp spring day, a small gun positioned on a ridge above. A crow is falling out of the sky into the bluff, its feathers sprayed as by an explosion. The first gun and the second gun are in position, the beginning and end of the bristling surround of thirty-five Prince Albert Volunteers, thirteen civilians and fifty-six policemen in position relative to the bluff and relative to the unnumbered whites astride their horses, standing up in their carts, staring and pointing across the valley, in position relative to the bluff and the unnumbered Indians squatting silent along the higher ridges of the Hills, motionless mounds, faceless against the Sunday morning sunlight edging between and over them down along the tree tips, down into the shadows of the bluff. Nothing moves. Beside the second gun the red-coated officer has flung a handful of grass into the motionless air, almost to the rim of the red sun.

And there is a voice. It is an incredible voice that rises from among the young poplars ripped of their spring bark, from among the dead somewhere lying there, out of the arm-deep pit shorter than a man; a voice rises over the exploding smoke and thunder of guns that reel back in their positions, worked over, serviced by the grimed motionless men in bright coats and glinting buttons, a voice so high and clear, so unbelievably high and strong in its unending wordless cry.

The voice of 'Gitchie-Manitou Wayo'—interpreted as 'voice of the Great Spirit'—that is, The Almighty Voice. His death chant no less incredible in its beauty than in its incomprehensible happiness.

I say 'wordless cry' because that is the way it sounds to me. I could be more accurate if I had a reliable interpreter who would make a reliable interpretation. For I do not, of course, understand the Cree myself.

THE QUESTION MARK IN THE CIRCLE

Wallace Stegner

I have sometimes been tempted to believe that I grew up on a gun-toting frontier. This temptation I trace to a stagecoach ride in the spring of 1914, and to a cowpuncher named Buck Murphy.

The stagecoach ran from Gull Lake, Saskatchewan, on the main line of the Canadian Pacific, to the town I shall call Whitemud, sixty miles southwest in the valley of the Whitemud or Frenchman River. The grade from Moose Jaw already reached to Whitemud, and steel was being laid, but no trains were yet running when the stage brought in my mother, my brother, and myself, plus a red-faced cowpuncher with a painful deference to ladies and a great affection for little children. I rode the sixty miles on Buck Murphy's lap, half anesthetized by his whiskey breath, and during the ride I confounded both my mother and Murphy by fishing from under his coat a six-shooter half as big as I was.

A little later Murphy was shot and killed by a Mountie in the streets of Shaunavon, up the line. As I heard later, the Mountie was scared and trigger-happy, and would have been in real trouble for an un-Mountie-like killing if Murphy had not been carrying a gun. But instead of visualizing it as it probably was—Murphy coming down the street in a buckboard, the Mountie on the corner, bad blood between them, a suspicious move, a shot, a scared team, a crowd collecting—I have been led by a lifetime of horse opera to imagine that death in standard walk-down detail. For years, growing up in more civilized places, I got a comfortable sense of status out of recalling that in my youth I had been a friend of badmen and an eyewitness to gunfights in wide streets between false-fronted saloons. Not even the streets and saloons, now that I test them, were authentic, for I don't think I was ever in Shaunavon in my boyhood, and I could not have reconstructed an image from Whitemud's streets because at the time of Murphy's death Whitemud didn't have any. It hardly even had houses: we ourselves were living in a derailed dining car.

Actually Murphy was an amiable, drunken, sentimental, perhaps dishonest, and generally harmless Montana cowboy like dozens of others. He may have been in Canada for reasons that would have interested Montana sheriffs, but more likely not; and if he had been, so were plenty of others who never thought of themselves as badmen. The Cypress Hills had always made a comfortable retiring place just a good day's ride north of the Line. Murphy would have carried a six-shooter mainly for reasons of brag; he would have worn it inside his coat because Canadian law forbade the carrying of sidearms. When Montana cattle outfits worked across the Line they learned to leave their guns in their bedrolls. In the American West men came before law, but in Saskatchewan the law was there before settlers, before even cattlemen, and not merely law but law enforcement. It was not characteristic that Buck Murphy should die in a gunfight, but if he had to die by violence it was entirely characteristic that he should be shot by a policeman.

The first settlement in the Cypress Hills country was a village of *métis* winterers, the second was a short-lived Hudson's Bay Company post on Chimney Coulee, the third was the Mounted Police headquarters at Fort Walsh, the fourth was a Mountie outpost erected on the site of the burned Hudson's Bay Company buildings to keep an eye on Sitting Bull and other Indians who congregated in that country in alarming numbers after the big troubles of the 1870's. The Mountie post on Chimney Coulee, later moved down onto the river, was the predecessor of the town of Whitemud. The overgrown foundation stones of its cabins remind a historian why there were no Boot Hills along the Frenchman. The place was too well policed.

So as I have learned more I have had to give up the illusion of a romantic gun-toting past, and it is hardly glamour that brings me back, a middle-aged pilgrim, to the village I last saw in 1920. Neither do I come back with the expectation of returning to a childhood wonderland—or I don't think I do. By most estimates, including most of the estimates of memory, Saskatchewan can be a pretty depressing country.

The Frenchman, a river more American than Canadian since it flows into the Milk and thence into the Missouri, has changed its name since my time to conform with American maps. We always called it the Whitemud, from the stratum of pure white kaolin exposed along its valley. Whitemud or Frenchman, the river is important in my memory, for it conditioned and contained the town. But memory, though vivid, is imprecise, without sure dimensions, and it is as much to test memory against adult observation as for any other reason that I return. What I remember are low bars overgrown with wild roses, cutbank bends, secret paths through the willows, fords across the shallows, swallows in the clay banks, days of indolence and adventure where space was as flexible as the mind's cunning and where time did not exist. That was at the heart of it, the sunken and sanctuary river valley. Out around, stretching in all directions from the benches to become coextensive with the disk of the world, went the uninterrupted prairie.

The geologist who surveyed southern Saskatchewan in the 1870s called it one of the most desolate and forbidding regions on earth. I can remember plenty of times when it seemed so to me and my family. Yet as I poke the car tentatively eastward into it from Medicine Hat, returning to my childhood through a green June, I look for desolation and can find none.

The plain spreads southward below the Trans-Canada Highway, an ocean of wind-troubled grass and grain. It has its remembered textures: winter wheat heavily headed, scoured and shadowed as if schools of fish move in it; spring wheat with its young seed-rows as precise as combings in a boy's wet hair; gray-brown summer fallow with the weeds disked under; and grass, the marvelous curly prairie wool tight to the earth's skin, straining the wind as the wheat does, but in its own way, secretly.

Prairie wool blue-green, spring wheat bright as new lawn, winter wheat gray-green at rest and slaty when the wind flaws it, roadside primroses as shy as prairie flowers are supposed to be, and as gentle to the eye as when in my boyhood we used to call them wild tulips, and by their coming date the beginning of summer.

On that monotonous surface with its occasional ship-like farm, its atolls of shelter-belt trees, its level ring of horizon, there is little to interrupt the eye. Roads run straight between parallel lines of fence until they intersect the circle of the horizon. It is landscape of circles, radii, perspective exercises—a country of geometry.

Across its empty miles pours the pushing and shouldering wind, a thing you tighten into as a trout tightens into fast water. It is a grassy, clean, exciting wind, with the smell of distance in it, and in its search for whatever it is looking for it turns over every wheat blade and head, every pale primrose, even the ground-hugging grass. It blows yellow-headed blackbirds and hawks and prairie sparrows around the air and ruffles the short tails of meadowlarks on fence posts. In collaboration with the light, it makes lovely and changeful what might otherwise be characterless.

It is a long way from characterless; 'overpowering' would be a better word. For over the segmented circle of earth is domed the biggest sky anywhere, which on days like this sheds down on range and wheat and summer fallow a light to set a painter wild, a light pure, glareless, and transparent. The horizon a dozen miles away is as clean a line as the nearest fence. There is no haze, neither the woolly gray of humid countries nor the blue atmosphere of the mountain West. Across the immense sky move navies of cumuli, fair-weather clouds, their bottoms as even as if they had scraped themselves flat against the flat earth.

The drama of this landscape is in the sky, pouring with light and always moving. The earth is passive. And yet the beauty I am struck by, both as present fact and as revived memory, is a fusion: this sky would not be so spectacular without this earth to change and glow and darken under it. And whatever the sky may do, however the earth is shaken or darkened, the Euclidean perfection abides. The very scale, the hugeness of simple forms, emphasizes stability. It is not hills and mountains which we should call eternal. Nature abhors an elevation as much as it abhors a vacuum; a hill is no sooner elevated than the forces of erosion begin tearing it down. These prairies are quiescent, close to static; looked at for any length of time, they begin to impose their awful perfection on the observer's mind. Eternity is a peneplain.

In a wet spring such as this, there is almost as much sky on the ground as in the air. The country is dotted with sloughs, every depression is full of water, the roadside ditches are canals. Grass and wheat grow to the water's edge and under it; they seem to grow right under the edges of the sky. In deep sloughs tules have rooted, and every such pond is dignified with mating mallards and the dark little automata that glide after them as if on strings.

The nesting mallards move in my memory, too, pulling after them shadowy, long-forgotten images. The picture of a drake standing on his head with his curly tailfeathers sticking up from a sheet of wind-flawed slough is tangled in my remembering senses with the feel of the grassy edge under my bare feet, the smell of mud, the push of the traveler wind, the weight of the sun, the look of the sky with its level-floored clouds made for the penetration of miraculous Beanstalks.

Desolate? Forbidding? There was never a country that in its good moments was more beautiful. Even in drouth or dust storm or blizzard it is the reverse of monotonous, once you have submitted to it with all the senses. You don't get out of the wind, but learn to lean and squint against it. You don't escape sky and sun, but wear them in your eyeballs and on your back. You become acutely aware of yourself. The world is very large, the sky even larger, and you are very small. But also the world is flat, empty, nearly abstract, and in its flatness you are a challenging upright thing, as sudden as an exclamation mark, as enigmatic as a question mark.

It is a country to breed mystical people, egocentric people, perhaps poetic people. But not humble ones. At noon the total sun pours on your single head; at sunrise or sunset you throw a shadow a hundred yards long. It was not prairie dwellers who invented the indifferent universe or impotent man. Puny you may feel there, and vulnerable, but not unnoticed. This is a land to mark the sparrow's fall.

IMMIGRANT

Lorna Uher

i have slipped
through the iron teeth
of your country

26. No immigrant shall be permitted to land in Canada, who is feeble-minded, an idiot or an epileptic, or who is insane, or who has had an attack of insanity within five years

On the wooden floor
i thrash and foam
biting through pencils
the rusted metal of plow shares
fingerbones
my eyes roll back
and i see myself
the inside of my head
my rivers my trees

27. who is afflicted with a loathsome disease, or with a disease which is contagious or infections which may become dangerous to the public health or widely disseminated

i hand out mouthmasks
to visitors at my house
but one by one i see them
pale sicken coil into their bodies
they look at me with white
hoar frost eyes
they touch to find their way
they gnaw on poplar branches
green fibres grow between
their growing teeth

28. who is a pauper, or destitute, or a professional beggar or vagrant or who is likely to become a public charge

i stand at the river's mouth
an earth cup in my hand
i extend it to all
who wish to bare themselves
to the river's tongue
the cup jingles
with gold rings
suspender buttons
old eyelashes

No immigrant i *shall be* am *permitted to land* your scourge *in Canada* your salvation

I Have a Message: "Western Canada Is Beckoning To You Now."

G. L. DODDS, REAL ESTATE DEALER

And Appraiser for the North of Scotland Canadian Mortgage Company, Limited, for twenty years at Wolseley, Saskatchewan, and Melita, Manitoba.

Address: Leland Hotel, Winnipeg, Manitoba, Canada.

ACROSTIC

INTENDING IMMIGRANT TO G. L. DODDS. ESQ.

G ive me the land for prosperous farms,
L and rich, that with its richness charms,
D emanding little toil.
O r, Mr Dodds, canst show me this
D ark fertile land, the best that is,
D eep, easy cultured soil?

S ay! where can I, on farming bent,
L ight on a spot to pitch my tent,
E xactly where't will pay?
L ittle care I where be the land,
A s long as it is good or grand,
N ot middling anyway.

THE REPLY OF MR G. L. DODDS.

D ear Sir! I have the place for you.
H ere, sunny Daysland, rich all through,
O n bright Alberta's Plain.
T here's black loam soil and water good,
E xcessive coal, abundant wood;
L and none can beat for grain.

W ith railroad running very near,
I ts climate good through all the year;
N or you for stock need fear
N o matter how the winds may blow
I n this fair land, or fall the snow,
P ut none in shelter here.

E nough I've said, and all is true;
G ood Sir, is this enough for you?

PRAIRIE SETTLERS

Mary Hiemstra

c. 1903-4

The men went away after a while and Dad went to look at his land. Mother said he counted every blade of grass every day, which was an exaggeration, but he never tired of walking across his acres. He was terribly proud of this new farm, and he inspected it as a king inspects his kingdom. When he returned from a walk his face was always bright and his voice hopeful.

'I never saw owt to compare with this place,' he said when he came home that afternoon. 'It's fair surprising the way it warms up. No fog, no drizzle, just sunshine. If you stand still you can see the grass growing. Another week and the trails will be passable, then work on the railroad will start. Once that's finished, Sally, we'll be rich in no time.' He took off his cap, the one he had brought from England, hung it on a peg, pulled his home-made chair close to the packing-box table, and waited for Mother to pour him some tea.

Mother paused with her hand on the handle of the little blue teapot and looked sharply at Dad. 'I thought you said we were going home as soon as the trails were passable?' she said.

'Well . . .' Dad looked uneasily at the brown log walls and the green trees not far from the open door. 'I thought maybe we might try it a bit longer now that the weather's warm,' he said.

'It won't be warm for ever.' Mother filled Dad's mug with steaming brown tea and handed it to him. 'And there'll be other winters.'

'But not as bad as the last, and when we get some breaking done—'

'The prairie doesn't plough easy.' Mother put sugar in her tea. 'And it won't be ploughed in a day either. It will take years, and a lot of things might happen. Have you forgotten how we nearly lost Jack last winter? Next time we might not be so lucky.'

'I was thinking on buying a farm for him and for the lasses as well, one of these days.' Dad stirred his tea, though he hadn't put any sugar in it.

'They may not want a farm.' Mother stirred her tea carefully. 'Farming's a hard life for a woman.'

'You don't think you could stick it another year?' Dad stopped stirring, lifted the spoon out of the brown tea and watched the drops fall off the tip of the spoon back into the mug. They made soft little plinks in the silence.

'It's that lonely. All winter and hardly a word to another woman.' Mother picked up her mug of tea, but her hand trembled and she put it down again.

'We might go to Lloydminster next winter.' The warm glow was going from Dad's voice.

'And live in a tent and have scurvy?'

'There might be houses by then.'

'But it's more likely there won't.' Mother's blue eyes were beginning to look angry.

'It's a shame to lose the farm after we've lived on it a whole year.'

'It isn't as if it was one of the bairns.' Mother glanced at Jack, busy in the wood-box.

'If we go,' Dad said slowly, looking at his spoon, 'the rest of the colony might go too. I wouldn't want to start something like that.'

'You're making excuses, that's all.' Mother voice trembled.

'No, I'm not. You heard what Watson said: nobody wants to be the first to go. They'll say we're running away.'

'I don't care what they say.' Mother flounced across the room and shut the door as if she couldn't bear the sight of Canada. 'I've had enough of this place,' she said.

'It's a shame to give up now,' Dad said. 'In another year the farm will be worth a thousand dollars, and when Jack grows up—'

'If we stay here he may not live to grow up,' Mother said.

'He has more chance of growing up here than he would have in England,' Dad said. 'All that soot. And if he did live, what then? He'd never be independent there the way he will be here. If we go back he'll allus have to work for somebody else.'

'It isn't Jack you're thinking of,' Mother said. 'It's you that doesn't like to work for somebody else.'

'No, I don't.' Dad frowned. 'And Jack won't, either, or the lasses. It's better to live on crusts and be independent than to live on beef and have to knuckle down to somebody for it. Not that we'll live on crusts if we stay here. This country's going to amount to something some day, and them that stays will be a lot better off than anybody in England ever thought of being. But if you want to go back, that's what we'll do.'

'You might be able to get a farm.' Mother sounded uncertain.

'I could if we had a bit of money,' Dad said thoughtfully. 'So I'll tell you what I think would be a good plan. You and the bairns go back now and I'll stay a while. I'll work in summer and live here in winter till I prove up, then I'll sell out and come back. I can make more money here than I can at home and I'll send you plenty to live on. You can get one of them cottages on Ramsden Street near Sam. Happen in a year or two you'll be tired of England. If you are you can come back here and Sam might come with you. There's going to be a lot of building when the railroad gets to Lloydminster, and that's in Sam's line. He allus wanted to get out of England. It might be a rare opportunity for him, and he'd be company for you. What do you think of it?'

A gurgling sound came from Mother's throat. Later she said Dad's wild idea fairly took her breath away, and for a minute she did look queer. Her face turned red and then white, and her blue eyes looked like glass, then all at once she exploded.

'Well!' she cried, and jumped out of her chair, her eyes full of sparks, her small fists clenched, her figure stiff, and her little chin lifted. 'So you're trying to get rid of me, are you? Let me tell you something, Walter Pinder, you aren't going to. Not that way or so easy. They're your children and you're going to look after them.'

'I'll be damned!' Dad said. 'I told you I'd send plenty of—'

'Don't think you can push your bairns off on me,' Mother interrupted, 'or on Sam, either.'

'I'm not. I—'

'Yes, you are.' Mother glared at Dad. 'You want to be rid of us and you know it. Well, your little scheme won't work.'

'I said I'd come home in two years.' Dad's voice was getting loud.

'And in two years you'll have another excuse.' Mother's voice was loud also.

'You're never satisfied.' Dad jumped up.

'And you never say what you mean.'

'You can go home if you want to,' Dad stormed.

'So you're turning me out!' Mother's round chin quivered.

'Good God! I thought you said you wanted to go?'

'I do. I wish I'd never seen Canada, but they're your bairns and you're going to look after them.'

'I allus intended to look after them.' Dad's eyebrows were low over his eyes and his mouth was thin.

'So it's me you don't want.' Mother's voice trembled and tears stood in her eyes. 'And after all I've gone through coming to this country with you.'

'Oh, for God's sake!' Dad grabbed his cap, crammed it on his head, and strode out, slamming the door after him.

'And that's all the thanks I get.' Mother sat down and look unhappily at the door for some time. Her eyes were open but she didn't seem to see or hear anything that went on in the little house. Lily and I fought over a piece of wood that looked like a doll and Jack hit his finger with the hammer and said, 'Damm't,' but Mother paid no attention. She seemed to be turning something over in her mind, first one way then another. 'I wonder if it's that Dukhobor?' she murmured at last, and her whole face frowned.

Still frowning, Mother got up and went outside and brought in a prairie chicken Dad had shot the day before and began to skin it. Lily and I watched her and asked what she was going to make. We rarely had meat for supper.

'Run and play,' Mother said absently and rolled the dark red meat in flour and put it in the frying-pan. Then she set the packing-box table, a job usually mine, and cut some slices of fresh bread, another treat. Mother said fresh bread wasn't good for us.

The kettle was singing cheerfully and the prairie chicken was sizzling merrily and filling the house with its rich meat smell when Dad finally opened the door. He had a few sticks of stove wood on his arm and he came in slowly and glanced around as if sizing up the situation before he spoke. 'Look's like supper's about ready,' he said at last and dropped the wood into the box by the stove. 'Smells good too. I won't be getting such meals when you go.'

Mother straightened her trim shoulders and tossed her little head, topped by its neat coil of hair. 'I'm not going,' she said primly. 'If you think you're going to bring that Dukhobor into my house you're mistaken.'

Dad looked as if the roof had fallen on him, then his eyes began to twinkle. 'I never thought of such a thing.' he said.

'You'd better not.' Mother poured boiling water from the black kettle into the blue teapot.

'Well, I'm glad you changed your mind.' Dad sat down at the packing-box table. He looked perfectly happy.

'It's for the sake of the bairns that I'm staying.' Mother served Dad a large piece of chicken. 'Out of sight is out of mind.'

Dad put a slice of bread in the chicken gravy and a little smile curved his lips. It wasn't because of the bairns that you gave Edmond Bastwo the slip that day at Cleckheaton,' he said. 'We hadn't any bairns then.'

'Me give him the slip!' Mother stared at Dad. 'I never did any such thing. He went to look for Emma—'

'You asked him to go and look for Emma and then you asked me to go and look at the bob-dollies,' Dad said, and his grey, ocean-flecked eyes sparkled.

'Tell the truth if you can,' Mother said. 'It was you that asked me to go and look at the bob-dollies.'

'Well, anyway, you went,' Dad said contentedly.

'And look where it got me.' Mother shook her pretty little head, but her voice sounded pleased and her eyes and her lips were smiling.

NOT A PENNY IN THE WORLD

We come to Calgary in 1898 and then we moved out of there about 10 miles and then my father died, so my mother she took a homestead. Oh yes, a woman could take up land then, but not many did. Not many. I don't know how she did it or how she ever got the idea she could do it. A wonderful woman, my mother, wonderful woman. Even today I don't know how she managed.

See, she had no experience. We weren't farm people. We'd come from the Falkland Islands, and if you know them there's nothing there to farm.

I don't know how in the world she ever got along. Three children, two sisters, and myself and not a penny in the world. Somehow she got a roof over our heads. A neighbor or two helped but she did it all, mostly. That's the kind of women there were then. I wish I had a picture of her to show you. Not a big woman but all this spirit. She knew she had to provide a home for the three of us and that's how she did it, right out on the prairie. She would work 18 hours a day. Absolutely.

At first she'd hire to get a little bit of plowing done when she could get a dollar or two. She'd sell eggs in High River, and sometimes women in the town would hire her for a day. She'd walk in to town, work all day, walk back. For just a few cents. Wages wasn't nothing in those days. Not too many people had money and those that had it were awfully close with it.

First she got an acre plowed and that became a garden. That's an awful lot of garden, but all of us worked in it. We didn't go to school much but we sure worked around the place. In that garden. Then the next year she got another acre plowed and so forth, and after that I was big enough to drive a team around and I plowed up the rest. I can't remember just where she got the horses. I think she must have borrowed them or maybe rented them, because I know we didn't own them. Horses in them days was expensive. So I was behind the plow. How old was I? Oh, 1905, let me see, I'd be about 10. Yes, I was 10 years old. It must have been quite a sight to see a 10-year-old boy behind a big team of horses plowing. It wasn't good land, it was fair land, some alkali, some sand, and I plowed up the whole shooting match.

Yes, I remember now. We rented the team from the money Mother used to make working for other people. She'd get a dollar and a half a day in harvest. She would cook, sometimes for as many as 21 men during harvest.

Between her and me we proved up that homestead and everybody was saying, 'Oh, they'll never make it.' But Mother just kept at it, working away and getting this done one year, that done the next year. A cow, more chickens, later a team. The neighbors were real good when they saw how hard we were all working, and they come and give us a hand.

It was my mother who did it. She just said she was going to have a home for us and that's all there was to it and she went and filed on that homestead. She'd never seen it but the map showed it was on a lake and she thought that would be nice. Having a home by a lake. She said, 'That's the place I want,' and she got it. And then she brought out all the things we had from the place west of Calgary and she rolled up her sleeves and pitched in. She worked 18 hours a day, that woman did. And when it was all over, all those years later when she had a nice farm, if you looked at her talking with other women in town on Saturday, just as quiet and gentle and lady-like, you wouldn't have believed that she could have done it. *As reported to* BARRY BROADFOOT

'KODAM'

J. F. C. Wright

1899

In the South Colony, 'rich' Dukhobors of Novatroitski village loaned $500 to 'poor' Dukhobors of Selkiper village. With this loan the villagers bought food, farm implements, horses. Within seven weeks, the 'rich' went to the 'poor' and took back the horses, saying that payment of the loan was too slow.

Soon after that, each village received a loan of $125 from money sent by Aylmer Maude in England. The Selkiper people bought two wagons and a horse. A few days later the Novatroitski creditors went again to the Selkiper debtors. They collected both wagons and the horse, saying, 'These are ours because you still owe us $58.99.'

'Yes,' said a Selkiper Dukhobor, 'but what of the $66.01 that is still ours? Yet you are taking everything from us.'

The Novatroitski men insisted that was not so. 'You used our money for seven weeks, buying horses with most of it. That was the same as using our horses, so now you must pay by letting us have the last two wagons and the horse.'

Thus the Novatroitski 'rich' went away with the wagons and horse, leaving the Selkiper 'poor' with little more than they had had before it all, but owing Aymler Maude $125.

News of incidents such as these spread, increasing confusion among the brothers. At the same time they became still more dubious of the good intentions of their Russian and English 'guides.' Yet, incongruously enough, 'Tolstoy's followers,' were expected to perform feats of legerdemain and conjure wagons and bags of flour from nothing.

Leon Sulerjitski, at Yorkton to meet a Quaker who was in Canada to visit the Christian Community of Universal Brotherhood, saw a Dukhobor riding an ox and leading another along the dusty main street. Both the lad and the oxen looked as if they had come from a distance.

'Sdorovo, Leo Alexandrovich. It is like this,' the boy began. 'I was sent to you by the elder of our village, because in our village soon there will be no flour left. So, I was sent to bring back some flour. Our neighbors will not haul flour for us now. They used to haul it, but they stopped. So, I was sent.'

'What do you expect me to do?' Sulerjitski asked. 'There is no general fund.'

'Well,' said the lad, blinking his naive and serious blue eyes, 'the elder told me not to come back without a wagon and flour. They said you would find a new wagon and flour, slava Bohu.'

One of the oxen coughed, and the other seemed to roll his round eyes as if to assist the appeal. This, coupled with the thought of the village elders waiting for the lad to return with a hundred sacks of flour, caused Sulerjitski to laugh aloud.

The lad's mouth opened in amazement. How could Leo Alexandrovich be so frivolous?

As if in answer to a prayer, the visiting Quaker came along the street. He had with him a small gift of money for the Christian Community of Universal Brotherhood. And so was the miracle performed. Slava Bohu!

The next morning, the lad, sitting on top of a load of flour in a new green and red wagon, left Yorkton for his village. When he arrived home, he related how 'Leo Alexandrovich likes to tease.' Of course Sulerjitski had known all the time where to get a wagon and a load of flour. How these Russian 'officers' like to joke!

Toward the end of July, women and children of the South Colony trudged through the long grass in search of wild strawberries. They gathered wild spinach too, the nurses, Anna Rabetz and E. Markova, encouraging them because there was indication of scurvy among the children who lacked fresh vegetables and milk.

In Thunder Hill Colony, even Nikolai Zibaroff was becoming disheartened. The men were leaving the railway grade, because they said, they could earn no more than six cents a day. Perplexed, Zibaroff sent a messenger to Sulerjitski, with a request that he find out the trouble.

With horse and buggy, Sulerjitski started over the trail to Cowan, and as he bumped over the shattered corduroy road he pondered on why the Dukhobors could earn no more than six cents a day. Twenty men came toward him through the lane of spruce trees. They marched dejectedly, their clothes mud-spattered and torn. 'Like remnants of Napoleon's retreat from Moscow,' he thought as he greeted them; he asked why were they leaving their work.

They looked at one another. A man in a tattered beshmet brushed a mosquito from the end of his flat nose and said, 'It is no use to stay. We earn only six cents a day.'

'Why is it the other men can make $1.50 a day on the same grade?' Sulerjitski asked.

'Well, Leo Alexandrovich, we have bad places to work. Wet ditches with many stones,' said one.

Sulerjitski, on questioning several others, received the same answer. 'Wet ditches with many stones,' as if repeating a mournful psalm. Puzzled, he drove on. The Dukhobors continued their weary retreat homeward.

Along the trail he met more men straggling back, and each group gave the same answer to his question.

When he reached the railway grade, not a Dukhobor remained at work. He found Turnbull, the civil engineer, and together they walked over the grade where the Dukhobors had been working.

'They would get together and talk,' said Turnbull, 'then a few would leave. I don't know what they were saying, of course, but you can see for yourself that this is not an especially hard section. Besides, they picked their own spots over a mile of right of way, and the good digging averages with the bad fairly well. When they first came they worked hard, threw up a lot of grade and made good wages as good and better than any of the men on the job.' Turnbull was as puzzled as Sulerjitski.

Still without a clue, Sulerjitski returned over the forty-five miles to Thunder Hill Colony. In the villages he found inertia and disinclination to discuss the railway grade enigma.

After a few days of persuasion, early in August, delegates from the thirteen villages reluctantly assembled in Mikhaelovka village. When the last notes of the opening psalm had floated over the goldenrod, desultory discussion began, one Dukhobor blaming another for the failure of the work.

'Wet ditches with many stones,' gave way to, 'Those people in the village of Stradaevka sent only their very young boys to the grade, leaving the strong men at home.'

'Somebody had to stay home and build the houses and barns,' defended a Stradaevka villager.

'All of us have homes to build, and that is no excuse,' replied another.

For hours accusations were passed back and forth with tedious lack of logic.

Sulerjitski, feeling the truth would come out if the discussion continued long enough, passed the time checking accounts from merchants of

Land Office. Some of these counter-check slips had no names of the Dukhobors who had received the merchandise. In these cases, all that the merchant knew was that the man was a Dukhobor and that he had promised the account would be paid from wages earned on the railway grade. Such was their reputation for monetary honesty.

'Postoi! Wait!' shouted Sulerjitski above the babble of voices. 'I will read the accounts to you.'

He read aloud the various items of sugar, boots, butter, socks; more sugar, butter—the delegates interrupted to ask one another, 'Who bought this? Who bought that? . . . Why so many pairs of gloves?'

'Butter, sugar,' Sulerjitski went on, then suddenly, 'two pounds of tobacco.'

'Tobacco!'

'What's that?'

'Who bought it?'

Elders looked at one another in astonishment.

'Someone among us smoking,' Legebokoff exclaimed, face like that of a Spanish inquisitor.

'Why does anyone need tobacco?'

'Who bought it?' again someone asked.

From a back bench came a guilty voice. 'The tobacco, it was bought for tooth medicine. It was—'

'So! That is what happens!' A man with a massive head thrust out his jaw at the culprit. 'Those who do not work, stroll about in low-cut shoes and smoke tabak—knowing they will have their tea with sugar in it from someone else's labor. Then those who go away to earn the money come home in worn-out boots and live on bread. What is the use of working if one lives in a commune?'

One after another, men rose to tell the meeting there was no use working when they could see no benefit from it. . . . 'It would be much better if the bolshoi commune for the thirteen Thunder Hill villages was done away with. . . . Each village should have its own commune. . . . Da, da, then we will know who is working and who is not. . . . What everyone is buying and why . . . where our wages are going. . . .'

Thus the mystery of six cents a day was solved. 'Wet ditches with many stones,' had been a fabrication agreed upon to conceal the real reason for quitting and to avoid, for as long as possible, the disagreeable ordeal of frank discussion.

The delegates decided that in future all money earned by the men of one village should be received and disbursed by the elders of that village —'no more large communes.' Vasili Chernenkoff was elected 'wholesale' treasurer; from wholesale firms in Winnipeg he was to purchase for all the villages, but only after each had told him its needs. Only the men who earned the money would have the right to say how it should be spent. A man leaving the grade before completion of the work would forfeit his right to vote concerning use of earnings.

The new economic policy of Thunder Hill Colony was received so enthusiastically that the men returned to the railway, and old men, women and children worked the harder plowing, hauling logs for stables, plastering houses with clay and piling firewood for the winter. On the grade there was keen competition between the various village groups. Civil Engineer Turnbull was surprised and satisfied. Could these be the same men who, two weeks before, had scratched the ground with their picks and used their shovels to lean on while they argued?

For two weeks the men kept up the tempo of hard work, but toward the end of August they slackened their pace, and began holding meetings again, to discuss leaving the grade and going south for the wheat harvest. Farmers near Winnipeg, they had heard, were paying $35 a month and board. 'All the Canadians have gone to work in the harvest; why is it necessary that we stay here?' said Feduk.

Nikolai Aldakimonich opposed going to the harvest fields. He had discovered that the railway fare to Winnipeg was more than nine dollars each, 'and to walk there would take one week.'

'Why can we not get more money here?' suggested another. 'We should ask the engineer.'

In the morning a delegation approached Turnbull, asking for sixteen cents a cubic yard—two cents more than the original contract. Turnbull refused. If they did not wish to work at the old rate, they could leave, and he would get other men for the job.

Another meeting was called. At the end of two hours discussion they decided to lie down in the shade of the spruce trees 'where we will rest, until we are promised sixteen cents.'

Except for a few flies zigzagging above it, the grade was deserted. Neither the ring of a pick nor the scrape of a shovel disturbed the afternoon air. The foreman, in a brown derby hat, came out of his tent, his horselike lips muttering, 'These bohunks . . . you never know what they are going to do next.' He shouted to the men, 'Why quit? Go to work.'

Ponderously a Dukhobor rose to his feet. '*Schestnawtsat*,' he said holding up his fingers on both hands, then closing them, then opening them to hold up all fingers of one hand and one finger of the other.

The foreman took his pipe out of his mouth. 'You won't get sixteen cents,' he said.

Turnbull telegraphed the Winnipeg office for men, but transient labour was feeding wheat sheaves into humming threshing machines, and no men were available at the wage rate offered by the railway.

For two days the Dukhobors rested, after which Turnbull offered them fifteen cents. They still asked for sixteen, but on the third day they agreed to fifteen and a half cents.

At Cowan, still end of commercial steel, twenty Dukhobors had finished a contract for unloading rails, and they wanted their money before joining the brothers on the grade. The English-speaking foreman had told them, through an interpreter that, as their money must come from Winnipeg, they would have to wait three days.

'Three days? In three days we will have eaten all our food,' said Kuzma.

'And we will lose the wages we would have if we were working with the brothers,' said another.

Kuzma had a suggestion. 'Possibly if we tell the foreman "Kodam," he will get the money for us.'

'What does that mean, "Kodam"?' asked Efrem.

'It means something to those Englishmen. When they are angry and in a hurry they always say, "Kodam,"' said Kuzma. 'Now we are angry at *him* and *we* want our money, dkoro!'

'Da, we should now go and tell the foreman "Kodam."'

The twenty men went to the foreman's car. Kuzma knocked on the car door.

'What do you want?' asked the foreman.

'Moni give,' said Kuzma, holding open his hands.

'I told you you must wait. Come-from-Winnipeg,' said the foreman. He paid no more attention to the Dukhobors but went along the cinder path toward the station.

'Kodam,' shouted Kuzma after him. 'Kodam, Kodam,' echoed the others.

'Kodam, kodam, kodam, kodam,' all joined the chorus, following the foreman to the station like twenty angry geese.

The foreman hurried. He had heard things about these Dukhobors. One could never tell what they would do. They might be peaceful, but what had they done to the fellow in Land Office who put ashes in their tea? It was the first time he had heard them in angry words.

'Kodam, kodam!'

Section men in the yard gaped at the spectacle. The locomotive engineer of the work train, oilcan in hand, paused by the wheels of his panting engine. The telegrapher thrust his head from the station window.

'We must get authority wired from Winnipeg to release their wages,' the foreman told the telegrapher. 'I don't want them hanging around here.'

'Telegram-money-come-today,' he called through the window to the Dukhobors.

That afternoon they received their wages. Thanking the foreman and bowing, they boarded a work train which would take them to within a few miles of where the brothers were working. As the train rocked along the new road-bed, the Dukhobors discussed the magic of the English word, 'Kodam.'

'Pravda,' Semon nodded, 'it is a very important word to the Anglichani.'

The train stopped at the gravel-pit switch, and they climbed out of the bunk car to trudge past rows of new ties and a giant shovel snorting white steam into the clear autumn air.

It was almost time to stop work for the day when they reached the first group of brothers working in the ditch, but the conventional greeting could not be deferred.

'Slava Bohu,' the Dukhobors in the ditch dropping their tools, returned the bow. The greeting proceeded. To hurry it was not the Christian way. Riley, the foreman's assistant, was intrigued with these ceremonies; each time they seemed to fascinate him more, and he fixed the Russian words in his memory. Next morning he felt ready to try it himself, and stopped ceremoniously on the grade.

'Sdorovo jevote,' he said, lifting his straw hat high above his red head and bowing from the waist.

With a clatter the Dukhobors dropped their shovels and picks.

'Slava Bohu,' they raised their caps and bowed.

'Spasi hospodi,' said Riley bowing.

'Spasi hospodi,' returned the spokesman.

'Nashi vam poklon pasilali,' continued Riley, which meant that all Riley's fold bowed to the God within the Dukhobors in the ditch.

'Spasi ich hospodi. May it please the Lord to save them,' the Dukhobors bowed.

Riley bowed once more, put on his straw hat, and, highly pleased with the success of his experiment, went along the grade to the foreman's office.

These greetings became a diversion which relieved the monotony of the camp. When the foreman first caught him at it, they both laughed. But later he warned Riley not to waste the men's time.

On a morning with a cool tang of fall in the air, Riley, unaware that the foreman was walking the grade not far behind him, stopped alongside a gang where big Kuzma was working.

'Sdorovo jevote,' he began, lifting his hat.

'Slava Bohu,' the Dukhobors dropped their tools.

'Spasi hos—'

'Say, Riley,' the foreman shouted, 'I thought I told you to stop that. . . . every time you do it you cut down a man's work by forty minutes. Leave those elephants to their work, I'm telling you. You're getting to be a "godam" nuisance.'

Riley argued with the foreman, the Dukhobors looking, disconcerted by this rude interruption of their ceremony.

Kuzma picked up his shovel, and remarked, 'Pravda, brothers, what they are now saying must be very important, both at once shouting "kodam!"'

DOUKHOBOR

John Newlove

When you die and your weathery corpse
lies on the chipped kitchen table,

the wind blowing the wood of your house
painted in shades of blue, farmer

out from Russia as the century turned,
died, and lay at the feet of the wars,

who will ever be able to say for you
what you thought at the sight of the Czar's horsemen

riding with whips among you, the sight
of the rifles burning in bonfires,

the long sea-voyage, strange customs endured,
officials changing your name

into the strange script that covered the stores,
the polite brown men who spoke no language

you understood and helped you
free your team from Saskatchewan river mud,

who will be able to say for you
just what you thought as the villages marched

naked to Eden and the English
went to war and came back again

with their funny ways, proud
to speak of killing each other, you, whose mind

refused the slaughter, refused the blood,
you who will lie in your house, stiff as winter,

dumb as an ox, unable to love,
while your women sob and offer the visitors tea?

GRANDFATHER

George Bowering

Grandfather
          Jabez Harry Bowering
strode across the Canadian prairie
hacking down trees
          & building churches
delivering personal baptist sermons in them
leading Holy holy holy lord god almighty songs in them
red haired man squared off in the pulpit
reading Saul on the road to Damascus at them

Left home
          big walled Bristol town
at age eight
          to make a living
buried his stubby fingers in root snarled earth
for a suit of clothes & seven hundred gruelly meals a year
taking an anabaptist cane across the back every day
for four years till he was whipt out of England

Twelve years old
        & across the ocean alone
to apocalyptic Canada
        Ontario of bone bending labor
six years on the road to Damascus till his eyes were blinded
with the blast of Christ & he wandered west
to Brandon among wheat kings & heathen Saturday nights
young red haired Bristol boy shoveling coal
in the basement of Brandon college five in the morning

Then built his first wooden church & married
a sick girl who bore two live children & died
leaving several pitiful letters & the Manitoba night

He moved west with another wife & built children & churches
Saskatchewan Alberta British Columbia Holy holy holy
lord god almighty
        struck his labored bones with pain
& left him a postmaster prodding grandchildren with crutches
another dead wife & a glass bowl of photographs
& holy books unopened save the bible by the bed

Till he died the day before his eighty fifth birthday
in a Catholic hospital of sheets white as his hair

THE PILOT'S MEASURE

Ralph Connor

It was Hi Kendal that announced the arrival of the missionary. I was standing at the door of my school, watching the children ride off home on their ponies, when Hi came loping along on his bronco in the loose-jointed cowboy style.

'Well,' he drawled out, bringing his bronco to a dead stop in a single bound, 'he's lit.'

'Lit? Where? What?' said I, looking round for an eagle or some other flying thing.

'Your blanked Sky Pilot; and he's a beauty, a pretty kid—looks too tender for this climate. Better not let him out on the range.' Hi was quite disgusted evidently.

'What's the matter with him, Hi?'

'Why, *he* ain't no parson! I don't go much on parsons, but when I calls for one I don't want no bantam chicken. No, siree, horse! I don't want no blankety-blank, pink-and-white complected nursery kid foolin' round my graveyard. If you're goin' to bring along a parson, why, bring him with his eyeteeth cut and his tail feathers on.'

That Hi was deeply disappointed was quite clear from the selection of the profanity with which he adorned this lengthy address. It was never the extent of his profanity, but the choice, that indicated Hi's interest in any subject.

Altogether, the outlook for the missionary was not encouraging. With the single exception of the Muirs, who really counted for little, nobody wanted him. To most of the reckless young bloods of the Company of the Noble Seven his presence was an offence; to others, simply a nuisance; while the Old Timer regarded his advent with something like dismay; and now Hi's impression of his personal appearance was not cheering.

My first sight of him did not reassure me. He was very slight, very young, very innocent, with a face that might do for an angel, except for the touch of humour in it, but which seemed strangely out of place among the rough, hard faces that were to be seen in the Swan Creek country. It was not a weak face, however. The forehead was high and square, the mouth firm, and the eyes were luminous, of some dark colour—violet, if there is such a colour in eyes—dreamy or sparkling, according to his mood; eyes for which a woman might find use, but which in a missionary's head appeared to me one of those extraordinary wastes of which Nature is sometimes guilty.

He was gazing far away into space infinitely beyond the Foothills and the blue line of the mountains behind them. He turned to me as I drew near, with eyes alight and face glowing.

'It is glorious,' he almost panted. 'You see this every day!' Then, recalling himself, he came eagerly toward me, stretching out his hand. 'You are the schoolmaster, I know. Do you know, it's a great thing? I wanted to be one, but I never could get the boys on. They always got me telling them tales. I was awfully disappointed. I am trying the next best thing. You see, I won't have to keep order, but I don't think I can preach very well. I am going to visit your school. Have you many scholars? Do you know, I think it's splendid? I wish I could do it.'

I had intended to be somewhat stiff with him, but his evident admiration of me made me quite forget this laudable intention, and as he talked on without waiting for an answer, his enthusiasm, his deference to my opinion, his charm of manner, his beautiful face, his luminous eyes, made him perfectly irresistible; and before I was aware I was listening to his plans for working his mission with eager interest. So eager was my interest, indeed, that before I was aware I found myself asking him to tea with me in my shack. But he declined, saying:

'I'd like to, awfully; but do you know, I think Latour expects me.'

This consideration of Latour's feelings almost upset me.

'You come with me,' he added, and I went.

Latour welcomed us with his grim old face wreathed in unusual smiles. The Pilot had been talking to him, too.

'I've got it, Latour!' he cried out as he entered; 'here you are,' and he broke into the beautiful French-Canadian *chanson*, 'A la Claire Fontaine,' to the old half-breed's almost tearful delight.

'Do you know,' he went on, 'I heard that first down the Mattawa,' and away he went into a story of an experience with French-Canadian raftsmen, mixing up his French and English in so charming a manner that Latour, who in his younger days long ago had been a shantyman himself, hardly knew whether he was standing on his beard or on his heels.

After tea I proposed a ride out to see the sunset from the nearest rising ground. Latour, with unexampled generosity, offered his own cayuse, 'Louis.'

'I can't ride well,' protested The Pilot.

'Ah! dat's good ponee, Louis,' urged Latour. 'He's quiet lak wan leetle mouse; he's ride lak—what you call?—wan horse-on-de-rock.' Under which persuasion the pony was accepted.

That evening I saw the Swan Creek country with new eyes—through the luminous eyes of The Pilot. We rode up the trail by the side of the Swan till we came to the coulee mouth, dark and full of mystery.

'Come on,' I said, 'we must get to the top for the sunset.'

He looked lingeringly into the deep shadows and asked; 'Anything live down there?'

'Coyotes and wolves and ghosts.'

'Ghosts?' he asked delightedly. 'Do you know, I was sure there were, and I'm quite sure I shall see them.'

Then we took the Porcupine trail and climbed for about two miles the gentle slope to the top of the first rising ground. There we stayed and watched the sun take his nightly plunge into the sea of mountains, now dimly visible. Behind us stretched the prairie, sweeping out level to the sky and cut by the winding coulee of the Swan. Great long shadows from the hills were lying upon its yellow face, and far at the distant edge the gray haze was deepening into purple. Before us lay the hills, softly curving like the shoulders of great sleeping monsters, their tops still bright, but the separating valleys full of shadow. And there, far beyond then, up against the sky, was the line of the mountains—blue, purple and gold, according as the light fell upon them. The sun had taken his plunge, but he had left behind him his robes of saffron and gold. We stood long without a word or movement, filling our hearts with the silence and the beauty, till the gold in the west began to grow dim. High above all, the night was stretching her star-pierced, blue canopy, and drawing slowly up from the east over the prairie and over the sleeping hills the soft folds of a purple haze. The great silence of the dying day had fallen upon the world and held us fast.

'Listen,' he said in a low tone, pointing to the hills. 'Can't you hear them breathe?' And, looking at their curving shoulders, I fancied I could see them slowly heaving as if in heavy sleep, and I was quite sure I could hear them breathe. I was under the spell of his voice and his eyes, and nature was all living to me then.

We rode back to the Stopping Place in silence, except for a word of mine now and then which he heeded not and, with hardly a good night, he left me at the door. I turned away feeling as if I had been in a strange country and among strange people.

How would he do with the Swan Creek folk? Could he make them see the hills breathe? Would they feel as I felt under his voice and eyes? What a curious mixture he was? I was doubtful about his first Sunday, and was surprised to find all my indifference as to his success or failure gone. It was a pity about the baseball match.* I would speak to some of the men about it tomorrow.

Hi might be disappointed in his appearance, but, as I turned into my shack and thought over my last two hours with The Pilot and how he had 'got' old Latour and myself, I began to think that Hi might be mistaken in his measure of The Pilot.

*The Pilot's first divine service was announced to take place after the annual baseball match.

HOW I LEARNED TO MAKE BREAD

Oh, I'll never forget that first year. I made a perfect fool of myself. A perfect fool.

Bread. My husband said a family needed bread, and I had a recipe book my mother had given me and it told how to make bread. But I just couldn't do it. I tried and tried but it wouldn't rise or it was sour or like lead or big air holes in it. Always something wrong. Well, my husband said, 'Why can't you make the barmy struff?' and I said I had never been taught. After all, in the town I had lived in the baker came around with his wagon and his hot box every morning and you just went out to the lane and chose bread and scones and whatever you wanted. Well Weyburn certainly wasn't England. I'll say that again. My husband told me to ask the neighbors and I said I didn't like the neighbor women. And I didn't. They were coarse. I wasn't putting myself on a pedestal. These women were coarse, gossips. Almost strumpets. Some of them, anyway.

We got this farm paper and there was a column that gave advice and it was printed by a woman called Millicent Miller. I'm sure that was the name. You wrote her a question and she'd answer it, so I wrote this woman—which wasn't her real name, I found out later—and lo and behold in about three weeks the paper came back and there was my letter printed, and with my name on it. Well, you can imagine how I felt. Other letters she printed had initials, like G.T. or B.R. I thought she'd do it with me, but there was Mary Watson, Weyburn, large as life. But there was a recipe to make bread, which as far as I could see was the same as the one in my book. So I just forgot about it that day. I didn't tell my husband, that's for certain.

Next morning there is a knock on the door and I look out and there's a Mrs Ratigan on the stoop. I knew her. She was one of the coarse ones. Irish. A big woman and even though I didn't have much to do with her on our street I believed her to be capable. She just looked like she was. In the store she was always wiping some child's nose or slapping another, but they obeyed her and that was something. Children were as much ruffians in those days as they are now.

When I opened the door she just barged in and said, 'Mary Watson. Weyburn. Bread. I read it,' and she sat down. Then she said, 'Nobody ever learned to make bread out of a book. It takes a mother to teach her daughter. Where's your mother?' I said in Guildford in England and she said, 'Fine. Leave her there. I'll be your mother this morning and we'll make bread.'

And we did. She stood beside me and told me how to mix and how to pour and how to get the heat up and how to punch and poke. When it was rising we sat around and drank tea and I even thought of giving her something in her tea out of my husband's cabinet, but decided I wouldn't. Then she said, 'The Good Lord never said a person always has to have Irish coffee. There's Irish tea, too, you know, dear.' I laughed and got up and got the brandy. I was getting to like her and when I came back with the bottle she poured a great whack in it, smiled, and said, 'If you weren't Anglican I would have said you were one of the true faith.'

She left about three in the afternoon. There wasn't much left in my husband's bottle but I didn't care. He'd forget about that when he saw that I'd learned to bake bread and buns. There were four nice loaves and some buns waiting for him under clean washcloths on the kitchen table when he came home from the store. I was that proud.

He never knew about the little ad I'd put in Millicent Miller's column in the paper. He only found about it years later and he said that half the town must have been laughing at me. I said no, I didn't guess so. I got some very nice smiles when I went shopping after that; people talked to me and I met some nice ladies. And besides, Mrs Ratigan told me that day if anybody laughed at me for what I'd done, she said she'd conk them on the snoot.

As reported to BARRY BROADFOOT

I WANTED TO SAY SOMETHING

Barry McKinnon

they came to conceive the land as enemy and fought
back with god and muscle and stupidity until the first winters
are thru, then spring and the promise enters again, the natural
cycle of trees beginning to bud and green beneath
the slough in the
                    hollow
                        (2 years later, 1910, he got his land/changed
                        beneath his
                                hand . . .

then, the mans task: horses, plows, and hired strangers—
and the fields stretched
                        natural before him
                                    (the thick soil   the enemy

lying flat
          and indians pushed farther east
by the government:

it all begins in innocence: the old news reels,
the chronicles.   shots of the plow, and
black earth cut deep
                              thru the grass
                                                  beneath the roots—earth
split in
          furrows
                    a trench for the
seed.

it all begins in innocence: grand father, mother and brothers, move
along the dawn,
                    the early sweat
                                        and horses too
as beasts of burden, scraping
                                        at the earth
with a purpose
                    inside the geometry of how a man conceives the land, all
without art or grace
and all meditation lacking

clarity

The plains, I think, are too big to be matched by hyperbole; if anything the subtle spaciousness of understatement is the norm.

LAURENCE RICOU

PHILIP WELL

Andrew Suknaski

prairie spring
and i stand here before a tire crimper
two huge vices held by a single bolt
(men of the prairies were grateful to a skilled man
who could use it and fix wooden wheels
when the craft flourished)

i stand here
and think of philip well found in his musty woodshed
this morning
by dunc mcpherson on the edge of wood mountain—
philip well lying silent by his rusty .22

and i ask my village: *who was this man?*
this man who left us

in 1914
well and my father walked south from moose jaw
to find their homesteads
they slept in haystacks along the way
and once nearly burned to death
waking in the belly of hell they were saved by mewling mice
and their song of agony—
a homesteader had struck a match and thought he
would teach them a lesson

well and father lived in a hillside and built fires
to heat stones each day in winter
they hunted and skinned animals to make fur blankets
threw redhot stones into their cellars
overlaid the stones with willows
and slept between hides

father once showed me a picture
nine black horses pulling a gang plough
philip well proudly riding behind (breaking
the homestead to make a home)

well quiet and softspoken
loved horses and trees and planted poplars around his shack
when the land began to drift away

in tough times well bought a tire crimper
and fixed wheels tanned hides and mended harnesses
for people

and later (having grown older and often not feeling well)
moved to wood mountain village
to be near people who could drive him to a doctor
if necessary

today in wood mountain
men's faces are altered by well's passing
while they drink coffee in jimmy hoy's cafe
no one remembers if well had a sweetheart
though someone remembers a school dance near
the montana border one christmas—
well drunk and sleeping on a bench in the corner
while the people danced
well lonelier than judas after the kiss
(the heart's sorrow like a wheel's iron ring
tightening around the brain till
the centre cannot hold and
the body breaks)

THE GREAT LONE LAND

I don't know who first got their hands on a copy of Butler's book on the Wild West, but all the young men in our town read it and they all wanted to come out to the Northwest Territories. Make their fortune.

This book by Butler caused a lot of excitement, but looking back on it I don't know why it should have because he had been writing about another time. Anyway, you know how a bunch of young men are when they get their mind on something. Instead of going to Montreal or Boston or Maine where a lot had gone to before, they all began hightailing it out to the West.

As reported to BARRY BROADFOOT

THE PRAIRIE

Sid Marty

Now but a bruise on the sidehill,
the sod hut they packed their love into
Little more than desire
kept out the sun and the rain
Not much more than love
did they have
there on the ravished plain

Here is their hard won house
abandoned now
that they built from the roots
coming out of the ground at last
to name every direction they wheeled in
and plant their landmark in the air,
to break the desolate arc
. . . but the name of the house is lost
like them

It is a secret kept by the neighbours
who survived
the politics of wind
and money

They will understand me
knowing how hard it is
to corral the wind

And you strangers

knowing only the highway,
you too
can at least imagine
in that extremity
as any desert
the sole relief of a tree

Hunting grouse
on the old abandoned farm,
we found a crabapple tree
heavy with fruit,
eaten only by deer

How many years ago
did the couple we'll say
were young
windburnt flowers
plant the dozen varieties
of trees

Act of love, to seed the prairie
among the buffalo beans,
the old dream shouldered aside

Sliced the turf, and watered green shoots
from mountain streams flowing
under deep black dirt
under the glacial debris

A thousand beaded pails
carried in the heat of summer
flashing of the metal
by the white alkali sloughs

Crabapples cured by frost taste sweet
tasting of cool nights
moonshine cider,
water, the depths of earth

The flavour of love savoured by strangers
lingers on in red crabapples
Though the passion of this house
has faded like a fiery old woman
hugging the wind in her spaces
beneath the open windows of the sky

2ND CONTINGENT OF SASKATOON'S. BRAVE BOYS

THE PRAIRIE AND THE WAR

Robert Stead

The following day Gander began hauling wheat to the elevators at Plainville. During the threshing season, and owing perhaps to the prospect of a rising market, Jackson Stake had hauled out a few loads in order to meet his need of ready cash and had then gone on with his fall ploughing. But now the ground was hard with frost and bleak with a thin fretwork of dusty snow. On the frozen prairie trails the rattle of an empty wagon could be heard for miles.

Gander harnessed a four-horse team—three old Clydesdales that had long since lost all but a flicker of fractiousness and young Jim, the colt, who could be counted upon to behave himself in such a preponderance of good company. Jim's first glimpse of the serious side of life had been in the fall ploughing There he bent a surprised and protesting shoulder into his collar, marvelling the while at the strange turn in events which had taken him from the freedom of the pasture field to the irksome monotony of dragging a wholly purposeless device up and down an interminable furrow. But discipline soon ground the imagination out of his soul as it does to other beasts of burden besides horses, and already he accepted straining on his traces as a distasteful but inevitable procedure.

The horses were harnessed in double tandem, two abreast, and Gander skilfully swung the rear team to position on either side of the wagon tongue. He slouched about their heads and heels in long, ungainly strides, but there was speed in his gracelessness; in a moment he had the tongue in the neck-yoke, the traces hitched to the whiffletrees. A word, a touch of the reins, and the four horses moved off as one, while Gander circled them around to the spot where the grain box had been dropped in the centre of the yard after its previous use. There were puffs, and grunts, and straining of hard muscles while father and son heaved the heavy box to position. Jackson Stake threw two scoop-shovels into the box while Gander, already up over the front wheel, directed his team toward a spot in the field where a strawstack raised its mountainous dome, half-crusted with snow, against the grey November sky.

'I'll have to get me some port'ble graineries,' said Jackson, who with as much alacrity as his son had climbed over the rear end of the box after the wagon was in motion. 'Skid 'em around wherever we want 'em.'

As they neared the mountain of straw a grain bin seemed to detach itself and stand a little to one side. It was a square box framed of boards to a height of seven or eight feet and tied together across the top with strands of heavy wire. Into this the grain had been spouted straight from the separator. When filled with wheat it was covered with a thick cap of straw to keep out rain and snow, and left to stand until a suitable time for marketing.

Beside the bin were two long-haired steers, licking up stray kernels that leaked out between the boards. Jackson Stake threw a shovel at them as a matter of principle, then got out, gathered up his shovel, and, again with his surprising alacrity, clambered onto the bin. Here the two men turned back the straw until they bared the golden bosom of the wheat below; thrust went the shovels into that chaste embrace; then, singing, the wheat slid into the great box, where it rattled like nails on the wooden floor. Thrust and swing, thrust and swing, went the shovels, while the golden tide slowly rose in the box. The men worked on, without conversation and with the precision of machines, until the box was full; then, when the flood lapped its very lip, they threw their shovels on board, and Jackson Stake, straightening his great frame, rested his hands on his kidneys in a way he had and twisted his back for relief.

'You take 'er in, Gander,' he said, 'an' don' let them rogues in Plainville rob you any more'n seems necessary.'

Gander threw his folded horse-blankets across the front of the load, settled himself into a comfortable, shapeless heap upon them, and snapped a sharp order to his team, which tightened their traces and swung off slowly toward the Plainville road.

It was a long, slow haul to the market town, under a sky curtained with grey clouds and shaking an occasional threatening snowflake in the air, by stark clumps of leafless poplars, along trails rutted smooth with the broad tires of many wagons, through a world in which nature had already hibernated for her long sleep until another spring. As Gander crouched on his blankets, his cap down about his ears, his collar up around them, he, too, might have been a lifeless thing but for the occasional automatic word of command or suggestion to his horses. It was a great opportunity to think, and in his way Gander made use of it. He wondered what price his load would bring, and how many bushels he carried in that heaving box. He wondered whether he would spend an hour or two in town; maybe get a haircut at the barber's shop and pick up the latest gossip in the poolroom. Perhaps, too, he thought a little of that dark cloud which hung over all the world, and even sometimes wrapped its noisome mists about his heart. And when he thought of that he thought of Jo Burge, and wondered. Gander had no definite idea about Jo Burge. Still, he supposed that sometime—That would be the natural thing, and Gander lived close to nature. Her beauties may fall upon blind eyes, her harmonies upon deaf ears, but her instincts, unerring, stir in every clod.

As he neared Plainville Gander became aware of other traffic on the road. Now and again an automobile or buggy overtook him, pulled out onto the rough prairie at the side, rutted with tracks made in wet weather and now corrugated into frozen ridges, and went bumping by. Other heavily-laden wagons in front and still others behind, the faster teams gradually overtaking the slower but unable to pass, resolved themselves into an irregular procession—the march of King Wheat into the gates of the world.

Gander drew up in the straggling street that skirted the railway track at Plainville. On his right a row of garages, livery stables, implement warehouses, grocery and hardware stores, offices; on his left the huge bulk of the grain elevators, each with its squat little engine room from which came the intermittent spit . . . spit . . . of the gasoline motor. The air was filled with the dust of wheat; around the elevators were drifts of chaff in which one or two outlaw cows of the town were browsing; from the railway track came the sound, like rushing water, of wheat being piped into cars for shipment, first to Fort William or Port Arthur and later to those hiving lands of Europe now so assiduously engaged in a business of their own, but a business which could not be carried on for long without the help of that little red kernel, mightier than siege guns and battleships. . . . Gander straightened into the attitude of a biped and awaited the verdict of the buyers.

They came presently, three of them, from the wagon just ahead. With a great show of competition they clambered up Gander's wheels and dug their hands into his ruddy load, sifting samples through their fingers, turning them over in their palms, smelling them, chewing a few kernels.

'All I can see is a Three Northern,' said one.

'Just what I was going to say,' said another.

'You beat me to it,' said the third with a gesture of annoyance.

'Then you better get somethin' done for your eyes, all of you,' said Gander. 'I can see a One Northern, and I ain't wearin' no glasses.'

The three buyers laughed as though Gander had perpetrated a great joke. But Gander wasn't laughing. His gorge was boiling within him. He had the farmer's deep-rooted sense of injustice over the fact that whenever he bought he had to pay the seller's price, but whenever he sold, the buyer dictated the figure. His gorge boiled none the cooler for the helplessness of his position.

'Take another look,' said Gander to the three buyers, who, for competitors, seemed to him to be on much too friendly terms with each other. 'Its a One Northern, or there ain't no such thing.'

'No, Gander,' said one who knew him. 'It's nice wheat, all right, but a little bleached, and you're lucky to get a Three out of it. Rusted, too. I dunno but I was a little rash in offering you Three for it; may not go any better than Four.'

'That's what I was thinking,' said the second.

'Yep. It's pretty risky,' said the third.

'Well, I'll ship it myself,' said Gander, with a show of finality. 'I'll get a bin an' ship it myself.'

'That's risky, too,' his acquaintance told him. 'The lakes'll be freezing up pretty soon, and if you don't get your car down before the close of navigation you're in for a bump. Besides, I don't know whether you can get a bin.'

Gander's inquiries proved this misgiving to be well founded. Individual bins, in which a farmer may store and ship his own wheat, were at a premium. The alternative of loading a car direct over the loading platform without making use of an elevator was out of the question; he had no car, and no idea when he could get one. He came back to the buyer who had made him the first offer.

'Guess I'll have to take your price, George, but it don' seem right. That wheat's better'n Three Northern.'

'You're all wrong, Gander,' the buyer said pleasantly.

'I'll be lucky if I get out on it. But I'll tell you what I'll do. I'll send a sample to Winnipeg for official grading—or you can do it—and if it goes higher than Three I'll pay you the difference, but if it goes lower you pay me the difference. That's fair, Gander.'

'Oh, take it!' said Gander, helplessly. This was not his world. He was a producer, not a seller.

Gander drove his team up the gangway into one of the elevators. He guided his four horses with a dexterity that was an art, bringing the great load to position to an inch. This was his world. The load was weighed as it stood in the wagon; the warehouseman touched a lever; the front end of the wagon went up, the rear end down; a trap door in the back of the wagon box was opened and the wheat rushed out in a golden stream into a hopper under the driveway. It was all over in a minute. Gander got his ticket, good for cash at the bank, and drove on.

He put his team in a livery stable, rubbing down their fetlocks and wiping the sweat out from under their collars before he left them, and then went to the Chinese restaurant to get a bite of dinner. The 'Chink's place' was a comparatively new establishment in Plainville. It rejoiced in a painted signboard, 'No Sing—Wun Lung,' which occasioned much local merriment. If the owner knew the reason for the amusement he gave no hint, but it is a good thing to have men come into your place of business smiling. Gander patronized the slant-eyed gentleman with the vocal disadvantages not on account of the wit in his signboard but in order to escape the tyranny of tablecloths and napkins with which the Palace Hotel insisted on encumbering its guests. Besides, the meals were ten cents cheaper.

Gander was bent industriously over pork and potatoes when two young men in uniform entered and took seats at the next table. He observed them under his eyebrows. Their faces were clean shaven and their hair was close cropped about the ears and up from the back of the neck—a fact that recalled Gander's own need of tonsorial attention. Their uniforms sat upon them snugly, and Gander could not but admit that they probably looked much more handsome than he, in his overalls and smock drawn tight over an old tweed suit which he had put on for warmth. And they appeared to be quite happy. If they were charged with the duty of saving the world from the Germans they evidently were not worried about it. Gander was no eavesdropper, but he would have had to stuff his fingers in his ears—those ears over which the hair straggled and curled—in order to avoid hearing some of their remarks. They seemed to be talking about girls. Yes, there was no doubt they were talking about girls.

No Sing or Wun Lung or both (no one seemed to know whether the name was singular or plural) combined a grocery business with his restaurant, and at this moment, as though to afford a proper setting for the military conversation, two young girls of Plainville came in to buy a can of salmon. Gander had no idea that the purchase of so trifling an atom of commerce could exhaust so much time, so much giggling, so much obvious desire to be observed. He had no delusions as to the audience for whose benefit this performance was presented. In a dusty, fly-specked mirror he could see his own humped profile, his shaggy locks, the long hair about his ears and neck, the fuzz on his lips and chin. . . .

With colour rising in his cheeks Gander gulped the remainder of his meal, paid for it, and hurried into the street. The sharp tang of the November air was a tonic and a stimulant. He walked by an implement warehouse and a garage and stopped in front of a barber's shop. For a moment he stood irresolute, then plunged inside and flopped into the empty chair.

'Haircut?' said the barber.

'Yep,' said Gander. 'Mow it good and short.'

'Military cut, eh?'

Gander wasn't very sure. 'Yep,' he hazarded.

'Thinking of joining up, maybe?' the barber suggested.

'Well, not today,' said Gander.

The barber's chair was by the window where the light was good, and further back were pool tables, with several young men playing at them, and a fringe of others seated on benches around the wall. Here again Gander noticed two or three men in khaki. Suddenly another in a smarter uniform came through the door, and as he did so the soldiers in the room sprang to their feet, clicking their heels together, squaring their shoulders and looking generally as though they had been petrified into an attitude of aggressive immobility.

'All right, men, carry on,' said the officer smartly, and the petrification suddenly ran limp again. Something in the voice stirred Gander's memory, and he studied the officer's face for a moment. It was Andy Lee, the clothes presser! And men springing to their feet, and clicking their heels!

'A little shampoo?' the barber suggested. 'Fine to take the dust out of the hair.'

'Sure; hop to it!' said Gander recklessly. He was in the intoxication of his first reaction to the war. Three-quarters of an hour later he walked out of the barber's shop, shampooed, shaved, massaged, scented, and with the pride of his soul somewhat restored.

He made some purchases for his mother at Sempter & Burton's; then, wishing to give his horses ample time to feed and rest, he loitered about the elevators. The gasoline engines fascinated him. They were so like and so unlike steam. Less human than steam, and more mechanical, but still somewhat on the same principle. Thumping faithfully away without supervision; that was the remarkable thing about them. Gander was looking forward to the day when he would persuade his father to buy a threshing mill, and wondering whether it would be steam or gasoline.

'Still,' he said, as though in answer to an argument within himself, 'when you got steam you got steam, but when you got one o' these chapunkers you don' know what you got.'

A freight train pulled in, picked up some cars, and pulled out again. Gander watched the huge engine struggling with its load. He caught a glimpse of the engineer up in his seat in the cab, a lever in his hand. That was power for you! That was life! Sometimes in the wildest flights of his imagination Gander thought of himself as a locomotive engineer.

When the horses were well rested he hitched up again and started for home. He was barely out of town when, in a vacant space, he saw four or five soldiers drilling. They were near the road, and Gander, curious, allowed his team to come to a stop. It seemed that four were drilling and the fifth was giving orders. Gander gathered also that the fifth was disappointed in the way in which his orders were being executed.

'Na-a-gh, I didn't say "Right turn," I said "Left turn."' Do you not know one side o' you from the other? Or will I have to tie a string on your fingers? A little silk bow, maybe. Now try it again, and see if you can all turn the same way for once.

'Left—turn!' The sergeant's voice snapped through the cold air. 'Quick—march! . . . Form two-deep! . . . Form—fours! Na-a-gh, I didn't say "Left turn"; I said "Form fours." As you were! *As-you-were!*'

The sergeant's voice indicated, as only a sergeant's voice can indicate, the hopelessness of instilling intelligence into heads so ill-designed to receive it. He explained this in a monologue of some length while Gander's Adam's apple hopped boisterously about, for had he not at this moment, in spite of the khaki, recognized the bucolic figure of Freddie Gordon? Gander chuckled outright. So this was war? Strutting about on a vacant lot, like a flock of mating prairie chickens! Being told you don't know one foot from another—and proving it! Taking the lip of that fresh guy, and not saying a word back at him! Ha!

At this moment Freddie Gordon, glancing toward the road, recognized the humped figure on the wagon, and Gander, with the most innocent of intentions, sang out cheerily, 'Lo Fred! How's she goin'?'

Freddie twisted his mouth as though to speak, but before any sound had been emitted the sergeant intervened. 'Silence!' he roared. 'Silence in the ranks! You're not gawkin' now on the street corner, me lads, remarkin' on the weather. 'Shun! As you were! 'Shun! As you were! 'Shun! As you were! Put some gimp into it! With the help o' God I'll make soldiers of you yet.' The sergeant's voice suggested an imprecation rather than a prayer. 'And *I'll* take care of your conversational duties for the time bein', me lads. 'Shun!'

The sergeant surveyed his four 'rookies,' now galvanized into a convulsive attitude supposed to represent attention. Suddenly his voice fell from its note of autocratic command to one of amiability. 'Stand at ease! Stand easy! Now I'll just interview our visitor.'

He came over to the wagon where Gander, despite a sudden impulse for flight, remained immobile.

'Well, me lad,' he said in a quite friendly manner, 'you seem interested. Perhaps you were thinkin' of joinin' up?'

'Not partic'lar,' said Gander.

'It's a great life, and you're a likely lookin' chap.'

But Gander was irritated by what he had seen and heard. It clashed with all his ideas of democracy. When Gander worked for his father, or Bill Powers, he counted himself as good a man as the boss. So did the boss. But here was a boss who said things to his men—well, if Bill Powers had said them to *his* men they would have given him directions to his ultimate destination.

'Do you have to learn that new-fangled square dance before you can kill a German?' said he.

'It's discipline, me lad, discipline. An army is built on discipline.'

'It may be what you call it, but it looks to me like a new kind o' square dance—an' I ain't much of a dancer,' Gander retorted. 'Giddap!' He chirped to his horses and left the astonished sergeant standing by the road.

As he wound his slow course homeward through the closing night Gander chuckled more than once over his smart repartee. 'I ain't much of a dancer,' he would say to himself. 'That got him. He didn't know what to say.'

But that was all on the surface. Down underneath was a gnawing sense—a sense that he was running away from something, that he was a fugitive, taking refuge on the farm! He actually experienced a feeling of escape from danger as he rumbled over the ridge beyond the school and the light in Double F's kitchen window came into view.

'But I can't do anythin' else,' he argued with himself. 'I promised both Dad and Mother I'd stick to 'em, an' I guess that's my job.'

He felt the cold air on his ears and neck, and turned his collar closer around them. From that he fell to thinking of the girls in the restaurant, and of how obviously they had ignored him, playing their little patter to the two men in uniform. And up through the grey night came a picture of Josephine Burge—Jo of his old school days, of his herding days, of the threshing gang where she had said, 'Maybe some day he'll wear a real VC.'

His happiness over the discomfiture of the sergeant seeped from him, and at supper he was more silent than usual. His father attributed his gloom to the after effects of a tonsorial spree which had cost him a dollar and a half.

In the literature of Saskatchewan and the other prairie provinces there is a sort of familiarity with forces that everywhere else are considered scourges. I remember a certain page by W. O. Mitchell in which he describes a snowstorm with a certain fellow-feeling, so that it is not easy to tell whether he saw this grandiose spectacle from the stage or from a very comfortable loge in the theatre: 'A tin can rolled in the street, a newspaper plastered itself against the base of a telephone pole'—the description begins like a simple, almost friendly thing.

EUGÈNE CLOUTIER

THE PLAY

Nellie McClung

'Sorry, sir,' said the man in the box-office of the Grand, 'but the house has been sold out for two days now. The standing room has gone too.'

'Can you tell me what this is all about, that every one is so crazy to see it?' the man at the wicket asked, with studied carelessness. He was a thick-set man, with dark glasses, and wore a battered hat, and a much bedraggled waterproof.

'The women here have got up a Parliament, and are showing tonight,' said the ticket-seller. 'They pretend that only women vote, and women only sit in Parliament. The men will come, asking for the vote, and they'll get turned down good and plenty, just like the old man turned them down.'

'Did the Premier turn them down?' asked the stranger. 'I didn't hear about it.'

'Did he? I guess, yes—he ripped into them in his own sweet way. Did you ever hear the old man rage? Boy! Well, the women have a girl here who is going to do his speech. She's the woman Premier, you understand, and she can talk just like him. She does everything except chew the dead cigar. The fellows in behind say it's the richest thing they ever heard. The old boy will have her shot at sunrise, for sure.'

'He won't hear her,' said the man in the waterproof, with sudden energy. 'He won't know anything about it.'

'Sure he will. The old man is an old blunderbuss, but he's too good a sport to stay away. They're decorating a box for him, and have his name on it. He can't stay away.'

'He can if he wants to,' snapped the other man. 'What does he care about this tommyrot—he'll take no notice of it.'

'Well,' said the man behind the wicket, 'I believe he'll come. But say, he sure started something when he got these women after him. They're the sharpest-tongued things you ever listened to, and they have their speeches all ready. The big show opens tonight, and every seat is sold. You may get a ticket though at the last minute, from some one who cannot come. There are always some who fail to show up at the last. I can save you a ticket if this happens. What name?'

'Jones,' said the gentleman in the waterproof. No doubt the irritation in his voice was caused by having to confess to such a common name. 'Robertson Jones. Be sure you have it right,' and he passed along the rail to make room for two women who also asked for tickets.

The directors of the Woman's Parliament knew the advertising value of a mystery, being students of humanity, and its odd little ways. They knew that people are attracted by the unknown; so in their advance notices they gave the names of all the women taking part in the play, but one. The part of the Premier—the star part—would be taken by a woman whose identity they were 'not at liberty to reveal.' Well-known press women were taking the other parts, and their pictures appeared on the posters, but no clue was given out as to the identity of the woman Premier.

Long before sundown, the people gathered at the theatre door, for the top gallery would open for rush seats at seven. Even the ticket holders had been warned that no seat would be held after eight o'clock.

Through the crowd came the burly and aggressive form of Robertson Jones, still wearing his dark glasses, and with a disfiguring strip of court plaster across his cheek. At the wicket he made inquiry for his ticket, and was told to stand back and wait. Tickets were held until eight o'clock.

In the lobby, flattening himself against the marble wall, he waited, with his hat well down over his face. Crowds of people, mostly women, surged past him, laughing, chattering, feeling in their ridiculous bags for their tickets, or the price of a box of chocolates at the counter, where two red-gold blondes presided.

Inside, as the doors swung open, he saw a young fellow in evening dress, giving out handbills, and an exclamation almost escaped him. He had forgotten all about Peter Neelands!

Robertson Jones, caught in the eddies of women, buffeted by them, his toes stepped upon, elbowed, crowded, grew more and more scornful of their intelligence, and would probably have worked his way out—if he could, but the impact of the crowd worked him forward.

'A silly, cackling hen-party,' he muttered to himself. 'I'll get out of this—it's no place for a man—Lord deliver me from a mob like this, with their crazy tittering. There ought to be a way to stop these things. It's demoralizing—it's unseemly.'

It was impossible to turn back, however, and he found himself swept inside. He thought of the side door as a way of escape, but to his surprise, he saw the whole Cabinet arriving there and filing into the boxes over which the colors of the Province were draped; every last one of them, in evening dress.

That was the first blow of the evening! Every one of them had said they would not go—quite scornfully—and spoke of it as 'The Old Maid's Convention'—Yet they came!

He wedged his way back to the box office, only to find that there was no ticket for him. Every one had been lifted. But he determined to stay.

Getting in again, he approached a man in a shabby suit, sitting in the last row.

'I'll give you five dollars for your seat,' he whispered.

'Holy smoke!' broke from the astonished seatholder, and then, recovering from his surprise, he said, 'Make it ten.'

'Shut up then, and get out—here's your money,' said Mr Jones harshly, and in the hurriedly vacated seat, he sat down heavily.

Behind the scenes, the leader of the Woman's Party gave Pearl her parting words:

'Don't spare him, Pearl,' she said, with her hand around the girl's shoulder, 'it is the only way. We have coaxed, argued, reasoned, we have shown him actual cases where the laws have worked great injustice to women. He is blind in his own conceit, and cannot be moved. This is the only way—we can break his power by ridicule—you can do it, Pearl. You can break down a wall of prejudice to-night that would take long years to wear away. Think of cases you know, Pearl, and strike hard. Better to hurt one, and save many! This is a play—but a deadly serious one! I must go now and make the curtain speech.'

'This is not the sort of Parliament we think should exist,' she said, before the curtain, 'this is the sort of Parliament we have at the present time—one sex making all the laws. We have a Parliament of women tonight, instead of men, just to show you how it looks from the other side. People seem to see a joke better sometimes when it is turned around.'

Robertson Jones shrugged his shoulders in disgust. What did they hope to gain, these freaks of women, with their little plays and set little speeches. Who listened or noticed? No one, positively no one.

Then the lights went out in the house, and the asbestos curtain came slowly down and slowly crept into the ceiling again, to re-assure the timorous, and the beautiful French garden, with its white statuary, and fountain, against the green trees, followed its plain asbestos sister, and the Woman's Parliament was revealed in session.

The Speaker, in purple velvet, with a sweeping plume in her three-cornered hat, sat on the throne; pages in uniform answered the many calls of the members, who, on the Government side were showing every sign of being bored, for the Opposition had the floor, and the honorable member from Mountain was again introducing her bill to give the father equal guardianship rights with the mother. She pleaded eloquently that two parents were not any too many for children to have. She readily granted that if there were to be but one parent, it would of course be the mother, but why skimp the child on parents? Let him have both. It was nature's way. She cited instances of grave injustice done to fathers from having no claim on their offspring.

The Government members gave her little attention. They read their papers, one of the Cabinet Ministers tatted, some of the younger members powdered their noses, many ate chocolates. Those who listened, did so to sneer at the honorable member from Mountain, insinuating she took this stand so she might stand well with the men. This brought a hearty laugh, and a great pounding of the desks.

When the vote was taken, the House divided along party lines. Yawningly the Government members cried 'No!'

Robertson Jones sniffed contemptuously; evidently this was a sort of Friday afternoon dialogue, popular at Snookum's Corners, but not likely to cause much of a flutter in the city.

There was a bill read to give dower rights to men, and the leader of the Opposition made a heated defence of the working man who devotes his life to his wife and family, and yet has no voice in the disposition of his property. His wife can sell it over his head, or will it away, as had sometimes been done.

The Attorney General, in a deeply sarcastic vein, asked the honorable lady if she thought the wife and mother would not deal fairly—even generously with her husband. Would she have the iron hand of the law intrude itself into the sacred precincts of the home, where little cherub faces gather round the hearth, under the glow of the glass-fringed hanging lamp. Would she dare to insinuate that love had to be buttressed by the law? Did not a man at the altar, in the sight of God and witnesses, endow his wife with all his goods? Well then—were those sacred words to be blasphemed by an unholy law which compelled her to give back what he had so lovingly given? When a man marries, cried the honorable Attorney General, he gives his wife his name—and his heart—and he gives them unconditionally. Are not these infinitely more than his property? The greater includes the less—the tail goes with the hide! The honorable leader of the Opposition was guilty of a gross offense against good taste, in opening this question again. Last session, the session before, and now this session, she has harped on this disagreeable theme. It has become positively indecent.

The honorable leader of the Opposition begged leave to withdraw her motion, which was reluctantly granted, and the business of the House went on.

A page brought in the word that a delegation of men were waiting to be heard.

Even the Opposition laughed. A delegation of men, seemed to be an old and never-failing joke.

Some one moved that the delegation be heard, and the House was resolved into a committee of the whole, with the First Minister in the chair.

The first minister rose to take the chair, and was greeted with a round of applause. Opera glasses came suddenly to many eyes, but the face they saw was not familiar. It was a young face, under iron gray hair, large dark eyes, and a genial and pleasant countenance.

For the first time in the evening, Mr Robertson Jones experienced a thrill of pleasure. At least the woman Premier was reasonably good looking. He looked harder at her. He decided she was certainly handsome, and evidently the youngest of the company.

The delegation of men was introduced and received—the House settled down to be courteous, and listen. Listening to delegations was part of the day's work, and had to be patiently borne.

The delegation presented its case through the leader, who urged that men be given the right to vote and sit in Parliament. The members of the Government smiled tolerantly. The First Minister shook her head slowly and absentmindedly forgot to stop. But the leader of the delegation went on.

The man who sat in the third seat from the back found the phrasing strangely familiar. He seemed to know what was coming. Sure enough, it was almost word for word the arguments the women had used when they came before the House. The audience was in a pleasant mood, and laughed at every point. It really did not seem to take much to amuse them.

When the delegation leader had finished, and the applause was over, there was a moment of intense silence. Every one leaned forward, edging over in their seats to get the best possible look.

The Woman Premier had risen. So intent was the audience in their study of her face, they forgot to applaud. What they saw was a tall, slight girl whose naturally brilliant coloring needed no make-up; brilliant dark eyes, set in a face whose coloring was vivid as a rose, a straight mouth with a whimsical smile. She gave the audience one friendly smile, and then turned to address the delegation.

She put her hands in front of her, locking her fingers with the thumbs straight up, gently moving them up and down, before she spoke.

The gesture was familiar. It was the Premier's own, and a howl of recognition came from the audience, beginning in the Cabinet Minister's box.

She tenderly teetered on her heels, waiting for them to quiet down, but that was the occasion for another outburst.

'Gentlemen of the Delegation,' she said, when she could be heard, 'I am glad to see you!'

The voice, a throaty contralto, had in it a cordial paternalism that was as familiar as the Premier's face.

'Glad to see you—come any time, and ask for anything you like. You are just as welcome this time as you were the last time! We like delegations—and I congratulate this delegation on their splendid, gentlemanly manners. If the men in England had come before their Parliament with the frank courtesy you have shown, they might still have been enjoying the privilege of meeting their representatives in this friendly way.'

'But, gentlemen, you are your own answer to the question; you are the product of an age which has not seen fit to bestow the gift you ask, and who can say that you are not splendid specimens of mankind? No! No! any system which can produce the virile, splendid type of men we have before us today, is good enough for me, and,' she added, drawing up her shoulders in perfect imitation of the Premier when he was about to be facetious, 'if it is good enough for me—it is good enough for anybody.'

The people gasped with the audacity of it! The impersonation was so good—it was weird—it was uncanny. Yet there was no word of disrespect. The Premier's nearest friends could not resent it.

Word for word, she proceeded with his speech, while the theatre rocked with laughter. She was in the Premier's most playful, God-bless-you mood, and simply radiated favors and goodwill. The delegation was flattered, complimented, patted on the head, as she dilated on their manly beauty and charm.

In the third seat from the back, Mr Robertson Jones had removed his dark glasses, and was breathing like a man with double pneumonia. A dull, red rage burned in his heart, not so much at anything the girl was saying, as the perfectly idiotic way the people laughed.

'I shouldn't laugh,' a woman ahead of him said, as she wiped her eyes, 'for my husband has a Government job and he may lose it if the Government members see me, but if I don't laugh, I'll choke. Better lose a job than choke.'

'But my dear young friends,' the Premier was saying, 'I am convinced you do not know what you are asking me to do;' her tone was didactic now; she was a patient Sunday School teacher, laboring with a class of erring boys, charitable to their many failings and frailties, hopeful of their ultimate destiny, 'you do not know what you ask. You have not thought of it, of course, with the natural thoughtlessness of your sex. You ask for something which may disrupt the whole course of civilization. Man's place is to provide for his family, a hard enough task in these strenuous days. We hear of women leaving home, and we hear it with deepest sorrow. Do you know why women leave home? There is a reason. Home is not made sufficiently attractive. Would letting politics enter the home help matters. Ah no! Politics would unsettle our men. Unsettled men mean unsettled bills—unsettled bills mean broken homes—broken vows—and then divorce.'

Her voice was heavy with sorrow, and full of apology for having mentioned anything so unpleasant.

Many of the audience had heard the Premier's speech, and almost all had read it, so not a point was lost.

An exalted mood was on her now—a mood that they all knew well. It had carried elections. It was the Premier's highest card. His friends called it his magnetic appeal.

'Man has a higher destiny than politics,' she cried, with the ring in her voice that they had heard so often, 'what is home without a bank account? The man who pays the grocer rules the world. Shall I call men away from the useful plow and harrow, to talk loud on street corners about things which do not concern them. Ah, no, I love the farm and the hallowed associations—the dear old farm, with the drowsy tinkle of cow-bells at even tide. There I see my father's kindly smile so full of blessing, hard-working, rough-handed man he was, maybe, but able to look the whole world in the face. . . . You ask me to change all this.'

Her voice shook with emotion, and drawing a huge white linen handkerchiefs from the folds of her gown, she cracked it by the corner like a whip, and blew her nose like a trumpet.

The last and most dignified member of the Cabinet, caved in at this, and the house shook with screams of laughter. They were in the mood now to laugh at anything she said.

'I wonder will she give us one of his rages,' whispered the Provincial Secretary to the Treasurer.

'I'm glad he's not here,' said the Minister of Municipalities, 'I'm afraid he would burst a blood vessel; I'm not sure but I will myself.'

'I am the chosen representative of the people, elected to the highest office this fair land has to offer. I must guard well its interests. No upsetting influence must mar our peaceful firesides. Do you never read, gentlemen?' she asked the delegation, with biting sarcasm, 'do you not know of the disgraceful happenings in countries cursed by manhood suffrage? Do you not know the fearful odium into which the polls have fallen—is it possible you do not know the origin of that offensive word "Poll-cat"; do you not know that men are creatures of habit—give them an inch—and they will steal the whole sub-division, and although it is quite true, as you say, the polls are only open once in four years—when men once get the habit—who knows where it will end—it is hard enough to keep them at home now! No, history is full of unhappy examples of men in public life; Nero, Herod, King John—you ask me to set these names before your young people. Politics has a blighting, demoralizing influence on men. It dominates them, hypnotizes them, pursues them even after their earthly career is over. Time and again it has been proven that men came back and voted—even after they were dead.'

The audience gasped at that—for in the Premier's own riding, there were names on the voters' lists, taken, it was alleged, from the tombstones.

'Do you ask me to disturb the sacred calm of our cemetries?' she asked, in an awe-striken tone—her big eyes filled with the horror of it. 'We are doing very well just as we are, very well indeed. Women are the best students of economy. Every woman is a student of political economy. We look very closely at every dollar of public money, to see if we couldn't make a better use of it ourselves, before we spend it. We run our elections as cheaply as they are run anywhere. We always endeavor to get the greatest number of votes for the least possible amount of money. That is political economy.'

There was an interruption then from the Opposition benches, a feeble protest from one of the private members.

The Premier's face darkened; her eyebrows came down suddenly; the veins in her neck swelled, and a perfect fury of words broke from her lips. She advanced threateningly on the unhappy member.

'You think you can instruct a person older than yourself, do you—you with the brains of a butterfly, the acumen of a bat; the backbone of a jelly-fish. You can tell me something, can you? I was managing governments when you were sitting in your high chair, drumming on a tin plate with a spoon.' Her voice boomed like a gun. 'You dare to tell me how a government should be conducted.'

The man in the third seat from the back held to the arm of the seat, with hands that were clammy with sweat. He wanted to get up and scream. The words, the voice, the gestures were as familiar as his own face in the glass.

Walking up and down, with her hands at right angles to her body, she stormed and blustered, turning eyes of rage on the audience, who rolled in their seats with delight.

'Who is she, Oh Lord. Who is she?' the Cabinet ministers asked each other for the hundredth time.

'But I must not lose my temper,' she said, calming herself and letting her voice drop, 'and I never do—never—except when I feel like it—and am pretty sure I can get away with it. I have studied self-control, as you all know—I have had to, in order that I may be a leader. If it were not for this fatal modesty, which on more than one occasion has almost blighted my political career, I would say I believe I have been a leader, a factor in building up this fair province; I would say that I believe I have written my name large across the face of this Province.'

The government supporters applauded loudly.

'But gentlemen,' turning again to the delegation, 'I am still of the opinion even after listening to your cleverly worded speeches, that I will go on just as I have been doing, without the help you so generously offer. My wish for this fair, flower-decked land is that I may long be spared to guide its destiny in world affairs. I know there is no one but me—I tremble when I think of what might happen these leaderless lambs—but I will go forward confidently, hoping that the good ship may come safely into port, with the same old skipper on the bridge. We are not worrying about the coming election, as you may think. We rest in confidence of the result, and will proudly unfurl, as we have these many years, the same old banner of the grand old party that had gone down many times to disgrace, but thank God, never to defeat.'

The curtain fell, as the last word was spoken, but rose again to show the 'House' standing, in their evening gowns. A bouquet of American beauty roses was handed up over the foot-lights to the Premier, who buried her face in them, with a sudden flood of loneliness. But the crowd was applauding, and again and again she was called forward.

The people came flocking in through the wings, pleading to be introduced to the 'Premier,' but she was gone.

In the crowd that ebbed slowly from the exits, no one noticed the stout gentleman with the dark glasses, who put his hat on before he reached the street, and seemed to be in great haste.

The comments of the people around him, jabbed him like poisoned arrows, and seared his heart like flame.

'I wonder was the Premier there,' one man asked, wiping the traces of merriment from his glasses, 'I've laughed till I'm sore—but I'm afraid he wouldn't see the same fun in it as I do':

'Well, if he's sport enough to laugh at this, I'll say he's some man,' said another.

'That girl sure has her nerve—there isn't a man in this city would dare do it.'

'She'll get his goat—if he ever hears her—I'd advise the old man to stay away.'

'That's holding a mirror up to public life all right.'

'But who is she?'

'The government will be well advised to pension that girl and get her out of the country—a few more sessions of the Women's Parliament, and the government can quit.'

He hurried out into the brilliantly lighted street, stung by the laughter and idle words. His heart was bursting with rage, blind, bitter choking. He had been laughed at, ridiculed, insulted—and the men, whom he had made—had sat by applauding.

John Graham had, all his life, dominated his family circle, his friends, his party, and for the last five years had ruled the Province. Success, applause, wealth, had come easily to him, and he had taken them as naturally as he accepted the breath of his nostrils. They were his. But on this bright night in May, as he went angrily down the back street, unconsciously striking the pavement with his cane, with angry blows, the echo of the people's laughter in his ears was bitter as the pains of death.

SATISFACTION GUARANTEED—THE 1928 EATON'S CATALOGUE

Fredelle Bruser Maynard

If anyone were to ask what books influenced my childhood, I wouldn't hesitate. Dickens—thought of as a single, tremendous entity, at once enlarging and illuminating the life of our prairie town; the *Book of Knowledge*; and the T. Eaton Co. catalogue. Perhaps the catalogue seems a curious choice, and yet in its way (which was sociological, not literary) it performed the functions of the other two. Like the *Book of Knowledge*, it was encyclopedic; like Dickens, it brought the world to my door. No one unfamiliar with the western plains can conceive of their unimaginable loneliness—the flat land beneath the bowl of sky. Summers, the endless undulations of wheat fields in a noon haze; winters, the great drifted expanse of furrowed snow ... a life austere as the grain elevators that stabbed the horizon and fierce as a wildcat's scream. My knowledge of absolutes—all absolutes—is based on that experience. When I first read *Samson Agonistes*—'O dark, dark, dark amid the blaze of noon, Irrecoverably dark, total eclipse Without all hope of day'—blindness pulsed behind my lids because I had known total eclipse: I had lived in Birch Hills, Saskatchewan. Total? Not quite. There were books, evidence of a world beyond. Dickens brought people; the *Book of Knowledge*, a rich salmagundi of puzzles, projects, information, romantic story; and the catalogue brought me *things*.

There were two issues of Eaton's catalogue—Spring and Summer, Fall and Winter. The fall issue was the important one. It came with goldenrod and the clicking of crickets, with pressing leaves (dun yellow and brown, never the extravagant blaze of eastern maples) and gathering great armfuls of wild purple asters. From early August I watched the post-office boxes until the magic day when every box, almost, showed the transverse line of a package-at-the-wicket card. Then I raced to get Papa so he could dial our box combination. Home with the brown-paper-covered book, I settled in.

There was only one room for catalogue reading—the kitchen—and one place, the kitchen table by the stove. I suppose that is why, when I think now of The Book, I can smell not only its thin browntone paper, but peach halves bubbling in sugar syrup, or the sharp, crisp tang of piccalilli. The taste of the catalogue is the taste of apples cold on the teeth, followed perhaps by a bowl of brazil nuts (which we called nigger toes) or tangerines (which we called Jap oranges). Though for many country families Eaton's was a chief source of goods, in our house the catalogue served no such practical purpose. I don't recall that we ever sent off a single order; our supplies came from Papa's store. The catalogue was a book to dream over, and the fact that I was not getting a new Eaton Beauty doll took nothing from my pleasure in studying her rosy smile and fringy eyelashes. My winter dresses—even my winter coat—would be made by Mama as usual. (Whatever the fashion, I wore variations of her plump-child theme: Peter Pan collar, yoke, and broad straight pleats to disguise a lack of waist.) Still I pored over the city flounces. I read the lists of books and records; even, as the season progressed, the pages of farm supplies. I played 'choose-ups' with friends, taking turns at wishing on the catalogue. And when the new copy came—double joy!—I got the old one to cut. (I never saw a commercial paper doll book until I was twelve—and I thought it, then, a sad substitute for Eaton's infinite variety.)

There aren't many copies of the Prairie Bible left. They were cut up, used as bed warmers (nicely toasted in the oven), even—after an elaborate process of page folding—as decorative doorstops. I suppose the great bulk of them ended up in outdoor privies. So it was with a sense of real discovery that I pounced on a copy that turned up not long ago, in the bottom of an old trunk. 1928. The Diamond Jubilee, celebrating Confederation's sixtieth anniversary, had come and gone in a blaze of firecrackers. Mackenzie King was Prime Minister; crops were good; a Dominion-Provincial conference had declared Canada's effective equality with the United Kingdom... and Eaton's was selling lamp wick at four cents a yard.

What strikes one first now about the old catalogue is its extraordinary innocence. Nothing even remotely approaches the modern concept of layout or design. Page after page is crowded with painstakingly realistic sketches—ladies in ladies' dresses, children in children's dresses, men in breeches or overalls. One feels, indeed, that the book had no 'composer' at all. It is as if some conscientious, unimaginative stock boy had passed along the supply room shelves and dutifully recorded what he found there. Text matches pictures in homely directness. 'Good Quality Flat Crepe,' 'Winter Comfort Assured,' 'Unusual Value,' 'For the Short, Stout Figure.' Was ever woman in this manner wooed? Everywhere, the plain prose emphasizes plainer virtues. Little is said about style, much about 'Cumfy Cut'; what matters is durability, warmth, value-for-the-money. The housewife who shops these pages does not much care what everyone else is wearing. She wants to be certain that what she buys now will be wearable for years to come. Even moderately frivolous garments are recommended in terms which emphasize feel, not look: 'fleecy, soft nap makes this dress warm and cosy.' Perhaps in the big department stores of Winnipeg and Toronto smart shoppers asked, 'What does Chanel say?' On the prairies, the lead question was likelier to be 'Do the merino combinations have a closed or open crotch?'

Reading catalogue prose now is a little like sitting down to a large crockery bowl of old-fashioned porridge. It is so heavy, so gray, in every way so unpretentious that one feels the stuff *must* be good. 'Here's a misses' extremely inexpensive dress that adequately meets the exacting needs of everyday wear during the Fall and Winter. It is fashioned in our factories of durable All-Wool English Crepe in a straight, simple style, with cosy long set-in sleeves trimly finished with cuffs. Good satisfaction for such a small outlay.' What is said, what is meant, and what is, are all very close together here. (The writer is saying, 'This dress is no big thrill, but it will do—and what can you expect at the price?') The golden age of euphemism has not dawned in 1928. 'Stout' is a common word; so is 'heavy' and 'elderly.' (The illustrator minces no lines. Models shown in 'approved styles for the larger woman' are size fifty-twos at least, broad of beam and shoulder and short of leg.) It is clear, too, that advertising copywriters have not yet teamed up with the psychologists and motivational researchers. One 'Interesting New Style, just the type that attends many happy little informal affairs' is offered in a choice of color combinations—Folly Red with Mother Goose, or Marron Glace with Mother Goose. For those who cannot trust their intuitions, a color table on the front cover provides the necessary clue: Mother Goose is 'Medium tan or sand but darker than grain.' The color table is a fascinating study in language as well as fashion trends. Very big in fall 1928 were Grasshopper Green, Monkeyskin, and Pinecone ('A medium brown, similar to dead leaves'). There are eight distinct varieties of gray (Battleship, Gull, Zinc, Gunmetal, and so forth), a color called Bran, one called Wigwam, and Drab (really). The liveliest-sounding shades carry dreadully inappropriate connotations: Grapenuts, Waffle, Muffin ('similar to Toast'). And there is Sedge. A skirt in Sedge, think of it, with Wigwam blouse and hat of Bran.

Occasionally the catalogue attempts loftier flights. Some dresses are 'beautiful' and 'splendid' as well as 'modest in every line.' One delicate costume, georgette and velvet, inspires a positively lyrical burst. 'A lovely "dress-up" frock, where Fashion works out her truest art in rich simplicity. No lovelier medium than the rich, softly hanging All-Silk Transparent Velvet, and no lovelier finish than the pretty shoulder flower and the stunning large brilliant clasp that fastens the wide all-around girdle and forms the heading for the soft-swaying flare of the new wrap-around skirt.' In a book where the norm is a housedress 'of strong, sturdy, wear-resisting Khaki cloth,' such prose seems decadent if not downright depraved, and one turns with relief from its oriental seductions to the elemental simplicities of Eaton's Extra-Large Fleece-Lined Bloomers: 'Has roomy gusset and well-sewn seams. Strong, serviceable elastic at waist and knees.'

Since the catalogue was primarily a clothing book, it preserves most obviously the fashions of its period, though the image is John Held modified by forty below zero and the McCormick tractor. The women in the flat, stylized illustrations are decidedly on the heavy side, but the heaviness is without any suggestion of sensuous ripeness. They are quite breastless, these large bovine females—and no wonder. The corset pages reveal horrifying Flex O Steel casings 'Strongly boned throughout to hold and give the figure a straight line.' Back and front laces, inner belts, hooks and clasps and elastic inserts are all calculated to reduce any discrepancy between bust, waist, and hips. For women whose figures resist equalizing, there is a rubber reducing brassiere. Legs, revealed to just knee level, are sexless as sausages. Beneath the neat bobs and cloches, faces are sweetly vacuous, with round eyes, round spots of rouge, and Betty Boop lips accented in bright lipstick. Little girls are miniature adults; the pre-schoolers, with their deep cloche hats and dropped waistlines, look like stout matrons on their way to a Ladies Aid Luncheon.

More interesting than fashion data is the evidence, in Eaton's catalogue, of opinion and attitude. Canada in 1928 would seem to have been spectacularly unaware of large elements in its cultural heritage: an 'Eskimo doll' is a run-of-the-mill doll in, of all things, a clown suit with pom-poms and ruff at the neck; the 'Indian crafts' feature tie holders, score pad covers, and cushion tops all decorated with the identical silhouette of a feathered chieftain (*circa* Tecumseh). As for minority groups other than the indigenous, the Negro appears, predictably, as exotic and ridiculous. A leading fashion color is 'Nigger Brown.' A featured toy, 'Hey, Hey,' is a comic-vaudeville representation of a Negro in cheap bright tin. The figure holds a squawking chicken. Wind it up, and 'the darkie shuffles along' with his stolen bird, while a small dog, yapping fiercely, attaches itself to the seat of his trousers. Another toy—'very amusing, sure to please' —features two dancing Negroes on a shanty-shaped box from whose windows peer little golliwog children. Again, the theme is See How They Jump.

If the old Eaton's catalogues provide indications of how the prairie farmer saw the rest of the world, they also, of course, reveal what his own world was like. It was *cold.* A sense of winter hardship rises from these pages like frosted breath on a January morning. Oh, there are lightweight church clothes and round-the-house clothes, surely. But the tone of the book is set by all those garments designed for long trudges through the whirling snow, for carrying in wood and carrying out feed to the barn. The children who wore these toques and jumbo sweaters with blanket cloth knickers and lumberjack-style knee stockings were not members of a car pool. If they were lucky, they might ride horseback, or scrunch over snow-packed roads in a horse-drawn sleigh. But mostly they walked—two, three, four miles in forty below weather, with books and a lard pail of lunch. 'Here,' says the catalogue of a sheepskin-lined model, 'is our Sub-Zero coat that we especially offer to the woman who lives on a farm, with a long ride to town . . . or the rural school teacher with a cold walk to school every morning.' Even the tams are made of double-knit wool; a page headed 'For Days That Are Chilly' features not only the expected mufflers and vests but a variety of cozy garments called hug-me-tights. And the underwear! From this section alone, social historians of the future might reconstruct the image of prairie life before the triumph of electricity and the gasoline engine. Over twenty pages of the 1928 catalogue are devoted to things-to-go-under-things. A few scanties (lustrous sateen bloomers, pongee boudoir caps with insert of satin ribbon), but for the rest, it is woolen all the way. There are shirts and drawers and combinations to enclose every inch of flesh. (The big brand name here, by an odd trick of association, is 'Wolsey,' every unshrinkable undergarment stamped with the cardinal's noble profile.) There are knee-warmers to go over the underwear and under the overstockings; abdominal protectors ('for maximum comfort and warmth during severe cold weather'); fleece-lined petticoats and knitted underpants. Just reading about these marvels is an experience in ultimate coziness, like sitting by a wood stove on a bitter night.

Precisely because prairie winters were so ferocious, the demands of prairie life so unremitting, farm women craved frivolity. This too Eaton's understood. The hats, for instance, are purest frippery, a tropical paradise of sequins, rhinestones, velvet, feathers, beads. 'Pretty Flowers, Ribbons, and Novelties' is a page of baubles for the woman who wore her husband's mackinaw to milk the cows. Here is a crepe de chine hankie, hand-painted. Here is a pair of shirred ribbon garters with rosebud trim, a decorated clothes hanger, a lace collar and cuff set (might perk up those sturdy, low-priced flannel frocks) and even—good heavens!—detachable georgette sleeves and a marabou stole. It must have been a comfort. (Looking at these absurdities, I remember a curiousness that intrigued me as a child. We of the twenties are personal. Stomachaches are the province not of Alka-Seltzer (the name chills), but of Mother Siegel, whose wise, benign countenance shines forth from every bottle of curative syrup. For kidney trouble, there is Dr A. W. Chase; for blood and nerves, Dr Williams (Pink Pills for Pale People). The medical schools of the period must have worked full time turning out pill vendors. Some, like the ambitious Dr Thomas, produced an Eclectric Oil (not electric, not eclectic) good for all diseases, internal and external, of horses and men. Sufferers not relieved by potions could turn, as a last resort, to a twenty-dollar wonder called the Signal Medical Battery, a Rube Goldberg construction which employed electric current to cure everything from headache to sore feet. (Accessories included a plug-in foot plate, a hair brush, two foot sponges, and one pair of cords. . . .)

The history of mail order in the West is full of drama—like the single gentleman who tried to order a bride from the underwear pages, and the townspeople who called their village 'Eatonia' in honor of their patron saint. It is easy to understand how such things were possible: the catalogue is a very personal book. A woman in Turtleford or Neepawa, ordering a bathing suit for her son, would surely feel that Eaton's *understood.* 'Nearly every boy wants a bathing suit, and at our low price [65¢], there is no reason why he shouldn't have one. They are light but strongly made and will stand up under the treatment the ordinary carefree boy gives a bathing suit.' Serious, friendly, sympathetic, aware, the catalogue writer gives advice on everything from buttonless combinations ('boys will slip out of it in a jiffy') to interior decorating. A page of living room furniture includes the reminder that this room is 'the heart of the home. Here the family meets as a family; here social contact is made with other families and individuals.' Even the order form rises above mere commerce: on the reverse side, Eaton's offers a thought-provoking essay. 'Are You Getting Ahead? Does money bring happiness? Perhaps not. Yet money poorly spent can bring unhappiness. . . . ' It is, in short, a dissertation calculated to give prodigals second thoughts about that new beaded lampshade, and one can only admire the company's altruism. Readers are encouraged to send special money problems to the Budget Director, some of whose sample budgets are printed in the back pages. (Suggested annual allotment for a farm family of six with a $2,600 income: $338 for food, $364 for clothing. 'Much depends on home sewing,' the Director adds crisply.) For problems not covered in the body of the book, there are free pamphlets available. Eaton's Farm News Service lists titles ranging from 'Swat the Fly' to 'Helping the Nervous, Irritable Child.'

No wonder farm families waited with such eagerness for The Book. It was department store, picture magazine and counseling service rolled into one, a friend in the city who knew your needs and could be trusted to serve them with absolute integrity. 'Customers reading the 'ads' may rely upon purchasing merchandise as represented—a spade is called a spade and not a silvered trowel.' Designed for customers on the remotest farms, without access to stores of any kind, Eaton's offered a total shopping service. From the catalogue in 1928 you could order a thimble, a single pair of shoelaces, a potholder, a dress buckle, a ball of twine, a collar button. And if you didn't like the thimble when it arrived, you could return it for prompt, cheerful refund. Abuses of Eaton's money-back guarantee were notorious—the dress returned after the dance, the broken toy—and there is just a touch of sad reproach in the catalogue's reminder that return of a used tube of toothpaste 'should not be necessary.'

Eaton's still serves the western farms, but the catalogue—like the farm—has gone electric. 'Walk in,' urges the text of a recent edition. 'Browse around. There's gear for every kind of action. But beware of the colour explosion . . . it's deafening! . . . We've picked the ripest plum, the coolest lime. What happened? Pow!' Youth dominates. The catalogue begins with its Junior Shop ('where the gad-about is simply mad-about the pop-in pant suit'), maintains throughout a young, bold, up-to-the-minute stance. Captions are saucy: 'My fair mini,' 'the mocking turtle,' 'Some like it striped,' 'A dress for all seasons.' Who cares about practicality? 'For the Big Freeze' there are silk stretch pants and fluffy fur hoods. Older women, demoted to mid-book, wear modified junior styles and are elegantly slender. ('Older,' like 'stout,' is a word unheard.) The underwear section is all puffs of lace. Though, presumably, the snows of today are deep as the snows of yesteryear, combinations in the good old Wolsey sense of the word have disappeared. Now there is snappy, with-it ski underwear 'available in lightning red.' Girdles emphasize ease rather than control; the bones are silent, and stomachs have turned into tummies. Instead of the rubber reducing brassiere, there is a fiberfill padded model which 'coaxes you into a fuller roundness.' '*You're shaped,*' the New Eaton's croons hypnotically. '*You're slim. You're smooth.*'

It's persuasive, the voice of today's Eaton's catalogue—persuasive and lively and various and richly toned. Why then do I miss the shy crudity of that fellow who used to write, with blunt pencil on heavy foolscap, no doubt, those touchingly sincere descriptions? 'We feel we are not overestimating its charms when we say this frock looks as though it cost several dollars more than our very moderate price.' 'You really cannot appreciate what a wonderful value this is unless you have attempted to make yourself a dress out of the same quality fine All-Wool Flannel that we have used here.' I miss him and I miss his quality merchandise—the felt shoes and leggings, the driving robes of Chinese dogskin, the Celluloid combs and razor strops and shoe button hooks with mother-of-pearl handles. Where are the wire armbands, the decorated hair receivers, and the smelling salts chunky in cut-glass bottles? Where are the curling tongs and marcel irons, the baby walkers and pen nibs? There's not a plowshare in the book, or a three-ring teat-slitter.

THE WIND OUR ENEMY

Anne Marriott

I

WIND

flattening its gaunt furious self against
the naked siding, knifing in the wounds
of time, pausing to tear aside the last
old scab of paint.

Wind
surging down the cocoa-coloured seams
of summer-fallow, darting in about
white hoofs and brown, snatching the sweaty cap
shielding red eyes.

Wind
filling the dry mouth with bitter dust
whipping the shoulders worry-bowed too soon,
soiling the water pail, and in grim prophecy
graying the hair.

II

The wheat in spring was like a giant's bolt of silk
Unrolled over the earth.
When the wind sprang
It rippled as if a great broad snake
Moved under the green sheet
Seeking its outward way to light.
In autumn it was an ocean of flecked gold
Sweet as a biscuit, breaking in crisp waves
That never shattered, never blurred in foam.
That was the last good year . . .

III

The wheat was embroidering
All the spring morning,
Frail threads needled by sunshine like thin gold.
A man's heart could love his land,
Smoothly self-yielding,
Its broad spread promising all his granaries might
    hold.
A woman's eyes could kiss the soil
From her kitchen window,
Turning its black depths to unchipped cups—a silk
    crepe dress—
(Two-ninety-eight, Sale Catalogue)
Pray sun's touch be gentleness,
Not a hot hand, scorching flesh it would caress.
But sky like a new tin pan
Hot from the oven
Seemed soldered to the earth by horizons of glare . . .

The third day he left the fields . . .

Heavy scraping footsteps
Spoke before his words, 'Crops dried out—
    everywhere—'

IV

They said, 'Sure, it'll rain next year!'
When that was dry, 'Well, next year anyway.'
Then, 'Next—'
But still the metal hardness of the sky
Softened only in mockery.
When lightning slashed and twanged

And thunder made the hot head surge with pain
Never a drop fell;
Always hard yellow sun conquered the storm.
So the soon sickly-familiar saying grew,
(Watching the futile clouds sneak down the north)
'Just empties goin' back!'
(Cold laughter bending parched lips in a smile
Bleak eyes denied.)

V

Horses were strong so strong men might love them,
Sides groomed to copper burning the sun,
Wind tangling wild manes, dust circling wild hoofs,
Turn the colts loose! Watch the two-year-olds run!
Then heart thrilled fast and the veins filled with glory
The feel of hard leather a fortune more sweet
Than a girl's silky lips. He was one with the thunder,
The flying, the rhythm, of untamed, unshod feet!

But now—
It makes a man white-sick to see them now,
Dull—heads sagging—crowding to the trough—
No more spirit than a barren cow.
The well's pumped dry to wash poor fodder down,
Straw and salt—and endless salt and straw—
(Thank God the winter's mild so far)
Dry Russian thistle crackling in the jaw—

The old mare found the thistle pile, ate till she bulged,
Then, crazily, she wandered in the yard,
Saw a water-drum, and staggering to its rim,
Plodded around it—on and on in hard,
Madly relentless circle.   Weaker—stumbling—
She fell quite suddenly, heaved once and lay.
(Nellie the kid's pet's gone, boys.
Hitch up the strongest team.   Haul her away.
Maybe we should have mortgaged all we had
Though it wasn't much, even in good years, and draw
Ploughs with a jolting tractor.
Still—you can't make gas of thistles or oat-straw.)

VI

Relief.
'God, we tried so hard to stand alone!'

Relief.
'Well, we can't let the kids go cold.'
They trudge away to school swinging half-empty
lard-pails,
to shiver in the schoolhouse (unpainted seven years),
learning from a blue-lipped girl
almost as starved as they.

Relief cars.
'Apples, they say, and clothes!'
The folks in town get their pick first,
Then their friends—
'Eight miles for us to go so likely we
won't get much—'
'Maybe we'll get the batteries charged up and have
the radio to kind of brighten things—'

Insurgents march in Spain

Japs bomb Chinese

Airliner lost

'Maybe we're not as badly off as some—'
'Maybe there'll be a war and we'll get paid to fight—'
'Maybe—'
'See if Eddie Cantor's on to-night!'

VII
People grew bored
Well-fed in the east and west
By stale, drought-area tales,
Bored by relief whinings,
Preferred their own troubles.
So those who still had stayed
On the scorched prairie,
Found even sympathy
Seeming to fail them
Like their own rainfall.

'Well—let's forget politics,
Forget the wind, our enemy!
Let's forget farming, boys,
Let's put on a dance tonight!

Mrs Smith'll bring a cake.
Mrs Olsen's coffee's swell!'

The small uneven schoolhouse floor
Scraped under big work-boots
Cleaned for the evening's fun,
Gasoline lamps whistled.
One Hungarian boy
Snapped at a shrill guitar,
A Swede from out north of town
Squeezed an accordion dry,
And a Scotchwoman from Ontario
Made the piano dance
In time to 'The Mocking-Bird'
And 'When I grow too Old to Dream,'
Only taking time off
To swing in a square-dance,
Between ten and half-past three.

Yet in the morning
Air peppered thick with dust,
All the night's happiness
Seemed far away, unreal
Like a lying mirage,
Or the icy-white glare
Of the alkali slough.

VIII

Presently the dark dust seemed to build a wall
That cut them off from east and west and north.
Kindness and honesty, things they used to know,
Seemed blown away and lost
In frantic soil.

At last they thought
Even God and Christ were hidden
By the false clouds.
—Dust-blinded to the staring parable,
Each wind-splintered timber like a pain-bent Cross.
Calloused, groping fingers, trembling
With overwork and fear,
Ceased trying to clutch at some faith in the dark,
Thin, sick courage fainted, lacking hope.
But tightened, tangled nerves scream to the brain

If there is no hope, give them forgetfulness!
The cheap light of the beer-parlour grins out,
Promising shoddy security for an hour.
The Finn who makes bad liquor in his barn
Grows fat on groaning emptiness of souls.

IX

The sun goes down. Earth like a thick black coin
Leans its round rim against the yellowed sky.
The air cools. Kerosene lamps are filled and lit
In dusty windows. Tired bodies crave to lie
In bed forever. Chores are done at last.
A thin horse neighs drearily. The chickens drowse,
Replete with grasshoppers that have gnawed and
  scraped
Shrivelled garden-leaves. No sound from the gaunt
  cows.

Poverty, hand in hand with fear, two great
Shrill-jointed skeletons stride loudly out
Across the pitiful fields, none to oppose.
Courage is roped with hunger, chained with doubt.
Only against the yellow sky, a part
Of the jetty silhouette of barn and house
Two figures stand, heads close, arms locked,
And suddenly some spirit seems to rouse
And gleam, like a thin sword, tarnished, bent,
But still shining in the spared beauty of moon,
As his strained voice says to her, 'We're not licked
  yet!
It must rain again—it *will*! Maybe—soon—'

X

Wind
  in a lonely laughterless shrill game
  with broken wash-boiler, bucket without
  a handle, Russian thistle, throwing up
  sections of soil.

  God, will it never rain again? What about
  those clouds out west? No, that's just dust, as thick
  and stifling now as winter underwear.
  No rain, no crop, no feed, no faith, only
  wind.

'YOU'LL NEVER SEE IT THIS WAY AGAIN'

'Just smell that breeze,' Dad said as we rounded a little grove. He inhaled deeply and I did the same. The warm air was both sweet and sharp: a delightful mixture of wild honeysuckle, roses, wild sweet peas, green grass, sap, tall slough plants, rich brown earth, and the yeasty odour of the silver wolf-willows. 'It's fair wonderful, isn't it?' Dad said as we jogged along again. 'Just like God's own garden.' We came to the top of a little rise and Dad let Nelly stop. Darkie stopped too, and we sat there for a while and looked at the beauty around us: at the poplars and willows both silver and green, and at the roses, wild mint, and harebells that were everywhere.

'Take a good look at it, Mary,' Dad said quietly. 'You'll never see it this way again.'

I did as I was told. I looked at the tall grass and the peavine and the soft green silk of the wild barley, but the sad note in Dad's voice puzzled me. How could the prairie change? I wondered. I did not realise then what an instrument of change a plough is.

The trees and willows are gone now, grubbed out and burned, and the roses and wild mint have been ploughed under. Wheat now grows where the chook-cherries and the violets bloomed. The wind is still sweet, but there is no wildness in it and it no longer seems to have wandered a great way over grass and trees and flowers. It now smells of dry straw and bread. The wild keen fragrance the wind knew in those days has gone for ever.

MARY HIEMSTRA

LANTERNS

Andrew Suknaski

the blizzard came
after the first frost—
the hired man left the house
with a lantern
to see how the cattle
were taking the storm
in the north pasture

my father found him
three days later
near the fence on the east side
of the pasture

the faithful dog froze
beside him—curled up
like a lover in the man's arms
(the broken lantern
lay near a stone   the glass shattered)

men freeze this way everywhere
when lanterns fall   a p a r t
(even within one's arms
inside the city's rim)

THE 'REGINA MANIFESTO'

Opening paragraphs from the platform of the Co-operative Commonwealth Federation, adopted at its First National Convention held at Regina, Sask., in July 1933. It was first drafted by F. H. Underhill and revised by other members of the League for Social Reconstruction.

The C.C.F. is a federation of organizations whose purpose is the establishment in Canada of a Co-operative Commonwealth in which the principle regulating production, distribution and exchange will be the supplying of human needs and not the making of profits.

We aim to replace the present capitalist system, with its inherent injustice and inhumanity, by a social order from which the domination and exploitation of one class by another will be eliminated, in which economic planning will supersede unregulated private enterprise and competition, and in which genuine democratic self-government, based upon economic equality will be possible. The present order is marked by glaring inequalities of wealth and opportunity, by chaotic waste and instability; and in an age of plenty it condemns the great mass of the people to poverty and insecurity. Power has become more and more concentrated into the hands of a small irresponsible minority of financiers and industrialists and to their predatory interests the majority are habitually sacrificed. When private profit is the main stimulus to economic effort, our society oscillates between periods of feverish prosperity in which the main benefits go to speculators and profiteers, and of catastrophic depression, in which the common man's normal state of insecurity and hardship is accentuated. We believe that these evils can be removed only in a planned and socialized economy in which our natural resources and the principal means of production and distribution are owned, controlled and operated by the people.

The new social order at which we aim is not one in which individuality will be crushed out by a system of regimentation. Nor shall we interfere with cultural rights of racial or religious minorities. What we seek is a proper collective organization of our economic resources such as will make possible a much greater degree of leisure and a much richer individual life for every citizen.

If the people have not suffered enough, it is their God-given right to suffer some more. WILLIAM ABERHART

REGINA RIOT

Robert Moon

1935

One of the most sombre episodes in Regina's history came in the middle of this decade [the thirties]. Relief camp strikers began a trek from British Columbia to Ottawa in early June 1935. They had simply wanted to place their complaints about camp conditions and about receiving relief rather than a work and wages programme before the federal government at Ottawa. On June 14th the long freight train bearing the 1,600 rolled into Regina from the west. The men formed fours and marched to the Stadium where they were to stay during the stop. Their leaders warned them there was to be: 'No hooliganism in Regina.'

Meanwhile the federal government ordered the RCMP to stop the march in the Queen City. In spite of this, it became evident the marchers did not intend submitting to the ultimatum to return to the B.C. relief camps. A mass meeting of 5,000 Reginans approved a resolution urging the then Prime Minister R. B. Bennett to remove all obstacles impeding the eastward trek. Regina service clubs offered to organize a voluntary motor cavalcade to carry the men toward the Manitoba border. Two federal cabinet ministers, Railways Minister R. J. Manion and Agriculture Minister Robert Weir, came west to negotiate with the strike leaders. With 10,000 milling about on downtown streets, a truce was arranged. Out of the discussions came a decision to send eight leaders to Ottawa to present demands. Nothing came out of the talks and they returned.

There was no doubt a move by rail would be blocked by police—four hundred of them were now mobilized in the city. The strikers decided to use trucks. Two truck-loads started east on the night of June 28th. They were stopped on the outskirts by steel-helmeted mounted policemen and five strikers were arrested. A tense week-end followed.

The RCMP then decided to arrest the strike leaders. They planned to go to a mass meeting of strikers and citizens on Market Square behind the police station. At dusk on July 1st, with speakers on the platform addressing the crowd a police whistle sounded and RCMP and city policemen swept onto the open ground where travelling carnivals occasionally pitch their tents today, where a weigh scale sits on one side, and where no one would suspect one of the worst street battles in Canadian history began.

When the police drove in, the crowd was thrown into a panic and surged back. The strikers, armed with clubs and pieces of cement and brick as if expecting a fight, then moved forward toward the police, who used tear gas bombs, quirts and the occasional pot shot. For the next three hours, lasting until eleven o'clock, the battle raged in chaos, wild confusion, bloodshed, and at time curious *bathos*. Mounted police on horseback rode through the streets. Automobiles were overturned. Downtown store windows were smashed—children sat in one, eating displayed candy while strikers and police fought hand to hand outside.

As the riot went on and before it finally subsided, there was a strange lull and in its midst there came a grim note of humour, as there is humour at some time in most tragedies. An old Englishman, a retired military man, cane in hand, walked stiffly across Market Square toward the fire hall where strikers were hurling rocks through windows.

'Chief,' he shouted, raising his cane. 'Get your revolver. Shoot those men.'

The men stopped their throwing to gaze in awe at the audacity of this unarmed old gentleman. The fire chief's mouth fell open. Had he owned a revolver, he would have obeyed the command.

During the riot thousands of dollars damage was done. One hundred and twenty were arrested. More than one hundred strikers, citizens and police were injured, half requiring hospitalization. One city detective was killed by a blow on the head from a club as he attempted to prevent marchers taking some wooden stakes piled on Market Square. No one was ever brought to justice for the killing.

The events leading up to the riot were tense enough. The method chosen by the police to arrest the leaders was ill-advised. The men themselves were ill-led, some leaders were Communist inspired. The combination had had all the elements of conflict. Five days later the strikers, appalled like everyone else by what had happened, swung aboard two west-bound freights and headed home.

The day had been one of the most tragic in recent Canadian times. Yet no one could have witnessed this combat, no one could have seen these men as they marched through the streets of cities they stopped at on their way east until riot stopped them at Regina without recognizing that here in this ill-dressed, ill-fed band was a dramatic witness to the depression times.

'Are we downhearted?' one would cry.

'No,' they all shouted back, not in carefully rehearsed, synchronized mass chorus as were uniformed young men in the military states of Europe of that era but with the voice of individuals. These were hard times in a democracy, but even in adversity there was hope.

There are some who say there is a direct connection between that sad July day of 1935 and the 1944 election of the Co-operative Commonwealth Federation—more commonly, CCF—government of Saskatchewan, the first Socialist administration in North America. There is not quite that but in the political factors of Saskatchewan today the depression is still a haunting spectre.

MANITOBA DROUGHT

Maara Haas

In the flutter of eyelids mothing a coal-oil lamp
her wrists' transparency is veined Iris
pulsating a crazy quilt of blue-bloused gardens,
riotous cotton roses and a snipped English sky.

Delirious with loneliness and now half blind
she does not turn sunflower and outgoing hands
when he comes through the door
bee-bumbling, awkward,
to shake like pollen the dust and goldenrod
from his bared arms and sun-stroked shoulders.

His appetites are fundamental,
a simple geometry of seasons:
green's sequence moving tractors, crops
as she is not

But spreading the quilt in her lap
will downward dip her face in the cool of colours
made lake and river drowning in fragrance,
While the lusting wind whispering obscenities
and LET ME IN, she smiles and is not shaken.

DAY AND NIGHT

Dorothy Livesay

1
Dawn, red and angry, whistles loud and sends
A geysered shaft of steam searching the air.
Scream after scream announces that the churn
Of life must move, the giant arm command.
Men in a stream, a human moving belt
Move into sockets, every one a bolt.
The fun begins, a humming whirring drum—
Men do a dance in time to the machines.

One step forward
Two steps back
Shove the lever,
Push it back

While Arnot whirls
A roundabout
And Geoghan shuffles
Bolts about

One step forward
Hear it crack
Smashing rhythm—
Two steps back.

Your heart-beat pounds
Against your throat
The roaring voices
Drown your shout

Across the way
A writhing whack
Sets you spinning
Two steps back—

One step forward
Two steps back.

2

Day and night rising and falling
Night and day shift gears and slip rattling
Down the runway, shot into storerooms
Where only eyes and a notebook remember
The record of evil, the sum of commitments.
We move as through sleep's revolving memories
Piling up hatred, stealing the remnants
Doors forever folding before us—
And where is the recompense, on what agenda
Will you set love down? Who knows of peace?

Day and night
Night and day
Light rips into ribbons
What we say

I called to love
Deep in dream:
Be with me in the daylight
As in gloom.

Be with me in the pounding
In the knives against my back
Set your voice resounding
Above the steel's whip crack.

High and sweet
Sweet and high
Hold, hold up the sunlight
In the sky!

Day and night
Night and day
Tear up all the silence
Find the words I could not say . . .

3

We were stoking coal in the furnaces; red hot
They gleamed, burning our skins away, his and mine.
We were working, together, night and day, and knew
Each other's stroke; and without words exchanged
An understanding about kids at home,
The landlord's jaw, wage-cuts and overtime.

We were like buddies, see? Until they said
That nigger is too smart the way he smiles
And sauces back the foreman; he might say
Too much one day, to others changing shifts.
Therefore they cut him down, who flowered at night
And raised me up, day hanging over night—
So furnaces could still consume our withered skin.

Shadrack, Mechak and Abednego
Turn in the furnace, whirling slow.

Lord, I'm burnin' in the fire
Lord, I'm steppin' on the coal
Lord, I'm blacker than my brother
Blow your breath down here.

Boss, I'm smothered in the darkness
Boss, I'm shrivellin' in the flames
Boss, I'm blacker than my brother
Blow your breath down here.

Shadrack, Mechak and Abednego
Burn in the furnace, whirling slow.

4
Up in the roller room, men swing steel
Swing it, zoom; and cut it, crash.
Up in the dark the welder's torch
Makes sparks fly like lightning's reel.

Now I remember storm on a field:
The trees bow tense before the blow
Even the jittering sparrow's talk
Ripples into the still tree shield.

We are in storm that has no cease
No lull before, no after time
When green with rain the grasses grow
And air is sweet with fresh increase.

We bear the burden home to bed
The furnace glows within our hearts:
Our bodies hammered through the night
Are welded into bitter bread.

Bitter, yes:
But listen, friend,
We are mightier
In the end

We have ears
Alert to seize
A weakness in
The foreman's ease.

We have eyes
To look across
The bosses' profit
At our loss.

Are you waiting?
Wait with us
Every evening
There's a hush

Use it not
For love's slow count:
Add up hate
And let it mount—

One step forward
Two steps back
Will soon be over:
Hear it crack!

The wheels may whirr
A roundabout
And neighbour's shuffle
Drown your shout

The wheel must limp
Till it hangs still
And crumpled men
Pour down the hill:

Day and night
Night and day—
Till life is turned
The other way!

LANDLADIES AND A WANT-AD HUSBAND

James Gray

The Winnipeg unemployed and everybody remotely connected with them were in a constant uproar about housing. The rental allowance varied slightly according to the size of the family. Kay and I and Patty qualified for $13 a month, which meant we could rent one unfurnished room. A large family might get up to $18 a month, but the allowance was never sufficient to pay the rent on a modern house. This meant that no family living in a rented house could stay in it when they went on relief. It meant that people buying homes lost them, because the rental allowances were insufficient to keep up the payments and taxes. Eventually, the home-buying class got a small break. When the debt-adjustments boards became operative, foreclosures were stopped if interest was paid. In some cases the unemployed were able to draw enough relief-rent to pay interest and taxes, if the house was very small and the family very large.

The economic results of relief rents were depressed housing values, and stagnation in the house-building industry. The social consequences were worse. Neuroses became endemic faster than psychiatrists could find labels for them. Hundreds of broken homes would have resulted from rooming-house congestion had it not been for relief regulations that discouraged separations. Husbands and wives, after a year on relief, might reach a stage where they could barely abide the sight of each other. But they went on living together because there was no practical alternative, except for the husband to hop a freight-train and leave the country, which frequently happened.

The rental department at the Woodyard was under continuous siege by landlords seeking to evict tenants, by tenants wanting permission to move to new quarters, by tenants looking for help to bring rooming-house feuds under control, and by optimists trying to persuade officialdom to make exceptions in their cases.

The delusion that it was possible to make a living by renting rooms was one of the most persistent of the depression. Every third house outside the better-off districts was adorned with a card advertising 'Unfurnished Rooms for Rent'. The signs never came down because the unemployed family that moved in this month would probably be moving out the month after next. Our landlord in the Furby Street house could have stood as the epitome of all the star-crossed landlords of the depression. The house contained seven rooms and a bath, and, by using some beaver-board partitions, he was able to cut the living-room in half and come up with seven rentable rooms for seven individual families.

The landlord and his wife slept on a cot in the kitchen. Kay and I and Patty had the largest bedroom, on the second floor. When we got a double bed, a bed for three-year-old Patty, a dresser, a kitchen table and three chairs into a twelve-by-twelve room, there was little room to move. In this room we cooked and ate and slept, as, of course, did all the others in their rooms. Everyone in the house, save the landlord, cooked on electric plates. When the storm windows went on, it was easily possible, on entering the house at meal-time, to tell what everyone was having for supper. The trick we discovered was to eat early, for if you waited until everyone else was eating, the conglomeration of odours jaded even the best appetite.

Our landlord lived in a state of perpetual hyper-hysteria. He was discovering, as hundreds of others were discovering, that running a rooming-house was a sure route to pauperism, if not to insanity. It was a matter of simple arithmetic. He paid $25 a month rent for the house, and his income from his seven tenants was $80 a month. At best, he had his rent free and $55 a month on which to live. His $55 surplus, however, was illusory from the beginning. Six families cooking on hotplates and using electric irons ran his light bill up to $25 a month. He had to buy fuel, which in this non-insulated barn of a house ran to $35 a month in winter. He had to pay another $3 or $4 a month for water. The very best he could do was to go behind $10 a month, if he and his wife didn't eat.

It was worse than that, however, because one of his tenants had stopped paying her rent. She was a prospective mother who lived in the tiny room at the back. No longer able to work, she was engaged in a seemingly hopeless campaign to get the soldier father of the impending child to marry her or at least support her. The other tenants fed her and tried to comfort her and for a while her plight occupied much of everybody's attention. The landlord, who was essentially a kindly man, was sympathetic, too. But, when the economic pressure on him became unbearable, he would rush up to her room, pound on her door, and demand his rent. Eventually, the army got the marriage arranged and the women in the house went on an orgy of trunk-ransacking in order to give the girl a proper send-off.

We all kept to ourselves, and we got along fairly well until winter set in, when the strain involved in keeping children cooped up in a rooming-house began to tell. Patty had a five-year-old playmate who lived downstairs. When they played together it had to be in the halls and on the stairs. When they played they naturally fought and cried, so the other tenants complained and shooed them out of the hallways. In an effort to keep peace in the house, Kay and I took turns riding Patty around the block in her sleigh, a Spartan regimen in a Winnipeg winter.

There were other, more difficult problems for which there was no such easy solution, problems common to all the rooming-houses in the city. There were hundreds of similar houses—old, old houses with broken-down furnaces and fouled-up hot-water systems. Life in the Furby Street *ménage* was complicated by a washing-machine, for the use of which the tenants paid twenty-five cents a week. The landlady could never keep track of who had paid and who still owed, and the faulty water-heater disrupted wash-day schedules. Such wash-day anarchy developed that by nightfall on Mondays half the tenants would not be speaking to the other half, and nobody would be talking to Mrs Landlord. As winter deepened, arguments over lack of heat and hot water intensified. Shouting matches could develop in a hallway and turn the house into bedlam. There was no such thing as a private argument in our rooming-house.

We spent the worst Christmas of our lives in the Furby Street house and decided to move. We then discovered landlords typical of another very large group—still-employed persons trying to overcome salary cuts by renting rooms. Kay located a room in a private home on Kelvin Street, but we were barely moved in before the landlady was pounding on the door demanding that we leave. She accused Kay of lying to her about Patty, of assuring her we had no children. She would positively have no children running in and out of her house, tracking in mud, soiling her wallpaper. We could stay the night, she said, but we would have to get out in the morning. Not on relief, we couldn't!

We reminded the lady she had signed a form to accept the relief rent, so there was no way in which we could be moved until at least a month was up. She stopped shouting at us and ran to the phone. She phoned the relief department, then she phoned the police, but she got no satisfaction anywhere. When her husband came home, the argument broke off for supper.

In the hiatus, Kay and I discovered that the room was hopeless anyway. Our bed, the dresser, and the kitchen table took up so much of the floor space that there was no place for the chairs. We sat on the edge of the bed to eat, with the chairs piled on the bed behind us. To sleep, we transferred the chairs from the bed to the top of the table. There was nothing for it but to find a much bigger room, if the Woodyard would let us move so quickly. Our conditional surrender only angered our landlady.

The woman's husband drove a delivery truck and they were early risers. Our room was on the second floor and there was an unoccupied third floor. At six o'clock next morning the lady put on a pair of heavy shoes and went into a tramping and stomping routine above our heads. While her coffee was boiling, she pounded back and forth with a clatter that rattled the windows and shook the ceiling. When we got up the bathroom door was locked, and it was a full hour before we discovered it was locked from the outside. I tried to pacify her by repeating our decision to leave as soon as we could and asked for the key to the bathroom. She let her blood pressure rise slowly before shouting that the bathroom would stay locked as long as we were in the house and so would the front door if we ever left.

I found a skeleton key and opened the bathroom door. Thereafter, every time we used the bathroom we left the hot water running. This brought the landlady rushing up the stairs, two at a time, to shut the tap and lock the door. That night when her husband came home, we arranged a truce by agreeing to move as soon as we could get arrangements made with the Woodyard. But as long as we stayed the lady did the clod-hopper dance over our beds in the morning.

There was a plentiful supply of rooms for rent during the depression; the only trouble was that they all tended to rent for the same price, regardless of size, location, or condition. At first relief tenants were regarded with suspicion, but they were quickly transformed by economic conditions into a preferred clientele. Rooms that might bring $10 a month or less from cash customers yielded $12 to $13 from people on relief. The first bit of information landladies always elicited from prospective tenants was whether they were on relief. The payment of relief-rent might have been slow, but it was sure, and that was unlikely to be true of some non-relief renters who paid cash but fell far in arrears. So eager did some landladies become to get relief tenants that they would offer to kick back a dollar or two a month to the tenant out of the relief rent.

Few people on relief were ever much more satisfied with landlords than the landlords were with tenants. Discussions of housing and landlords bulked large in any gathering of the unemployed. There was a deadly sameness to the stories that were told and underlying them all was the yearning for the perfect landlady. We eventually found her in an old cottage on Chalmers Avenue. She was seventy-seven years old and had lived all her adult life in this little house, which her first husband had built. Though she had come out to Canada in the '80s, there was still a trace of the English Midlands in her speech. She was a handsome and well-preserved old lady.

The house itself was badly run down. The almost flat roof was high at the front and sloped towards the rear. One storey in height, the house had no foundation or basement and was simply set on beams resting on the ground. It had last been painted perhaps twenty years before, and the paint might have been red or orange or yellow. It was simply a nondescript rust colour when we moved in. The original structure had probably contained two rooms, but more rooms had been added as time passed until it contained five. What sold us on it was that we could have two rooms, one to eat and cook in and one to sleep in. Another advantage was the yard, where Patty could play. We had the exclusive use of the front door, which opened into our kitchen-living-room.

Our landlady lived alone on the old-age pension and had been married at least twice and perhaps three times. She had little equity left in her house for it was plastered with hospital liens and she was several years behind in her taxes. From her $20-a-month pension, repairs were out of the question. We had this brought forcefully to our attention soon after we moved in. The toilet was located on the west side of the house in a little closet off the kitchen. The door from our kitchen into her living-room was also on the west side of the house. But the door leading from her living-room into her kitchen was on the east side. To get from our quarters to the kitchen it was necessary to cut diagonally across her living-room. The old lady always went to bed soon after dark and slept in a room off the living-room to the east. In order to ease our passage through her room, she had moved all her furniture to one side. We learned to make the journey in the dark and so got into the habit of closing our door quickly to keep the light from awakening her.

On the night in question I had taken off my shoes and was heading for the toilet in the dark. It was raining heavily. On my second step my foot landed in a pan of water. I swore, thrashed around, and my other foot kicked a jam-pail full of water. In the stillness of the house I must have sounded like an invading burglar. The old lady awoke and came out of her room full of apologies.

'Oh, I forgot to tell you about the pails. How stupid of me! Did you hurt yourself? Now, how did I ever forget to tell you about the pails?'

It transpired that the roof had been leaking for years. Unable to make repairs, she had done the next best thing—caught the water as it dripped through. She knew where every leak was located and when rain threatened she took down half a dozen empty jam-tins and a couple of pans. She knew so precisely where to set each tin that she seldom had a drop of water to wipe up after a rain.

This house, we were to discover that winter, was one of the most uninsulated houses in the city of Winnipeg. For both heating and cooking we acquired a small kitchen range with burned-out grates. The stove would boil water and fry eggs, but the oven was almost useless. When winter came, we were in trouble about heat. The only fuel we were given was cordwood. The fire-box in the stove was so small that the wood had to be chopped exceedingly fine in order to be burned in it. Nothing disappears quicker than fine-cut wood in a stove on a cold winter day.

On cold nights, Kay and I took turns staying up late. One of us would stay up till after midnight and get such a roaring fire going that the top of the stove would be red hot. A full kettle of water would be boiling madly when the stove was shut off and the lights put out. By five o'clock the next morning the water in the kettle on the stove would be frozen solid. The walls of the room were decorated with medallions of frost the size of pennies where the moisture had gathered on all the nail-heads. There was one corner where this frost never melted and the medallions grew larger and larger as winter passed.

To keep warm, Kay and Patty and I slept in the same bed. We piled on every blanket and quilt we owned. On top of them we put our overcoats. I put my socks under my pillow when I went to bed and put my hat on a chair within reach. When at last I had screwed up enough courage to get up, I would reach under the pillow, retrieve the socks and put them on. Then I'd slip the bed-clothes expertly aside and get into my overcoat. Towards the end of the winter I could put on my overcoat without getting out of bed and often without waking Kay. In a single motion I would be into my pants and out to the kitchen. Once the match was touched to the paper, I was back into bed again. Sometimes, on a very cold morning, I'd be in and out several times before the house was warm enough to live in.

We had not lived long in the little house on Chalmers Avenue before we began to notice our landlady's wide circle of gentleman friends. We had to be in and out of her kitchen a good deal, and during the first month she must have introduced us to half a dozen old codgers having tea with her. Strangely, we never saw the same one twice. It was not until several months later that she volunteered a rather simple explanation. She had been advertising for a husband, and these were prospective suitors who came in response to her newspaper advertisement:

> 'Refined English lady, owner of small, comfortable home, in receipt of old-age pension, would like to meet refined gentleman, old-age pensioner, object matrimony. Write particulars to Box 1621, Free Press.'

Her earlier advertisement had not produced a suitable husband, and she was about to try again. She had long since passed the point of surviving on the old-age pension. Our rent helped, but she still couldn't manage and she wasn't going to try any longer. She would insert another advert, she said, if I would take it to the *Free Press* for her. She wanted to assure us, however, that if she was successful it need make no difference to us. She was not going to marry just anybody. She would make sure that the man she got was sober and quiet and would not disturb us. We would just go on living as her tenants, and she hoped as her friends, as long as we cared to stay.

So it was that I took the advertisement to the newspaper and we sat back to await developments. She got perhaps a dozen replies and the winnowing process began. The technique employed was simple. The applicants were asked to call on a given afternoon. The lady made tea, and they sat and talked for an hour or so. If first impressions had been mutually favourable, the old geezer would be invited to return on another afternoon for another cup of tea. If she had drawn a blank, so to speak, he was rejected in the friendliest possible manner. She would invent insuperable differences in taste, temperament, or religion as a bar to union. On the other hand, if she was favourably impressed but the gentleman was not, he would simply not show up for the second date. While this system made courtship much slower than it might have been otherwise, our landlady preferred it that way.

During the next several weeks there was a parade of ancient Romeos to our house. Some of them were spry old fellows who scarcely seemed over sixty. Others looked like lost apostles and came hobbling up on canes. We could have told them that they would not do, for no suitor not sound of wind and limb had a chance of capturing her hand. Often after the suitors left, she would waylay Kay or me and ask for our judgment.

'That was Mr Armitage,' she would say. 'What did you think of *him*?'

With our landlady it was always best to be as vague as possible, so we would mumble something non-committal.

'Yes, he is rather nice in some ways, but he likes bacon and eggs for breakfast. He said his first wife was a wonderful cook and when they lived on the farm he always had bacon and eggs for breakfast, sometimes porridge too. He wanted to know if I liked bacon and eggs, and I can hardly stand tea on my stomach in the morning. Anyway, I'm such a poor cook that I'm afraid he would be disappointed. But he was nice and clean, wasn't he? I always say that if a man is clean that is about all you can ask for. Still, he'd always be thinking of his first wife's cooking. It's too bad, he was quite a nice man.'

If her prospects got over the first hurdle of personality, she went to work on the state of their bodies. She was particularly on the look-out for asthma, which had carried off her last husband. One old fellow got over several hurdles without her discovering that he had a heart condition. He was dropped like a cat in a bag off a bridge.

They came and they went and it seemed for a while that the search was going to go on forever. But one day an aged Lochinvar turned up to sweep her off her feet. His resemblance to cartoonist Bruce Bairnsfather's 'Old Bill' was quite remarkable, for he had the same straggling moustache and round face. He was a bit on the small side and did not look at all like a seventy-year-old. As it turned out, he was not seventy and did not get an old-age pension. His son, with whom he lived, talked him into answering the advertisement and came around to inspect and approve his future stepmother. The son promised his father that he would provide him with $20 a month until he got his pension in a couple of years. He reneged on this promise, and the old lady was to discover to her sorrow that she could have taken almost any one of the other applicants and been ahead of the game.

The old man, however, was a forceful character and swept her off to the altar. The week before the marriage was as hectic as if it was to be her first leap into the matrimonial pool instead of her third, for certain, and perhaps her fourth. She was ecstatically happy and did a thorough house-cleaning job with high enthusiasm. She fixed over her best dress for the wedding and became as flighty as a June-bug. She would make tea and forget to drink it or neglect to put tea in the pot and drink half a cup of hot water before discovering her mistake. She and her intended would hold hands under the table, billing and cooing like a couple of pigeons.

'Don't mind us, Mr Gray,' she said when I blundered in on them with a kettle for water. 'We are just a couple of silly kids.' In the evening they would walk around the back garden holding hands and laughing, completely oblivious of the amusement they were causing in the neighbourhood.

Love in such riotous bloom in December was amusing indeed. But what were we laughing at? What was so funny about a social order that drove a nice old lady to advertise for a husband in order to stay alive in our community? And not only her. There were dozens of others who sought the same solution for their problems every week. Was this to be our own fate, everybody's fate, fifty years down the same road? It was a melancholy question that was difficult enough to think about without having to live with it. After more than a year on relief, there was no comfort for Kay and me in any of the visible portents. A week after the wedding we went looking for other rooms.

THE SALE

Frederick Philip Grove

A young man was driving over the sand-flats along the margin of the Big Marsh, with a two-horse team hitched to a wagon.

The trail wound along, and he trotted his horses; they knew the road, he looked about. Before he had gone very far, others followed behind him: wagons, buggies, and similar vehicles; the farther he went, the more there were of them; every side-trail contributed its quotum as tributaries empty into a river: the bush was disgorging its population. On a farm near the town to the south-west, an auction sale was to be held; stock was to be sold, implements, household goods: a big sale.

When the driver came out on the highway from the north, the procession became a trek: cars, wagons, buggies from everywhere.

About ten o'clock, he reached the corner where the highway bent west into town; and he left it. In fact, it would have been impossible to follow it any longer; for from town, too, a stream of vehicles was coming: cars mostly; townpeople do not drive buggies and wagons.

Moreover, townpeople are inconsiderate. Henceforth, as the young man turned east along a new grade, he found that the wagon and buggy traffic was crowded off the road into the ditch, or, beyond it, on to the grass sward that bordered the road allowance. He glared at these people who drove in cars; his horses dodged and danced; but there was nothing to it; the cars retained the right-of-way.

Finally he saw the place where the sale was to be held. There were a number of long, unpainted buildings, barn, cow stable, granary, shed; the house, standing well back from the road, painted a dirty-drab colour, stood in the centre; in front, the huge yard was a litter and array of implements and machinery, displayed in rows radiating from an improvised platform of planks placed on trestles; beyond, the stock was crowded into horse and cow lots. Near the house his eye discovered a long, extemporized table at one end of which cups and plates were piled in huge stacks.

And through it all milled the crowd, looking, appraising, examining things.

The young man found a place, outside the yard, and tied his horses to the fence. Then he entered through the gate and lost himself in the multitude. He had to go where he was pushed; there was no choice. He surrendered himself.

At last he came near the platform and managed to push through to the centre, detaching himself from the laughing, joking derisive current of humanity. He knew what he wanted to buy if he got a chance; there was no use in allowing himself to be pushed about. Most of the rest were there in order to be in a crowd and to enjoy the show.

At the foot of the platform, a group of men stood conversing, some of whom he recognized. Altmann was there, the erstwhile owner of the property to be sold, an old, bearded man, portly, unctuous, but bearing on his face an expression which showed that he was looking darkly into the future: what might it hold? The past had been failure. His two sons were there, too: strapping young men who, you would think, might have pulled their father out of his hole if they had cared to. Every now and then a passer-by in the crowd called to them with a joke, and they responded. The smile with which they did so showed that they were not vitally interested in this affair; but the frown with which, a moment later, they glanced at the platform betrayed also that they felt dazed at the disaster which had overtaken their father. Redcliff, Altmann's son-in-law, also was there, a slim, pockmarked man who tried to step out of everybody's way with an apologetic smile and a shrug of his shoulders.

Opposite these stood an enormous man, six feet three inches tall and of lateral dimensions to match; his face was red and clean-shaven; its colour gave it a beefy expression. That was Mr Gunn, the chief creditor, the former owner of farm and outfit.

Next him stood Mr Macdonnell, the banker from town, who held a large sheaf of papers in his hand.

On the platform, two tables were arranged, one strewn with writing materials weighted down with stones. On the other lay a block of wood with a hammer on top.

Between platform and house a space was roped off, apparently to display the goods that were to be sold.

As the young man looked about, he saw many people perched on wagons and implements; some had even climbed into the tops of the few poplar trees along the fence; young boys were crouching on the fence-posts.

There was a note of impatience in the crowd. The opening of the sale had been advertised for ten o'clock; and it was almost eleven now.

Shouts rang across the multitude. 'Anfangen!' a German shouted. 'Crank her up, will you!' And, answering to this, a third voice yelled, 'Hi, there! Why don't you fellows get a self-starter?'

The young man edged up to the group at the platform.

'No,' he heard the banker say. 'We can't postpone. We have got the crowd. Let somebody start. Nicholson will come after awhile. They have had rain at Balfour. He must be delayed with his car.'

From that, the young man gathered that the auctioneer who was to conduct the sale had not arrived; for his name was Nicholson.

'I won't let some bungler spoil the whole thing,' the big man protested in singularly high-pitched notes, like those of a boy who has not yet changed his voice.

'Let's sell the trash first,' Mr Macdonnell urged. 'The household stuff. We must amuse the crowd. Keep them in good humour. Draw it out till Nicholson comes. He'll sell the big things, implements and livestock. We'll send a car into town and have somebody phone; see whether he's on the way. If we wait another hour, the people will go home; we'll never get such a crowd again. Say, Mr Gunn, I've got just the man. He isn't an auctioneer; but he'll josh them along: fellow by name of Cundy. He's here. He speaks some German, too. Half the crowd is foreign, anyway.'

A number of other people were patiently waiting nearby. Like the young man they knew what they wanted; they meant business; and they were willing to wait their chance.

In the milling crowd, the young man caught sight of such as he knew, some being his neighbours. There was Nielsen, the Dane, towering above those who surrounded him, laughing and indulging in antics as was his wont. That giant was not on the outside of a crowd; he mixed in; he was one of the rest. There were Dowdle, Finlay, Gowerluk, the Ruthenian, and many others. The young man, seeing how they all mingled and partook in the spirit of the crowd, began to feel lonesome and wished he had not come.

Suddenly a commotion arose. Somewhere in the crowd a voice started up a song, a popular tune at the time:

'We're marching; we're marching;

We'll soon go home . . . '

And immediately after that, a car was started on the road, just outside the fence; its engine roared; then subsided; then roared again, this time in low gear. Horses plunged and strained at their ropes.

For a second, the crowd went silent, looking and listening.

The car shot away towards town.

At the platform, the discussion came to a head. Before the lull in the general noise had again been drowned in the bedlam of voices, shouts, and laughter, Mr Macdonnell jumped on the platform, slim and active; and, raising his hand in a demand for silence, he sang out, 'Cundy!'

Laughing and uproarious, the crowd took up the shout. 'Cundy! Cundeeee!' Anything in the line of a diversion was welcome. On all sides people yelled, till the shout for Cundy was unanimous.

As soon as he had the chance, Cundy answered by yodling. He was a tall, slender man with a black moustache. Laughing, joking, replying to the teasing crowd, he pushed his way forward to the platform, reaching it at the exact spot where the young man stood. Lithe and energetic, Mr Macdonnell sprang down to meet him.

'Cundy,' he said, 'Nicholson, the auctioneer, is delayed. We've got to get this crowd started. We want you to open the sale.'

Cundy went serious for a moment. 'You don't say so,' he said.

'I'm sure you can do it,' Macdonnell replied persuasively.

'I've never done it before,' Cundy objected, still serious. Then he laughed. 'You don't mean to say that a hick like myself can get up there . . . '

'Hick nothing!' Macdonnell laughed. ' 'You are one of the ablest men in the district.'

'I sure am,' Cundy crowed, falling back into his usual tone. 'I'm hanged if I don't try it.'

A minute or so later he stood on the platform.

One of the Altmann boys seized a bell. Macdonnell, acting as clerk of the sale, sat down at the smaller table and put his papers in order.

'Start with the trash,' he prompted. 'Josh them along. Gain time. That's the main thing.'

The bell rang out; the crowd rearranged itself, facing the platform.

Cundy yodeled, and everybody laughed. Then a silence fell.

Cundy looked down over the crowd and began to speak, giving a brief introduction about the circumstances which had led to this sale, praising Altmann as one of the best farmers in the district.

The audience soon grew restless again; all this did not interest them.

Cundy, feeling his way, changed his method. He told them that Altmann had brought about this sale for their special benefit, sacrificing his possessions so others could enjoy what he had enjoyed. Incidentally, he talked up the stock, the implements, the machinery, and even the household junk.

He drew a few laughs. The crowd was in a recipient mood and became expectant. This was something new.

At the place where the household goods were piled, a thin German with a hatchet shaped face was holding an ordinary pail to the light. Just as Cundy wound up with a few remarks about the unparalleled opportunities which offered, this German said in a nagging voice, 'There's something wrong with everything in this yard. This pail leaks.'

In the silence which had followed Cundy's last words, his voice rang out so that most people heard him. Some laughed.

'Silence!' someone shouted.

But Cundy had fixed a glassy eye on the German as if he had been waiting for just that remark. 'Pletz!' he sang out. 'Hand me that pail.'

One of the Altmann boys jumped for it and handed it up. Again the crowd laughed.

Cundy raised the pail high over his head.

'Ladies and gentlemen,' he shouted with the full force of his lungs, 'You have heard what he said. I have a pail here, a good pail, galvanised inside and out . . . ' Handling it and showing it about. 'I am going to sell it. I am going to sell it to one of you. One of you is going to be the lucky man. Don't think for a moment that this is an ordinary pail. Far from it. It's quite a peculiar pail. Pletz here has told you. It LEAKS. It's like one of them big farms around here. You pour the money in; and you don't need to pour it out. The water in this pail pours out by itself.'

A roar went up from the crowd; but so far it came chiefly from the children and the young boys.

'Ladies and gentlemen,' Cundy went on when silence was restored. 'I am waiting for bids.'

'That's the sutff,' Macdonnell whispered in the momentary silence which followed; and he looked back at Gunn, the giant, winking.

'Five cents,' somebody shouted in derision.

'Swat the fly!' Cundy roared.

The crowd yelled.

But bidding began in earnest.

'Ten cents.'—'Fifteen.'—'Twenty-five.'—'Fifty.'—'Sixty.'

Cundy acted indignation. 'Such a pail,' he shouted, 'can be bought at the stores for eighty cents. But at that price I can't give you the leak. Mark my words. You don't get the leak. If you don't come ahead and bid, I shall have to sell the leak separately, ladies and gentlemen. I might sell you the pail alone for sixty cents. But I can't throw the leak in at that price... A dollar, I hear?... That sounds more likely... A dollar and ten... A dollar a quarter... Thirty... Thirty-five... Ladies and gentlemen, I am bid a dollar and thirty-five. A dollar and fifty... Seventy-five ... Do I hear eighty? Eighty... A dollar and eighty it is... Ladies and gentlemen, one dollar and eighty cents... A leaking pail... A dollar and eighty... Going, going, gone!' And he brought the hammer down on the block of wood, with a tremendous whack, jumping into the air and yodling. 'That man there,' he added in a business-like whisper to Macdonnell, pointing.

The crowd roared and whistled and applauded as at a show.

The man who had made the last but one bid looked up and shouted to Cundy, 'I'm sorry I couldn't bid more...'

'That's all right,' Cundy said; and, bending forward as if to impart a secret, the crowd going silent, he said in a whisper loud enough for everyone to hear it, 'The other fellow paid all it is worth.'

The crowd went raving with laughter.

The bell rang out.

'Ladies and gentleman!' Cundy yelled. 'I'm not an auctioneer. I'm an honest farmer. This is my first appearance on the platform; or you might be afraid that you wouldn't get value. But I'm not on to the tricks of the trade. There's my good friend Pletz. You all know him. I can see by the tip of his slender nose that he has something to tell you. I shall merely follow his lead. It may seem to some of you as if he were grumbling. Don't rely on appearances. He is merely trying to tell you about the good points of everything. There he is looking at a washing machine. Well, Pletz, darling, what have you to say?'

The crowd listened breathlessly.

'Shucks!' Pletz said. 'This is a mere pile of junk. The wringer board is loose...'

'You heard him,' Cundy shouted triumphantly. 'I'd never have noticed it. This washing machine not only helps the woman to do her washing. It keeps the man busy, too, meanwhile, putting bolts in. So he has something to grumble about. Hand it up, boys. Hand it up. I am going to sell it.'

The washing machine brought twelve dollars and fifty cents.

Pletz, as if in despair, sat down on a plank placed over two blocks of wood; and it broke under him.

'What?' Cundy sang out. 'Did I hear a plank in the Liberal platform breaking?'

The Liberal party had just got into power; and the crowd went frantic.

And thus it went on. For two hours Cundy kept talking, talking, getting money sometimes for what was not worth taking home. The little items began to total up to a respectable sum.

It was not so much a sale as a show. It was the townpeople who bought, mostly young folk; they were willing to pay for being entertained. The older people and the farmers sat and stood about, humped up, wary, patiently waiting for the time when all this tom-foolery would be over.

Meanwhile the car had returned from town. Nicholson, the auctioneer, would be there; but it would not be early. He had had a sale the day before, at Valley Stream, south of Balfour; and he had been rained in. He would have to come by the train; and the train would be late.

At half past one Cundy called a recess for luncheon.

The young man still stood at the foot of the platform when the crowd ebbed away towards the improvised buffet in front of the house. Everybody was laughing, shouting, joking again.

Altmann, Gunn, Macdonnell surrounded Cundy, congratulating and praising.

'You are hitting them in the right spot,' Macdonnell said. 'The stock next.'

'Well,' Cundy said. 'Nicholson will be here.'

'You go on, Mr Cundy,' said Gunn. 'I'll fix it with Nicholson. You've got the crowd going. You are my man.'

So, at two o'clock, when the bell was rung, the Altmann boys brought a calf into the ring; then a team of horses; more calves; a cow.

Cundy harped on Pletz. He called on him every time. Pletz was angry; he disliked it; he threatened to leave; he swore. The crowd merely laughed at him; and they pushed him forward whenever he tried to withdraw. Cundy played him like a fish he had hooked. He treated him like a spoiled child that needs to be humoured, that might refuse to do what he asked him to do but would give in at last. Everybody felt that Cundy was playing him up, waiting and watching for an opportunity to sacrifice him on the altar of his wit.

At last that opportunity came.

A cow was led forward; and the bell rang out.

'Sh!' Cundy said, putting his finger on his lips. 'Sh! Listen!'

And sure enough, through the silence that ensued, Pletz's nagging voice was heard. 'Too bad,' he said. 'This isn't a sale. It's a hold-up. That cow has only three teats.'

Triumphantly Cundy raised himself on his toes. Reproachfully he looked at the man and held up a hand, commanding silence. Then he hissed through the side of his mouth, like the villain in a bad play. 'Shame, man, shut up! Your mother had only two; and *she* raised a big calf!'

Bedlam broke loose. The cow, in the bidding which followed, brought sixty-five dollars.

A car rushed along the road. The auctioneer had arrived, a flashy, slick man of middle age. Gunn met him at the gate, began to argue, implored; in vain. Nicholson insisted on proceeding with the sale himself. Cundy held no license, he said. The fees on all that had been sold would be his . . .

Cundy yielded his place without raising any objection. The sale proceeded. But the interest of the crowd was gone.

The young man waited. So did others who had come with a definite object in view. They sat or stood about, humped up, tired out, but patient. Prices which had run unreasonably high now ran unreasonably low.

A five o'clock two buggy horses were brought into the enclosure. Under the monotonous drone of the auctioneer's voice the bidding started. It stopped at seventy-five dollars for the team.

The young man, who had straightened out and listened, hesitated.

Somebody shouted, 'Eighty!'—a desultory, half-hearted bid. The team was easily worth a hundred and fifty dollars. One of them was a mare, not more than five or six years old.

'Eighty dollars I am bid for the team . . . 'Eighty dollars,' the voice from the platform droned. 'Going . . . Going . . . '

'Eighty-five,' the young man said, clearing his throat.

'Eighty-five I am bid. Eighty five dollars . . . Eighty-five! . . . Going, going, gone!'

The young man stepped excitedly up to Macdonnell's table. 'The democrat,' he said. 'I want the democrat.'

'All right. Just a moment. Wait till it is put up.'

And, as the young man stood there, ready to give his cheque, he noticed that the crowd was dispersing and thinning out. Few people had come because they wanted to buy this or that. The sale was a social event, an occasion for fun and entertainment. Cundy had furnished that. This man did not. Money was plentiful with townpeople those days; there was the post-war boom. So long as they were amused, they spent recklessly. The moment they felt bored, they closed their pockets and went home. Those that were still holding out were hardheaded farmers, hunters for bargains.

Half an hour later, the young man had bidden the democrat in for forty-five dollars; and the double driving harness for eighteen.

He, too, withdrew. At the gate, he ran into a neighbour.

'Buy anything?' he asked.

'Yeh,' answered the neighbour. 'A cutting-box. Got it cheap . . . '

Cundy came out through the gate, accompanied by Nielsen, the big Dane.

'If that fake of an auctioneer hadn't come at last,' Nielsen was saying, 'Altmann might have been shut of his debts.'

'You bet,' Cundy agreed. 'I'd easily have joshed another thousand out of the crowd. Well, can't be helped. Come on. Where's my car?'

The young man tied the newly bought horses, hitched to the democrat, behind his wagon and started for home.

He was tired of the day's work of doing nothing; but he was happy in thinking that he was taking home what he had come for. He thought of his young wife at home and of his three children. They would be able to go to town now whenever they wished; it would no longer take a whole day.

And again he thought of the old man, Altmann, who had hoped no doubt that there would be a surplus from this sale over and above his indebtedness and who had been disappointed. Himself, a young man, was driving home with an outfit which he had bought for half its value while others carried leaking pails not worth a cent.

He shrugged his shoulders. 'One man's bread is the other man's poison' he muttered as he shook the lines over his horses' backs.

F. P. GROVE: THE FINDING

Robert Kroetsch

I

Dreaming the well-born   hobo of yourself
against the bourgeois father   dreaming Europe
if only to find   a place to be from

the hobo tragedian   pitching bundles
riding a freight   to the impossible city
the fallen archangel   of Brandon or Winnipeg

in all your harvesting   real
or imagined   did you really find
four aged stallions   neigh

in your cold undertaking   on those trails north
in all the (dreamed) nights   in stooks
in haystacks   dreaming the purified dreamer

who lured you   to a new man (back
to the fatal earth)   inventing (beyond
America) a new world   did you find

did you dream   the French priest who hauled you
out of your *fleurs du mal*   and headlong
into a hundred drafts   real

or imagined   of the sought form
(there are no models)   and always
(there are only models)   alone

2
alone in the cutter   in the blizzard
two horses   hauling you into the snow
that buries the road   burying the forest

the layered mind   exfoliating
back to the barren sea   (Greek to us,
Grove)   back to the blank sun

and musing snow to yourself   new
to the old rite of burial   the snow
lifting the taught man   into the coyote self

the silence of sight   'as if I were not myself
who yet am I'   riding the drifted snow
to your own plummeting   alone and alone

the *wirklichkeit*   of the word itself
the name under the name   the sought
and calamitous edge   of the white earth

the horses   pawing the empty fall
the hot breath on the zero day   the man
seeing the new man so vainly   alone

we say with your waiting wife   (but she
was the world   before you invented it
old liar)   'You had a hard trip?'

HOUSES

Douglas Barbour

Flat pine, bare
grey often, and the empty
windows: these are
silent sentinels

out of the past,

                    boyhood
sleeping in such rooms
beneath thin quilts, faded
linoleum on the floors

                              (or
fifty years gone, the thin
flare of oil wicks, night
in Spring, ruts in deep mud
animal sounds by the trough: at sun up
all rise, biscuits
bacon, milk and the day
to plough, the heavy steps).

they are few and far
between thin lines of trees
to break the flat still spaces

          (seventy-five years
when Grandfather brought seeds,
saw in his mind
the inch of shade on a barren map).

We see the still houses,
they might be empty

as we pass.

STILL STANDS THE HOUSE

Gwen Pharis Ringwood

CAST

Ruth Warren
Arthur Manning
Hester Warren
Bruce Warren

SCENE

A living room.

The icy wind of a northern blizzard sweeps across the prairie, lashes about the old Warren farmhouse, and howls insistently at the door and windows. But the Warren house was built to withstand the menace of the Canadian winter and scornfully suffers the storm to shriek about the chimney corner, to knock at the door and rattle the windows in a wild attempt to force an entrance.

The living room of this house has about it a faded austerity, a decayed elegance that is as remote and cheerless as a hearth in which no fire is ever laid. The room has made a stern and solemn pact with the past. Once it held the warm surge of life; but as the years have gone by, it has settled in a rigid pattern of neat, uncompromising severity.

As if in defiance of the room, the frost has covered the window in the rear wall with a wild and exotic design. Beside the window is an imposing leather armchair, turned toward the handsome coal stove in the Right corner. A footstool is near the chair. A door at the Center of the rear wall leads to the snow-sheeted world outside. Along the Left wall, between a closed door to the bedroom (now unused) and an open door to a kitchen, is a mahogany sideboard. Above it is a portrait of old Martin Warren, who built this house and lived in it until his death. The portrait is of a stern and handsome man in his early fifties, and in the expression of the eyes the artist has caught something of his unconquerable will.

An open staircase, winding to the bedrooms upstairs, extends into the room at Right. There is a rocking chair by the stove with a small stand-table beside it. A mahogany dining table and two matching chairs are placed at a convenient distance from the side-board and the kitchen door. The figured wall paper is cracked and faded. The dark rug, the heavy curtains, and the tablecloth show signs of much wear, but there is nothing of cheapness about them.

Two coal oil lanterns have been left beside the kitchen door. Blooming bravely on the table, in contrast to its surroundings, is a pot of lavender hyacinths.

Ruth Warren is standing near the outside door, talking to Arthur Manning, who is about to leave. Ruth is small, fair-haired, and pretty, twenty-five or twenty-six years of age. There is more strength in her than her rather delicate appearance would indicate. She wears a soft blue house-dress, with a light wool cardigan over it. Manning is a middle-aged man of prosperous appearance. He wears a heavy overcoat over a dark business suit. His hat, gloves and scarf are on the armchair.

RUTH: Do you think you'd better try to go back tonight, Mr Manning? The roads may be drifted.

MANNING: It's a bad blizzard, all right, but I don't think I'll have any trouble. There's a heater in the car, and I've just had the engine checked over.

RUTH: You'll be welcome if you care to spend the night.

MANNING: Thank you, but I'm afraid I've got to get back to town. I'd hate to try it in an old car, but this one of mine can pull through anything.

RUTH: I've never seen a storm come up so quickly.

MANNING: These prairie blizzards are no joke. One of my sheepherders got lost in one last year, just half a mile from the house. He froze to death out there trying to find his way.

RUTH: How frightful!

MANNING: One of the ranch hands found him the next morning. Poor old fellow—he'd herded for me for twenty years. I never knew how he came to be out in a storm like that.

RUTH: They say when a person gets lost he begins to go round in a circle, although it seems straight ahead.

MANNING: Yes, I've always heard that. The winters are the one thing I've got against this country.

RUTH: (*Wistfully*) I used to like them in town. We went skating on the river and tobogganing. But out here it's different.

MANNING: If Bruce sells the farm and takes this irrigated place near town, you won't notice the winter so much, Mrs Warren.

RUTH: No. I hope he does take your offer, Mr Manning. I want him to.

MANNING: He'll never get a better. Five thousand dollars and an irrigated quarter[1] is a good price for a dryland farm these days.

RUTH: If only we didn't have to decide so soon.

MANNING: I talked it all over with Bruce in town a couple of weeks ago, and I think he's pretty well made up his mind. All he needs to do is sign the papers.

RUTH: I thought he'd have until spring to decide.

MANNING: I've got orders to close the deal before I go South next week. You tell Bruce I'll come by tomorrow or the next day, and we can get it all settled.

RUTH: I'll tell him. I hope he does take it, Mr Manning.

MANNING: I know you do and you're right. I think all he needs is a little persuading. He's had a hard time here these dry years.

RUTH: I don't know what Hester will say.

MANNING: I understand she's very much attached to the place. Is it true that she never leaves the farm?

[1] Quarter-section, 160 acres or one-fourth of a square mile; a common farm area in the West.

RUTH: Not often.

MANNING: She'd be better off where she could get out more.

RUTH: I don't know.

MANNING: I suppose all those years out here, keeping house for Bruce and her father, were pretty hard on her.

RUTH: The house has come to mean so much to her. But maybe she won't mind. (*Smiling hopefully*) We'll see.

The door to the bedroom, Left, is opened quietly, and Hester Warren enters the room. She closes and locks the door behind her and stands looking at the two in the room with cold surmise. Hester is forty years old. She is tall, dark and unsmiling. The stern rigidity of her body, the bitter austerity of her mouth, and the almost arrogant dignity of her carriage seem to make her a part of the room she enters. There is bitter resentment in her dark eyes as she confronts Ruth and Manning. She holds a leather-bound Bible close to her breast.

RUTH: (*Startled*) Why, Hester! I thought you never unlocked that door.

HESTER: (*Quietly*) No. I keep Father's room as it was.

RUTH: Then why were you—

HESTER: I was reading in Father's room. I heard a stranger.

RUTH: You know Mr Manning, Hester.

MANNING: (*With forced friendliness*) I don't suppose you remember me, Miss Warren.

HESTER: (*Without moving*) How do you do?

MANNING: (*Embarrassed at her coldness and anxious to get away*) Well, I'll be getting on home. I'll leave these papers for Bruce to sign, Mrs Warren. Tell him I'll come by tomorrow. He'll find it's all there, just as we talked about it. (*He lays the document on the table.*)

RUTH: Thank you, Mr Manning.

MANNING: (*Turning to go*) Take care of yourselves. Good-night. (*To Hester*) Good-night, Miss Warren.

Hester barely nods.

RUTH: You're sure you ought to try it in the storm?

MANNING: Sure. There's no danger if I go right away. (*He goes out.*)

RUTH: (*Calling after him as she shuts the door*) Good-night.

Hester watches Manning out and, as Ruth returns, she looks at her suspiciously. There is a silence which Hester finally breaks.

HESTER: What did he want here?

RUTH: (*Uncomfortable under Hester's scrutiny*) He just left some papers for Bruce to look over, Hester. He was in a hurry so he didn't wait to see Bruce.

HESTER: I see. What has Arthur Manning got to do with Bruce?

RUTH: It's something to do with the farm, Hester. I'll put these away. (*She starts to take up the document on the table, but Hester is before her.*)

HESTER: (*After a long look at the document*) A deed of sale. (*Turning angrily upon Ruth*) So this is what you've been hiding from me.

RUTH: (*Quickly*) Oh, no! Nothing's settled, Hester. Mr Manning made an offer and Bruce wants to think it over. That's all.

HESTER: (*Her eyes betraying her intense agitation*) Bruce isn't going to sell this place!

RUTH: It's just an offer. Nothing has been decided.

HESTER: Your hand's in this! You've been after him to leave here.

RUTH: (*Trying to conciliate her*) Let's not quarrel. You can talk to Bruce about it, Hester.

HESTER: You hate this house, I know that.

RUTH: No. (*Facing Hester firmly*) But I think Bruce ought to sell.

HESTER: You married him. You made your choice.

RUTH: (*Quietly*) I've not regretted that. It's just that we're so cut off and lonely here; and this is the best offer we could get. But let me put these away. (*Indicating the deed of sale*) We'll talk about it later, the three of us.

HESTER: (*Allowing Ruth to take the papers*) You may as well burn them. He isn't going to sell.

RUTH: Please, Hester—we'll discuss it when Bruce comes. (*She places the document on the sideboard, then crosses to the stove.*) I'll build up the fire.

HESTER: (*Takes the Bible to the sideboard and places it under her father's portrait. She stands looking up at the portrait.*) This house will not be sold. I won't allow it.

RUTH: (*Puts some coal on the fire. Shivering*) It's so cold it almost frightens me. The thermometer has dropped ten degrees within the hour.

HESTER: I hope Bruce knows enough to get the stock in. They'll freeze where they stand if they're left out tonight. (*She moves to the window and takes her knitting from the ledge.*)

RUTH: He'll have them in. (*Crossing to the table*) Look, Hester, how the hyacinths have bloomed. I could smell them when I came in the room just now.

HESTER: Hyacinths always seem like death to me.

RUTH: (*Her voice is young and vibrant.*) Oh, no. They're birth, they're spring! They say in Greece you find them growing wild in April. (*She takes an old Wedgwood bowl from the sideboard, preparing to set the pot of hyacinths in it.*)

HESTER: (*In a dry, unfriendly tone*) I've asked you not to use that Wedgwood bowl. It was my grandmother's. I don't want it broken.

RUTH: I'm sorry. (*Replacing the bowl, she gets a plain one from inside the sideboard.*) I thought the hyacinths would look so pretty in it, but I'll use the plain one.

HESTER: You've gone to as much trouble for that plant as if it were a child. (*Hester sits in the rocking chair by the stove.*)

RUTH: (*Placing the hyacinths in the bowl*) They're so sweet. I like to touch them.

HESTER: They'll freeze tonight, I'm thinking.

RUTH: Not in here. We'll have to keep the fire up anyway. (*Leaving the bowl of hyacinths on the table, Ruth returns to the sideboard, taking some bright chintz from the drawer. She holds it up for Hester to see.*) I've almost finished the curtains, Hester.

HESTER: (*Tonelessly*) You have?

RUTH: Don't you think they'll make this room more cheerful?

HESTER: The ones we have seem good enough to me.

RUTH: But they're so old.

HESTER: (*Coldly*) Old things have beauty when you've eyes to see it. That velvet has a richness that you can't buy now.

RUTH: (*Moving to the window*) I want to make the room gay and happy for spring. You'll see how much difference these will make.

HESTER: I've no doubt. (*Hester rises and goes to the table to avoid looking at the curtains.*)

RUTH: (*Measuring the chintz with the curtains at the window*) I wonder if I have them wide enough.

The wind rises. As if the sound had quelled her pleasure in the bright curtains, Ruth turns slowly away from the window. A touch of hysteria creeps into her voice.

RUTH: The wind swirls and shrieks and raises such queer echoes in this old house! It seems to laugh at us in here, thinking we're safe, hugging the stove! As if it knew it could blow out the light and the fire and—(*Getting hold of herself*) I've never seen a blizzard when it was as cold as this. Have you, Hester?

HESTER: (*Knitting*) Bruce was born on a night like this.

Throughout this scene Hester seldom looks at Ruth but gives all her attention to her knitting. She seems reluctant to talk and yet impelled to do so.

RUTH: I didn't know.

HESTER: Father had to ride for the doctor while I stayed here with Mother.

RUTH: Alone?

HESTER: Yes. I was rubbing Father's hands with snow when we heard the baby crying. Then we helped the doctor bathe him.

RUTH: You were such a little girl to do so much.

HESTER: After Mother died I did it all.

RUTH: I know, but it was too hard for a child. I don't see how you managed.

HESTER: Father always helped me with the washing.

RUTH: Not many men would stay in from the field to do that.

HESTER: No. (*Her knitting drops to her lap, and for a moment she is lost in the past.*) 'We'll have to lean on one another now, Daughter.'—Those were his words.—And that's the way it was. I was beside him until—I never left him.

RUTH: (*At Hester's side*) You've never talked of him like this before.

HESTER: (*Unconscious of Ruth*) He always liked the snow. (*Her eyes are on the portrait of her father.*) He called it a moving shroud, a winding-sheet that the wind lifts and raises and lets fall again.

RUTH: It is like that.

HESTER: He'd come in and say, 'The snow lies deep on the summer fallow, Hester. That means a good crop next year.'

RUTH: I know. It's glorious in the fall with the wheat like gold on the hills. No wonder he loved it.

HESTER: (*Called out of her dream, she abruptly resumes her knitting.*) There hasn't been much wheat out there these last years.

RUTH: That isn't Bruce's fault, Hester.

HESTER: You have to love a place to make things grow. The land knows when you don't care about it and Bruce doesn't care about it any more. Not like Father did.

RUTH: (*Her hands raised to touch the portrait above the sideboard*) I wish I'd known your father.

HESTER: (*Rising and facing Ruth with a sudden and terrible anger*) Don't touch that picture. It's mine.

RUTH: (*Startled, she faces Hester*) Why, Hester—

HESTER: Can't I have anything of my own? Must you put your fingers on everything I have?

RUTH: (*Moving to Hester*) Hester, you know I didn't mean—What is the matter with you?

HESTER: I won't have you touch it.

RUTH: (*Gently*) Do you hate my being here so much?

HESTER: (*Turning away*) You've more right here than I have now, I suppose.

RUTH: (*Crossing over to the stove*) You make me feel that I've no right at all.

HESTER: (*A martyr now*) I'm sorry if you don't approve my ways. I can go, if that's what you want.

RUTH: (*Pleading*) Please—I've never had a sister, and when Bruce told me he had one, I thought we'd be such friends—

HESTER: (*Sitting in the chair by the stove*) We're not a family to put words to everything we feel. (*She resumes her knitting.*)

RUTH: (*Trying to bridge the gulf between them*) I get too excited over things: I know it. Bruce tells me I sound affected when I say too much about the way I feel, the way I like people—or the sky in the evening. I—

HESTER: (*Without looking up*) Did you get the separator put up? Or shall I do it?

RUTH: (*Discouraged, Ruth turns away, and going to the table, sits down with her sewing.*) It's ready for the milk when Bruce brings it. I put it together this morning.

HESTER: The lanterns are empty.

RUTH: I'll fill them in a minute.

HESTER: When I managed this house, I always filled the lanterns right after supper. Then they were ready.

RUTH: (*Impatiently*) I said I'd fill them, Hester, and I will. They're both there in the corner. (*She indicates the lanterns at the end of the sideboard.*)

HESTER: Bruce didn't take one, then?

RUTH: No.

HESTER: You'd better put a lamp in the window.

RUTH: (*Lights a small lamp on the sideboard and takes it to the window*) I wish he'd come. It's strange how women feel safer when their men are near, close enough to touch, isn't it? No matter how strong you think you are. (*As she speaks, Ruth drapes some of the chintz over the armchair.*)

HESTER: I can't say that I need my strength from Bruce, or could get it if I needed it.

RUTH: That's because he's still a little boy to you. (*A pause. Then Ruth speaks hesitantly*) Hester—

HESTER: Yes?

RUTH: Will you mind the baby in the house?

HESTER: (*After a silence, constrainedly*) No, I won't mind. I'll keep out of the way.

RUTH: (*Warmly, commanding a response*) I don't want you to. You'll love him, Hester.

HESTER: (*Harshly*) I loved Bruce, but I got no thanks for it. He feels I stand in his way now.

RUTH: (*Suddenly aware that Hester has needed and wanted love*) You musn't say that. It isn't true.

HESTER: When he was little, after Mother died, he'd come tugging at my hand—He'd get hold of my little finger and say, 'Come, Hettie—come and look.' Everything was 'Hettie' then.

RUTH: (*Eagerly, moving to Hester*) It will be like that again. This baby will be almost like your own.

HESTER: (*As if Ruth's words were an implied reproach*) I could have married, and married well if I'd had a mind to.

RUTH: I know that. I've wondered why you didn't, Hester.

HESTER: The young men used to ride over here on Sunday, but I stopped that. (*A pause*) I never saw a man I'd let touch me. Maybe you don't mind that kind of thing. I do.

RUTH: (*Involuntarily; it is a cry*) No! (*Attempting to put her arms around Hester*) What hurt you?

HESTER: (*Rising*) Don't try your soft ways on me. (*She moves behind the armchair, her hand falls caressingly on the back of the chair.*) I couldn't leave Bruce and Father alone. My duty was here in this house. So I stayed. (*Hester notices the chintz material draped over the chair and, taking it up, turns to Ruth angrily.*) What do you intend to do with this?

RUTH: I thought—there's enough left to make covers for the chair to match the curtains—

HESTER: (*Throwing the chintz down*) This is Father's chair. I won't have it changed.

RUTH: I'm sorry, Hester. (*With spirit*) Must we keep everything the same forever?

HESTER: There's nothing in this house that isn't good, that wasn't bought with care and pride by one of us who loved it. This stuff is cheap and gaudy.

RUTH: It isn't dull and falling apart with age.

HESTER: Before my father died, when he was ill, he sat here in this chair where he could see them threshing from the window. It was the first time since he came here that he'd not been in the fields at harvest. Now you come—you who never knew him, who never saw him—and you won't rest until—

RUTH: Hester!

HESTER: You've got no right to touch it! (*Her hands grip the back of the old chair as she stands rigid, her eyes blazing.*)

Bruce Warren enters from outside, carrying a pail of milk. He is tall and dark, about thirty years old, sensitive and bitter. His vain struggle to make the farm pay since his father's death has left him with an oppressive sense of failure. He is proud and quick to resent an imagined reproach. He has dark hair, his shoulders are a little stooped, and he moves restlessly and abruptly. Despite his moodiness, he is extremely likeable. He is dressed warmly in dark trousers, a sweater under his heavy leather coat; he wears gloves, cap and high boots. He brushes the snow from his coat as he enters.

BRUCE: (*Carrying the milk into the kitchen*) Is the separator up, Ruth?

RUTH: Yes, it's all ready, Bruce. Wait, I'll help you. (*She follows him into the kitchen.*)

Hester stands at the chair a moment after they have gone; her eyes fall on the table. Slowly she goes towards it, as if drawn by something she hated. She looks down at the lavender blooms for a moment. Then with a quick, angry gesture, she crushes one of the stalks. She turns away and is winding up her wool when Bruce and Ruth return.

RUTH: You must be frozen.

BRUCE: (*Taking off his coat and gloves*) I'm cold, all right. God, it's a blizzard: thirty-eight below, and a high wind. (*He throws his coat over a chair at the table.*)

RUTH: (*With pride*) Did you see the hyacinths? They've bloomed since yesterday.

BRUCE: (*Smiling*) Yes, they're pretty. (*Touching them, he notices the broken stalk.*) Looks like one of them's broken.

RUTH: Where? (*She sees it.*) Oh, it is! And that one hadn't bloomed yet! I wonder—It wasn't broken when I—(*Ruth turns accusingly to Hester*) Hester!

HESTER: (*Returns Ruth's look calmly. Coldly.*) Yes?

RUTH: Hester, did you—

BRUCE: (*Going over to the fire*) Oh, Ruth, don't make such a fuss about it. It can't be helped.

HESTER: I'll take care of the milk. (*She takes the small lamp from the window.*)

RUTH: I'll do it.

HESTER: (*Moving toward the kitchen*) You turn the separator so slow the cream's as thin as water.

RUTH: (*Stung to reply*) That's not true. You never give me a chance to—

BRUCE: (*Irritably*) For God's sake, don't quarrel about it. (*He sits in the chair by the stove.*)

HESTER: I don't intend to quarrel. (*She goes into the kitchen.*)

Ruth follows Hester to the door. The sound of the separator comes from the kitchen. Ruth turns wearily, takes up the pot of hyacinths, and places them on the stand near the stove. Then sits on the footstool.

RUTH: It's always that way.

BRUCE: (*Gazing moodily at the stove*) Why don't you two try to get along?

A silence.

RUTH: Did you put the stock in? (*The question is merely something to fill the empty space of silence between them.*)

BRUCE: Yes. That black mare may foal tonight. I'll have to look at her later on.

RUTH: It's bitter weather for a little colt to be born.

BRUCE: Yes.

Another silence. Finally Ruth, to throw off the tension between them, gets up and moves her footstool over to his chair.

RUTH: I'm glad you're here. I've been lonesome for you.

BRUCE: (*Putting his hand on hers*) I'm glad to be here.

RUTH: I thought of you out at the barn, trying to work in this cold.

BRUCE: I was all right. I'd hate to walk far tonight, though. You can't see your hand before your face.

RUTH: (*After a look at the kitchen*) Hester's been so strange again these last few days, Bruce.

BRUCE: I know it's hard, Ruth.

RUTH: It's like it was when I first came here. At everything I touch, she cries out like I'd hurt her somehow.

BRUCE: Hester has to do things her own way. She's always been like that.

RUTH: If only she could like me a little. I think she almost does sometimes, but then—

BRUCE: You think too much about her.

RUTH: Maybe it's because we've been shut in so close. I'm almost afraid of her lately.

BRUCE: She's not had an easy life, Ruth.

RUTH: I know that. She talked about your father almost constantly today.

BRUCE: His death hit us both hard. Dad ran the farm, decided everything.

RUTH: It's been six years, Bruce.

BRUCE: There are things you don't count out by years.

RUTH: He wouldn't want you to go on remembering forever.

BRUCE: (*Looking at the floor*) No.

RUTH: You should get free of this house. It's not good for you to stay here. It's not good for Hester. (*Getting up, she crosses to the sideboard and returns with the deed of sale, which she hands to Bruce.*) Mr Manning left this for you. He's coming back tomorrow for it, when you've signed it.

BRUCE: (*Takes the papers. Annoyed by her assurance*) He doesn't need to get so excited. I haven't decided to sign yet. He said he wouldn't need to know till spring. (*He goes over to the lamp at the table and studies the document.*)

RUTH: His company gave him orders to close the deal this week or let it go.

BRUCE: This week?

RUTH: That's what he said.

BRUCE: Well, I'll think about it.

RUTH: You'll have to decide tonight, Bruce. No one else will offer you as much. Five thousand dollars and an irrigated farm a mile from town seems a good price.

BRUCE: I'm not complaining about the deal. It's fair.

RUTH: (*Urgently*) You're going to take it, aren't you, Bruce?

BRUCE: I don't know. God, I don't know. (*He throws the document on the table.*) I don't want to sell, Ruth. I think I'll try it another year.

RUTH: Bruce, you've struggled here too long now. You haven't had a crop, a good crop, in five years.

BRUCE: I need to be told that!

RUTH: It's not your fault. But you've told me you ought to give it up, that it's too dry here.

BRUCE: We may get a crop this year. We're due for one.

RUTH: If you take this offer, we'll be nearer town. We'll have water on the place. We can have a garden, and trees growing.

BRUCE: That's about what those irrigated farms are—gardens.

RUTH: And, Bruce, it wouldn't be so lonely there, so cruelly lonely.

BRUCE: I told you how it was before you came.

RUTH: (*Resenting his tone*) You didn't tell me you worshipped a house. That you made a god of a house and a section of land. You didn't tell me that!

BRUCE: (*Angrily*) You didn't tell me that you'd moon at a window for your old friends, either. (*He stands up and throws the deed of sale on the table.*)

RUTH: How could I help it here?

BRUCE: And you didn't tell me that you'd be afraid of having a child. What kind of a woman are you that you don't want your child?

RUTH: That's not true.

BRUCE: No? You cried when you knew, didn't you?

RUTH: Bruce!

BRUCE: (*Going blindly on*) What makes you feel the way you do, then? Other women have children without so much fuss. Other women are glad.

RUTH: (*Intensely angry*) Don't speak to me like that. Keep your land. Eat and sleep and dream land, I don't care!

BRUCE: (*Turning to the portrait of his father*) My father came out here and took a homestead. He broke the prairie with one plough and a team of horses. He built a house to live in out of the sod. You didn't know that, did you? He and Mother lived here in a sod shanty and struggled to make things grow. Then they built a one-room shack; and when the good years came, they built this house. The finest in the country! I thought my son would have it.

RUTH: (*Moving to him*) What is there left to give a son? A house that stirs with ghosts! A piece of worn-out land where the rain never comes.

BRUCE: That's not all. I don't suppose you can understand.

RUTH: (*Turning away from him, deeply hurt*) No. I don't suppose I can. You give me little chance to know how you feel about things.

BRUCE: (*His anger gone*) Ruth, I didn't mean that. But you've always lived in town. (*He goes to the window and stands looking out for a moment, then turns.*) Those rocks along the fence out there, I picked up every one of them with my own hands and carried them with my own hands across the field and piled them there. I've ploughed that southern slope along the coulee[2] every year since I was twelve. (*His voice is torn with a kind of shame for his emotions.*) I feel about the land like Hester does about the house, I guess. I don't want to leave it. I don't want to give it up.

RUTH: (*Gently*) But it's poor land, Bruce.

Bruce sits down, gazing gloomily at the fire. Hester comes in from the kitchen with a small lamp and places it on the sideboard. Then she sits at the table, taking up her knitting. As Bruce speaks, she watches him intently.

BRUCE: Yes, it's strange that in a soil that won't grow trees a man can put roots down, but he can.

RUTH: (*At his side*) You'd feel the same about another place, after a little while.

BRUCE: I don't know. When I saw the wind last spring blowing the dirt away, the dirt I'd ploughed and harrowed and sowed to grain, I felt as though a part of myself was blowing away in the dust. Even, now, with the land three feet under snow, I can look out and feel it waiting for the seed I've saved for it.

RUTH: But if we go, we'll be nearer other people, not cut off from everything that lives.

BRUCE: You need people, don't you?

HESTER: Yes. She needs them. I've seen her at the window looking toward the town. Day after day she stands there.

[2] A steep and narrow valley cut by a stream.

Bruce and Ruth, absorbed in the conflict between them, had forgotten Hester's presence. At Hester's words, Ruth turns on them both, flaming with anger.

RUTH: You two. You're so *perfect*!

HESTER: (*Knitting*) We could always stand alone, the three of us. We didn't need to turn to every stranger who held his hand out.

RUTH: No! You'd sit in this husk of a house, living like shadows, until these four walls closed in on you, buried you.

HESTER: I never stood at a window, looking down the road that leads to town.

RUTH: (*The pent-up hysteria of the day and the longing of months breaks through, tumbling out in her words.*) It's not for myself I look down that road, Hester. It's for the child I'm going to have. You're right, Bruce, I am afraid. It's not what you think, though, not for myself. You two and your father lived so long in this dark house that you forgot there's a world beating outside, forgot that people laugh and play sometimes. And you've shut me out! (*There is a catch in her voice.*) I never would have trampled on your thoughts if you'd given them to me. But as it is, I might as well not be a person. You'd like a shadow better that wouldn't touch your house. A child would die here. A child can't live with shadows.

BRUCE: (*Much disturbed, Bruce rises and goes to her.*) Ruth! I didn't know you hated it so much.

RUTH: I thought it would change. I thought I could change it. You know now.

BRUCE: (*Quietly*) Yes.

RUTH: (*Pleading*) If we go, I'll *want* this child, Bruce. Don't you see? But I'm not happy here. What kind of a life will our child have? He'll be old before he's out of school. (*She looks at the hyacinth on the stand.*) He'll be like this hyacinth that's broken before it bloomed.

BRUCE: (*Goes to the table and stands looking down at the deed of sale. His voice is tired and flat, but resolved.*) All right. I'll tell Manning I'll let him have the place.

HESTER: (*Turning quickly to Bruce*) What do you mean?

BRUCE: I'm going to sell the farm to Manning. He was here today.

HESTER: (*Standing up, her eyes blazing*) You can't sell this house.

BRUCE: (*Looking at the deed of sale*) Oh, Ruth's right. We can't make a living on the place. (*He sits down, leafing through the document.*) It's too dry. And too far from school.

HESTER: It wasn't too far for you to go, or me.

BRUCE: (*Irritably*) Do you think I want to sell?

HESTER: *She* does. But she can't do it. (*Her voice is low.*) This house belongs to me.

BRUCE: Hester, don't start that again! I wish to God the land had been divided differently, but it wasn't.

HESTER: Father meant for us to stay here and keep things as they were when he was with us.

BRUCE: The soil wasn't blowing away when he was farming it.

HESTER: He meant for me to have the house.

RUTH: You'll go with us where we go, Hester.

HESTER: (*To Ruth*) You came here. You plotted with him to take this house from me. But it's mine!

BRUCE: (*His voice cracks through the room*) Stop that, Hester! I love this place as much as you do, but I'm selling it. I'm selling it, I tell you. (*As he speaks, he gets up abruptly and, taking up his coat, puts it on.*)

Hester sinks slowly into the chair, staring. Ruth tries to put her hand on Bruce's arm.

RUTH: Bruce! Not that way! Not for me. If it's that way, I don't care enough.

BRUCE: (*Shaking himself free*) Oh, leave me alone!

RUTH: Bruce!

BRUCE: (*Going to the door*) I'll be glad when it's over, I suppose.

RUTH: Where are you going?

BRUCE: (*Taking his cap and gloves*) To look at that mare.

RUTH: Bruce!

But he has gone.

HESTER: (*Getting up, she goes to her father's chair and stands behind it, facing Ruth; she moves and speaks as if she were in a dream.*) This is my house. I won't have strangers in it.

RUTH: (*At the table, without looking at Hester*) Oh, Hester! I didn't want it to be this way. I tried—

HESTER: (*As if she were speaking to a stranger*) Why did you come here?

RUTH: I've hurt you. But I'm right about this. I know I'm right.

HESTER: There isn't any room for you.

RUTH: Can't you see? It's for all of us.

Hester comes toward Ruth with a strange, blazing anger in her face.

HESTER: I know your kind. You tempted him with your bright hair.

RUTH: Hester!

HESTER: Your body anointed with jasmine for his pleasure.

RUTH: Hester, don't say such things!

HESTER: Oh, I know what you are! You and women like you. You put a dream around him with your arms, a sinful dream.

RUTH: (*Drawing back*) Hester!

HESTER: You lift your white face to every stranger like you offered him a cup to drink from. (*Turning from Ruth, as if she had forgotten her presence, Hester looks fondly at the room.*) I'll never leave this house.

BRUCE: (*Opens the door and comes in quickly and stormily. He goes into the kitchen as he speaks.*) That mare's got out. She jumped the corral. I'll have to go after her.

RUTH: (*Concerned*) Bruce, where will she be?

BRUCE: (*Returning with an old blanket*) She'll be in the snowshed by the coulee. She always goes there when she's about to foal.

Hester sits in the chair by the stove, her knitting in her hand. She pays no attention to the others.

RUTH: But you can't go after her in this storm.

BRUCE: I'll take this old blanket to cover the colt, if it's born yet. Where's the lantern? (*He sees the two lanterns by the kitchen door and, taking one of them to the table, lights it.*)

RUTH: It's three miles, Bruce. You mustn't go on foot, It's dangerous.

BRUCE: I'll have to. She'd never live through the night, or the colt either. (*He turns to go.*) You'd better go to bed. Good-night, Hester.

RUTH: Let me come with you.

BRUCE: No. (*Then, as he looks at her, all resentment leaves him. He puts down the lantern, goes to her, and takes her in his arms.*) Ruth, forget what I said. You know I didn't mean—

RUTH: (*Softly*) I said things I didn't mean, too—

BRUCE: I love you, Ruth. You know it, don't you?

RUTH: Bruce!

He kisses her, and for a moment their love is a flame in the room.

BRUCE: Don't worry. I won't be long.

RUTH: I'll wait.

Bruce goes out. Ruth follows him to the door, and, as it closes, she stands against it for a moment. There is a silence. Hester is slowly unravelling her knitting but is unaware of it. The black wool falls in spirals about her chair.

HESTER: (*Suddenly*) It's an old house. I was born here. (*Then in a strange, calm voice that seems to come from a long distance*) You shouldn't let Bruce be so much alone. You lose him that way. He comes back to *us* then. He'll see you don't belong here unless you keep your hand on him all the time.

Ruth looks curiously at Hester but does not give her all her attention.

HESTER: (*Suddenly becomes harsh*) This is my house. You can't change it. (*Ruth starts to say something but remains silent.*) Father gave it to me. There isn't any room for you. (*In a high, childlike tone, like the sound of a violin string breaking*) No room. (*She shakes her head gravely.*)

RUTH: (*Aware that something is wrong*) Hester—

HESTER: (*As if she were telling an often-recited story to a stranger*) I stayed home when mother died and kept house for my little brother and my father. (*Her voice grows stronger.*) I was very beautiful, they said. My hair fell to my knees, and it was black as a furrow turned in spring. (*Proudly*) I can have a husband any time I want, but my duty is here with Father. You see how it is. I can't leave him.

RUTH: (*Goes quickly to Hester. With anxiety and gentleness*) Hester, what are you talking about?

HESTER: That's Father's chair. I'll put his Bible out. (*She starts from her chair.*)

RUTH: (*Preventing her*) Hester, your father's not here—not for six years. You speak of him as if you thought—Hester—

HESTER: (*Ignoring Ruth but remaining seated*) When I was a girl I always filled the lanterns after supper. Then I was ready for his coming.

RUTH: (*In terror*) Hester, I didn't fill them! I didn't fill the lanterns! (*She runs to the kitchen door and takes up the remaining lantern.*)

HESTER: (*Calmly*) Father called me the wise virgin[3] then.

RUTH: Hester, Bruce took one! He thought I'd filled them. It will burn out and he'll be lost in the blizzard.

HESTER: I always filled them.

RUTH: (*Setting the lantern on the table*) I've got to go out after Bruce. If he gets down to the coulee and the lantern goes out, he'll never find the way back. I'll have to hurry! Where's the coal oil?

Ruth goes to the kitchen and returns with a can of coal oil and a pair of galoshes. Heather watches her closely. As Ruth comes in with the oil, Hester slowly rises and goes to her.

HESTER: I'll fill the lantern for you, Ruth.

RUTH: (*Trying to remove the top of the can*) I can't get the top off. My hands are shaking so.

HESTER: (*Taking the oil can from Ruth*) I'll fill it for you.

RUTH: Please, Hester. While I get my things on! (*Giving Hester the oil can, Ruth runs to the footstool and hurriedly puts on her galoshes.*) I'm afraid that lantern will last just long enough to get him out there. He'll be across the field before I even get outside. (*She runs up the stairs.*)

HESTER: (*Standing motionless, the oil can in her hand*) You're going now. That's right. I told you you should go.

Ruth disappears up the stairs. Hester moves a step towards the lantern, taking off the top of the coal oil can. She hesitates and looks for a long moment after Ruth. With the strange lucidity of madness, slowly, deliberately, she places the top back again on the can and, moving behind the table, sets it on the floor without filling the lantern. Ruth hurries down the stairs excited and alarmed. She has on heavy clothes and is putting on her gloves.

RUTH: Is it ready? (*Hester nods*) Will you light it for me, Hester? Please. (*Hester lights the lantern.*) I'll put the light at the window. (*She crosses with the small lamp and places it at the window.*) Hurry, Hester! (*With a sob*) Oh, if only I can find him!

Hester crosses to Ruth and gives her the lantern. Ruth takes the lantern and goes out. A gust of wind carries the snow into the room and blows shut the door after her. Hester goes to the window.

HESTER: (*Her voice is like an echo*) The snow lies deep on the summer fallow—The snow is a moving shroud—a winding sheet that the wind lifts and

[3] St Matthew, xxv: 1-4.

raises and lets fall again. (*Turning from the window*) They've gone. They won't be back now. (*With an intense excitement, Hester blows out the lamp at the window and pulls down the shades. Her eyes fall on the bowl of hyacinths in the corner. Slowly she goes to it, takes it up and, holding it away from her, carries it to the door. Opening the door, she sets the flowers outside. She closes the door and locks it. Her eyes blazing with excitement, she stands with her arms across the door as if shutting the world out. Then softly she moves to the door of her father's bedroom, unlocks it, and goes in, returning at once with a pair of men's bedroom slippers. Leaving the bedroom door open, she crosses to the sideboard, takes up the Bible and, going to her father's chair, places the slippers beside it. She speaks very softly.*) I put your slippers out. (*She draws the footstool up to the chair.*) Everything will be the same now, Father. (*She opens the Bible.*) I'll read to you, Father. I'll read the one you like. (*She reads with quiet contentment.*) 'And the winds blew, and beat upon the house; and it fell not: for it was founded upon a rock.'[4]

The wind moans through the old house as the curtain falls.

[4] St Matthew vii: 25.

A FIELD OF WHEAT

Sinclair Ross

It was the best crop of wheat that John had ever grown; sturdy, higher than the knee, the heads long and filling well; a still, heat-hushed mile of it, undulating into a shimmer of summer-colts and crushed horizon blue. Martha finished pulling the little patch of mustard that John had told her about at noon, stood a minute with her shoulders strained back to ease the muscles that were sore from bending, then bunched up her apron filled with the yellow-blossomed weeds and started towards the road. She walked carefully, placing her feet edgeways between the rows of wheat to avoid trampling and crushing the stalks. The road was only a few rods distant, but several times she stopped before reaching it, holding her apron with one hand and with the other stroking the blades of grain that pressed close against her skirts, luxuriant and tall. Once she looked back, her eyes shaded, across the wheat to the dark fallow land beside it. John was there; she could see the long, slow-settling plume of dust thrown up by the horses and the harrow-cart. He was a fool for work, John. This year he was farming the whole section of land without help, managing with two outfits of horses, one for the morning and one for the afternoon; six, and sometimes even seven hours a shift.

It was John who gave such allure to the wheat. She thought of him hunched black and sweaty on the harrow-cart, twelve hours a day, smothering in dust, shoulders sagged wearily beneath the glare of sun. Her fingers touched the stalks of grain again and tightened on a supple blade until they made it squeak like a mouse. A crop like this was coming to him. He had had his share of failures and set-backs, if ever a man had, twenty times over.

Martha was thirty-seven. She had clinched with the body and substance of life; had loved, borne children—a boy had died—and yet the quickest aches of life, travail, heartbrokenness, they had never wrung as the wheat wrung. For the wheat allowed no respite. Wasting and unending it was struggle, struggle against wind and insects, drought and weeds. Not an heroic struggle to give a man courage and resolve, but a frantic, unavailing one. They were only poor, taunted, driven things; it was the wheat that was invincible. They only dreaded, built bright futures; waited for the first glint of green, watched timorous and eager while it thickened, merged, and at last leaned bravely to a ripple in the wind; then followed every slip of cloud into the horizon, turned to the wheat and away again. And it died tantalizingly sometimes, slowly: there would be a cool day, a pittance of rain.

Or perhaps it lived, perhaps the rain came, June, July, even into August, hope climbing, wish-patterns painted on the future. And then one day a clench and tremble to John's hand; his voice faltering, dull.

Grasshoppers perhaps, sawflies or rust; no matter, they would grovel for a while, stand back helpless, then go on again. Go on in bitterness and cowardice, because there was nothing else but going-on.

She had loved John, for these sixteen years had stood close watching while he died—slowly, tantalizingly, as the parched wheat died. He had grown unkempt, ugly, morose. His voice was gruff, contentious, never broke into the deep, strong laughter that used to make her feel she was living at the heart of things. John was gone, love was gone; there was only wheat.

She plucked a blade; her eyes travelled hungrily up and down the field. Serene now, all its sting and torment sheathed. Beautiful, more beautiful than Annabelle's poppies, than her sunsets. Theirs—all of it. Three hundred acres ready to give perhaps a little of what it had taken from her—John, his love, his lips unclenched.

Three hundred acres. Bushels, thousands of bushels, she wouldn't even try to think how many. And prices up this year. It would make him young again, lift his head, give him spirit. Maybe he would shave twice a week as he used to when they were first married, buy new clothes, believe in himself again.

She walked down the road towards the house, her steps quickening to the pace of her thoughts until the sweat clung to her face like little beads of oil. It was the children now, Joe and Annabelle: this winter perhaps they could send them to school in town and let them take music lessons. Annabelle, anyway. At a pinch Joe could wait a while; he was only eight. It wouldn't take Annabelle long to pick up her notes; already she played hymn tunes by ear on the organ. She was bright, a real little lady for manners; among town people she would learn a lot. The farm was no place to bring her up. Running wild and barefoot, what would she be like in a few years? Who would ever want to marry her but some stupid country lout?

John had never been to school himself; he knew what it meant to go through life with nothing but his muscles to depend upon; and that was it, dread that Annabelle and Joe would be handicapped as he was, that was what had darkened him, made him harsh and dour. That was why he breasted the sun and dust a frantic, dogged fool, to spare them, to help them to a life that offered more than sweat and debts. Martha knew. He was a slow, inarticulate man, but she knew. Sometimes it even vexed her, brought a wrinkle of jealousy, his anxiety about the children, his sense of responsibility where they were concerned. He never seemed to feel that he owed her anything, never worried about her future. She could sweat, grow flat-footed and shapeless, but that never bothered him.

Her thoughts were on their old, trudging way, the way they always went; but then she halted suddenly, and with her eyes across the wheat again found freshening promise in its quiet expanse. The children must come first, but she and John—mightn't there be a little of life left for them too? A man was young at thirty-nine. And if she didn't have to work so hard, if she could get some new clothes, maybe some of the creams and things that other women had. . . .

As she passed through the gate, Annabelle raced across the yard to meet her. 'Do you know what Joe's done? He's taken off all his clothes and he's in the trough with Nipper!' She was a lanky girl, sunburned, barefoot, her face oval and regular, but spoiled by an expression that strained her mouth and brows into a reproachful primness. It was Martha who had taught her the expression, dinning manners and politeness into her, trying to make her better than the other little girls who went to the country school. She went on, her eyes wide and aghast, 'And when I told him to come out he stood right up, all bare, and I had to come away.'

'Well, you tell him he'd better be out before I get there.'

'But how can I tell him? He's all bare.'

Then Joe ran up, nothing on but little cotton knee-pants, strings of green scum from the water-trough still sticking to his face and arms. 'She's been peekin'.' He pointed at Annabelle. 'Nipper and me just got into the trough to get cooled off, and she wouldn't mind her own business.'

'Don't you tell lies about me.' Annabelle pounced on him and slapped his bare back. 'You're just a dirty little pig anyway, and the horses don't want to drink after you've been in the trough.'

Joe squealed, and excited by the scuffle Nipper yelped and spattered Martha with a spray of water from his coat and tail. She reached out to cuff him, missed, and then to satisfy the itch in her fingers seized Joe and boxed his ears. 'You put your shirt on and then go and pick peas for supper. Hurry now, both of you, and only the fat ones, mind. No, not you, Annabelle.' There was something about Annabelle's face, burned and countrified, that changed Martha's mind. 'You shell the peas when he gets them. You're in the sun too much as it is.'

'But I've got a poppy out and if he goes to the garden by himself he'll pick it—just for spite.' Annabelle spun round, and leaving the perplexity in her voice behind her, bolted for the garden. The next minute, before Martha had even reached the house, she was back again triumphant, a big fringed pink and purple poppy in her hand. Sitting down on the doorstep to admire the gaudy petals, she complained to herself, 'They go so fast—the first little winds blows them all away.' On her face, lengthening it, was bitten deeply the enigma of the flowers and the naked seed-pods. Why did the beauty flash and the bony stalks remain?

Martha had clothes to iron, and biscuits to bake for supper; Annabelle and Joe quarrelled about the peas until she shelled them herself. It was hot—heat so intense and breathless that it weighed like a solid. An ominous darkness came with it, gradual and unnoticed. All at once she turned away from the stove and stood strained, inert. The silence seemed to gather itself, hold its breath. She tried to speak to Nipper and the children, all three sprawled in a heap alongside the house, but the hush over everything was like a raised finger, forbidding her.

A long immobile minute; suddenly a bewildering awarenes that the light was choked; and then, muffled, still distant, but charged with resolution, climaxing the stillness, a slow, long brooding heave of thunder.

Martha darted to the door, stumbled down the step and around the corner of the house. To the west there was no sky, only a gulf of blackness, so black that the landscape seemed slipping down the neck of a funnel. Above, almost overhead, a heavy, hard-lined bank of cloud swept its way across the sun-white blue in august, impassive fury.

'Annabelle!' She wanted to scream a warning, but it was a bare whisper. In front of her the blackness split—an abrupt, unforked gash of light as if angry hands had snatched to seal the rent.

'Annabelle! Quick—inside—!' Deep in the funnel shaggy thunder rolled, emerged and shook itself, then with hurtling strides leaped up to drum and burst itself on the advancing peak of cloud.

'Joe, come back here!' He was off in pursuit of Nipper, who had broken away from Annabelle when she tried to pull him into the house. 'Before I warm you!'

Her voice broke. She stared into the blackness. There it was—the hail again—the same white twisting little cloud against the black one—just as she had seen it four years ago.

She craned her neck, looking to see whether John was coming. The wheat, the acres and acres of it, green and tall, if only he had put some insurance on it. Damned mule—just work and work. No head himself and too stubborn to listen to anyone else.

There was a swift gust of wind, thunder in a splintering avalanche, the ragged hail-cloud low and close. She wheeled, with a push sent Annabelle toppling into the house, and then ran to the stable to throw open the big doors. John would turn the horses loose—surely he would. She put a brace against one of the doors, and bashed the end into the ground with her foot. Surely—but he was a fool—such a fool at times. It would be just like him to risk a runaway for the sake of getting to the end of the field.

The first big drops of rain were spitting at her before she reached the house. Quietly, breathing hard, she closed the door, numb for a minute, afraid to think or move. At the other side of the kitchen Annabelle was tussling with Joe, trying to make him go down cellar with her. Frightened a little by her mother's excitement, but not really able to grasp the imminence of danger, she was set on exploiting the event; and to be compelled to seize her little brother and carry him down cellar struck her imagination as a superb way of crystallizing for all time the dreadfulness of the storm and her own dramatic part in it. But Martha shouted at her hoarsely, 'Go and get pillows. Here, Joe, quick, up on the table.' She snatched him off his feet and set him on the table beside the window. 'Be ready now when the hail starts, to hold the pillow tight against the glass. You, Annabelle, stay upstairs at the west window in my room.'

The horses were coming, all six at a break-neck gallop, terrified by the thunder and the whip stripes John had given them when he turned them loose. They swept past the house, shaking the earth, their harness jangling tinny against the brattle of thunder, and collided headlong at the stable door.

John, too; through Joe's legs Martha caught sight of his long, scarecrow shape stooped low before the rain. Distractedly, without purpose, she ran upstairs two steps at a time to Annabelle. 'Don't be scared, here comes your father!' Her own voice shook, craven. 'Why don't you rest your arms? It hasn't started yet.'

As she spoke there was a sharp, crunching blow on the roof, its sound abruptly dead, sickening, like a weapon that has sunk deep into flesh. Wildly she shook her hands, motioning Annabelle back to the window, and started for the stairs. Again the blow came; then swiftly a stuttered dozen of them.

She reached the kitchen just as John burst in. With their eyes screwed up against the pommelling roar of the hail they stared at each other. They were deafened, pinioned, crushed. His face was a livid blank, one cheek smeared with blood where a jagged stone had struck him. Taut with fear, her throat aching, she turned away and looked through Joe's legs again. It was like a furious fountain, the stones bouncing high and clashing with those behind them. They had buried the earth, blotted out the horizon; there was nothing but their crazy spew of whiteness. She cowered away, put her hands to her ears.

Then the window broke, and Joe and the pillow tumbled off the table before the howling inrush of the storm. The stones clattered on the floor and bounded up to the ceiling, lit on the stove and threw out sizzling steam. The wind whisked pots and kettles off their hooks, tugged at and whirled the sodden curtains, crashed down a shelf of lamps and crockery. John pushed Martha and Joe into the next room and shut the door. There they found Annabelle huddled at the foot of the stairs, round-eyed, biting her nails in terror. The window she had been holding was broken too; and she had run away without closing the bedroom door, leaving a wild tide of wind upstairs to rage unchecked. It was rocking the whole house, straining at the walls. Martha ran up to close the door, and came down whimpering.

There was hail heaped on the bed, the pictures were blown off the walls and broken, the floor was swimming; the water would soak through and spoil all the ceilings.

John's face quietened her. They are crowded together, silent, averting their eyes from one another. Martha wanted to cry again, but dared not. Joe, awed to calmness, kept looking furtively at the trickle of blood on his father's face. Annabelle's eyes went wide and glassy as suddenly she began to wonder about Nipper. In the excitement and terror of the storm they had all forgotten him.

When at last they could go outside they stumbled over his body on the step. He had run away from Joe before the storm started, crawled back to the house when he saw John go in, and crouching down against the door had been beaten lifeless. Martha held back the children, while John picked up the mangled heap and hurried away with it to the stable.

Neither Joe nor Annabelle cried. It was too annihilating, too much like a blow. They clung tightly to Martha's skirts, staring across the flayed yard and garden. The sun came out, sharp and brilliant on the drifts of hail. There was an icy wind that made them shiver in their thin cotton clothes. 'No, it's too cold on your feet.' Martha motioned them back to the step as she started towards the gate to join John. 'I want to go with your father to look at the wheat. There's nothing anyway to see.'

Nothing but the glitter of sun on hailstones. Nothing but their wheat crushed into little rags of muddy slime. Here and there an isolated straw standing bolt upright in headless defiance. Martha and John walked to the far end of the field. There was no sound but their shoes slipping and rattling on the pebbles of ice. Both of them wanted to speak, to break the atmosphere of calamity that hung over them, but the words they could find were too small for the sparkling serenity of wasted field. Even as waste it was indomitable. It tethered them to itself, so that they could not feel or comprehend. It had come and gone, that was all; before its tremendousness and havoc they were prostrate. They had not yet risen to cry out or protest.

It was when they were nearly back to the house that Martha started to whimper. 'I can't go on any longer; I can't, John. There's no use, we've tried.' With one hand she clutched him and with the other held her apron to her mouth. 'It's driving me out of my mind. I'm so tired—heart-sick of it all. Can't you see?'

He laid his big hands on her shoulders. They looked at each other for a few seconds, then she dropped her head weakly against his greasy smock. Presently he roused her. 'Here come Joe and Annabelle!' The pressure of his hands tightened. His bristly cheek touched her hair and forehead. 'Straighten up, quick, before they see you!'

It was more of him than she had had for years. 'Yes, John, I know—I'm all right now.' There was a wistful little pull in her voice as if she would have had him hold her there, but hurriedly instead she began to dry her eyes with her apron. 'And tell Joe you'll get him another dog.'

Then he left her and she went back to the house. Mounting within her was a resolve, a bravery. It was the warming sunlight, the strength and nearness of John, a feeling of mattering, belonging. Swung far upwards by the rush and swell of recaptured life, she was suddenly as far above the desolation of the storm as a little while ago she had been abject before it. But in the house she was alone; there was no sunlight, only a cold wind through the broken window; and she crumpled again.

She tried to face the kitchen, to get the floor dried and the broken lamps swept up. But it was not the kitchen; it was tomorrow, next week, next year. The going on, the waste of life, the hopelessness.

Her hands fought the broom a moment, twisting the handle as if trying to unscrew the rusted cap of a jar; then abruptly she let it fall and strode outside. All very fine for John: he'd talk about education for Joe and Annabelle, and she could worry where the clothes were to come from so that they could go clean and decent even to the country school. It made no difference that she had wanted to take out hail insurance. He was the one that looked after things. She was just his wife; it wasn't for her to open her mouth. He'd pat her shoulder and let her come back to this. They'd be brave, go on again, forget about the crop. Go on, go on—next year and the next—go on till they were both ready for the scrap-heap. But she'd had enough. This time he'd go on alone.

Not that she meant it. Not that she failed to understand what John was going through. It was just rebellion. Rebellion because their wheat was beaten to the ground, because there was this brutal, callous finish to everything she had planned, because she had will and needs and flesh, because she was alive. Rebellion, not John at all—but how rebel against a summer storm, how find the throat of a cloud?

So at a jerky little run she set off for the stable, for John. Just that she might release and spend herself, no matter against whom or what, unloose the fury that clawed within her, strike back a blow for the one that had flattened her.

The stable was quiet, only the push of hay as the horses nosed through the mangers, the lazy rub of their flanks and hips against the stall partitions; and before its quietness her anger subsided, took time for breath. She advanced slowly, almost on tiptoe, peering past the horses' rumps for a glimpse of John. To the last stall, back again. And then there was a sound different from the stable sounds. She paused.

She had not seen him the first time she passed because he was pressed against one of the horses, his head pushed into the big deep hollow of its neck and shoulder, one hand hooked by the fingers in the mane, his own shoulders drawn up and shaking. She stared, thrust out her head incredulously, moved her lips, but stood silent. John sobbing there, against the horse. It was the strangest, most frightening moment of her life. He had always been so strong and grim; had just kept on as if he couldn't feel, as if there was a bull's hide over him, and now he was beaten.

She crept away. It would be unbearable to watch his humiliation if he looked up and saw her. Joe was wandering about the yard, thinking about Nipper and disconsolately sucking hailstones, but she fled past him, head down, stricken with guilty shame as if it were she who had been caught broken and afraid. He had always been so strong, a brute at times in his strength, and now—

Now—why now that it had come to this, he might never be able to get a grip of himself again. He might not want to keep on working, not if he were really beaten. If he lost heart, if he didn't care about Joe and Annabelle any more. Weeds and pests, drought and hail—it took so much fight for a man to hold his own against them all, just to hold his own, let alone make headway.

'Look at the sky!' It was Annabelle again, breathless and ecstatic. 'The far one—look how it's opened like a fan!'

Withdrawn now in the eastern sky the storm clouds towered, gold-capped and flushed in the late sunlight, high still pyramids of snowiness and shadow. And one that Annabelle pointed to, apart, the farthest away of them all, this one in bronzed slow splendour spread up mountains high to a vast, plateau-like summit.

Martha hurried inside. She started the fire again, then nailed a blanket over the broken window and lit the big brass parlour lamp—the only one the storm had spared. Her hands were quick and tense. John would need a good supper tonight. The biscuits were water-soaked, but she still had the peas. He liked peas. Lucky that they had picked them when they did. This winter they wouldn't have so much as an onion or potato.

SAINT SAMMY

W. O. Mitchell

1

The first day after Mr Candy's visit was not the day. As soon as he lifted the sacking from the front of the piano box in which he lived, and looked out across the prairie sweeping to the horizon's bare finality, Saint Sammy, Jehovah's hired man, knew that it wasn't the day. The Lord had been busy; for one thing, He had been lightening and darkening His earth by slipping the slow edges of cloud shadows over the prairie.

The second day after Mr Candy's visit was not the day. Saint Sammy knew it wasn't, as he walked to the corner of the poplar-pole corral he had built on to the piano box. The second day was not the day, he decided as he walked with his left shoulder high, walking as though he had a spring under his right heel. Far to the east the Lord was occupied with a honing wind and a black dust storm that needed His attention. True, it had been on a day like this ten years ago that the Lord had come to him the first time. That had been the bad hail year when he had stood on the edge of his ruined crop looking at the countless broken wheat heads lying down their stalks.

As he had stared, the wind, turning upon itself in sudden fury, had built up a black body for itself out of the topsoil and had come whirling toward him in a smoking funnel that snatched up tumbleweeds, lifting them and rolling them over in its heart. The voice of the Lord had spoken to him:—

'Sammy, Sammy, ontuh your fifty-bushel crop have I sent hailstones the size-a baseballs. The year before did I send the cutworm which creepeth, and before that the sawfly which saweth, and before that the hoppers which hoppeth and the rust which rusteth, and every year the drought to make sure.

'Be you not downcast, for I have prepared a place for you. Take with you Miriam and Immaculate Holstein, and also them Clydes. Go you to Magnus Petersen, who is even now pumping full his stock trought, and he will give ontuh you his south eighty for pasture, and there you will live to the end of your days when I shall take you up in the twinkling of an eye.

'But I say ontuh you, Sammy, I say this—don't ever sell them Clydes, for without them ye shall not enter. I will take them up with you when I shall fill the air with cherubim and serubim from here to the correction line, and they shall have britching studded with diamonds and emeralds, and their halter shanks shall be of purest gold.

'Even as I did ontuh Elisha and Elijah and John will I speak ontuh you just like now. So git, Sammy—git to Magnus Petersen before he has finished of pumping full the stock trought and shall commence of stooking his oats which I have made ready for him.

'There will you find the box of Miss Henchbaw's piano which Magnus will give ontuh you together with his stone boat for hauling it.

'Hail, Saint Sammy!' the Lord had said. 'Hail, Jehovah's Hired Man!'

Although the second day after Mr Candy's visit was just such a day as the one ten years before, it was not the day. The wind was too far to the east.

The third day was not the day. That day there was no frightened feeling in the pit of Saint Sammy's stomach. So the third day was not the day.

Nor was the fourth day. That day was the Lord's hail day; He was mixing up a batch of hail. Hail to the Lord that was mixing hail! Hail to the little green frog that leaped to plop the stillness! Hail to his long leaf feet trailing, and his snout and the bump eyes that nudged the slough scum! Hail to Saint Sammy, too!

2

Today, the fifth day, was the day. As he watched Habbakuk and Haggai cropping the grass by the empty wagon, and the others, Hannah, Naomi, Ruth, Hosea, Joel, Malachi, and the colts, Corinthians One and Two, in a far corner of the pasture, Saint Sammy knew that today the Lord would punish Mr Candy. The Lord wouldn't let him get the Clydes.

As he began to walk over the prairie toward the Lord's corner of the pasture, he was aware of a rising wind in the grasses, and the stitching ring of crickets was in his ears like the pulsing of his own blood. He heard a meadow lark sing. A gopher squeaked.

Whatever the Lord did to him, it would serve Mr Candy right; he ought to have known better than to fool around with the Lord and Saint Sammy. Going to church, passing the collection plate, wouldn't help him now. It hadn't helped the Pharisees. After the Lord had smited him for coveting the Clydes, Mr Candy wouldn't be called the Flax King any longer.

Today was the Lord's smiting day. It was a perfect smiting day.

Ahead of him the sun haloed the soft heads of foxtails bending now in the growing wind; it glistened from the amber wings of a dragonfly hovering; it gleamed on the surface of the slough. High in the sky a goshawk hung, over the prairie, flat as the palm of a suppliant hand, inscrutable and unsmiling, patched with dark summer fallow, strung long with the black crosses of telephone poles marching to the prairie's rim.

The vengeance of the Lord on Mr Candy would be awful. Mr Candy would wish he'd never tried to get Saint Sammy's horses; he'd wish he had never ordered them off the Petersen pasture.. The vengeance of the Lord would be enough to give a gopher the heartburn.

Saint Sammy thought of the day that Mr Candy had called on him.

'Come ontuh me!' Saint Sammy had called as Mr Candy crawled under the barbed wire. 'Come ontuh me where I dwell in the midst-a the jack rabbits an' badger an' weasel an' skunk! Come ontuh me with the creepin' critter that hath life an' the whole host-a them about me—minus one, Lot's wife! Lot knew her an' she was with calf an' she up an' died! The Lord hath visited me with a plague-a rheumatism, so I aint' bin able tuh git the bresh tuh burn her!'

'I come to see was you gonna sell them Clydes.'

'Over the breadth-a the earth there ain't no horses like mine!' cried Saint Sammy. 'An' the voice-a the Lord come ontuh me sayin', "Sammy, Sammy, don't you sell them Clydes!" An' moreover I say ontuh you, I ain't!'

'Like I thought. Figgered to give you one chance. You ain't takin' it. You got a week to git off-a here.'

Saint Sammy's mouth made a round, dark well in his beard, and the wilderness of panic was in his mild blue eyes. 'All-a this here land was give ontuh me, an' the herb there-off for my critters! Magnus Petersen he—'

'Sold her.'

'But, the Lord, He wouldn't—'

'Blaspheemy ain't gonna do you no good! Sell or git off. My land now. Them horses ain't no good to anybody—way they are. You ain't broke 'em. You don't work 'em. Sell or git off!'

'But—Magnus wouldn't—'

'He did.'

'From here to the ridge there ain't no pasture for—The Lord hath mighty lightnin', Ab Candy!'

'Mebbe He has.'

'An' He moves in—'

'Sell or git off!'

'The Lord hit a man I knew an' it come to pass between the well an' the back stoop an' the Lord's fearful lightnin' burnt every stitch of clothes from off him an' left him standin' bare-naked with a bucket of water in each hand—once.'

'I got no time to—'

'An' his wife she arose an' she went for to emp'y the slop pail an' she was sore afraid when she saw him standin' there an' she yelled an' he come to with a great start an' he spilt the water from them red-hot buckets over him an' got scalded nigh ontuh death.'

'You got a week.'

'The Lord will—'

'Sell or git off!'

3

After Mr Candy had gone, Saint Sammy had been afraid. He went into his piano box and lay there. He plunged his hand deep into the raw sheep's wool and binder twine bits that made his nest, and brought out the tin box filled with broken glass and pebbles and twigs and bolts and empty matchboxes and the underwear labels he had been saving for years. He counted them as he always did when troubled. Count your labels, count them one by one.

It hadn't helped. He had put the red and blue underwear labels back, and for a long time he watched the wedge face of a field mouse just outside the piano-box opening.

When the fence-post shadows lay long over the prairie and the whole pasture was transfigured with the light of dying day, he went out to milk Miriam and turn the calf loose on Immaculate. Then he started across the prairie to Mr Candy's. He found him in the act of rolling gasoline barrels off his truck beside the barn.

'Whatta you want?'

'I've come to see would you—Ain't there any way me an' my critters could dwell on—'

'Just sell them ten head-a horses—stay as long as you please.'

'But—'

'You got a week till I drill her fer flax.'

'The Lord might knock your flax flatter'n a platter full-a—'

'You heard.'

Saint Sammy's long arm came slowly up, and the finger pointing at Mr Candy trembled. 'The glory of the Lord come out-a the east, an' His voice was like the wind through the smooth-on Barley field!'

On Mr Candy's face there was a faint look of discomfort; he enjoyed the reputation of being a religious man, and for many years had served as deacon in the district's Baptist church. 'Now, don't you go startin' none-a that—'

'An' the voice-a the Lord come ontuh me sayin', "I kin do the droughtin' out an' the hailin' out an' the rustin' an' the blowin' an' the hopperin' out till Ab Candy's good an' tired out!" An' she shall come to pass—'

Mr Candy reached behind him and knocked his knuckles against the handle of the manure fork leaning against the barn. He *was* a religious man, and years of prairie farming had deepened in him a faith in fate as effective as that of Greek drama. There had been a mental struggle before he had gone to Magnus Petersen about Saint Sammy's pasture. He wanted the Clydes badly.

'Sorra an' sighin' shall come to Ab Candy, for he hath played the sinner in the sight-a the Lord, an' it shall come to pass the horned owl mourneth an' the kiyoot howleth!'

Saint Sammy's arm had come down.

For a long time after Saint Sammy had left, Mr Candy stood by his barn, a particularly dilapidated building that shouldered alarmingly out to one side, its gray boards warped and cracked and gaping inches.

As he walked back to his house he looked up to the evening sky, where high clouds still caught the lingering light of day and held it unexpected there. His Baptist conscience told him that the Clydes were only horses after all. A killdeer sadly called. He must remember to put lightning rods on the house and barn. About the fields, fences, buildings, there was a clarity that was not theirs throughout the day. The church could use new pews.

Clear as a coin, the sun had sunk to leave an orange stain behind on clouds above the prairie's western line.

4

And now, the fifth day, Saint Sammy in the Lord's corner of the pasture waited for His coming. He looked down at the skeleton by the fence, with its whitened rib-bones clutching emptiness. In and out of the teeth an ant crawled, disappeared over the rim of an eye socket, reappeared, and began a long pilgrimage down the spools of the backbone. A short distance away a weasel looked out from his pulpit hole, his head and his toy ears bolt upright in Presbyterian propriety.

The rising wind was tossing the prairie grasses now, stirring Saint Sammy's long and tangled beard, lifting the gray hair that hung womanly to his shoulders from the cap tipped forward on his head—a child's cap with quartering creases that ran down from the cloth button at its centre. A yellow butterfly came pelting past to pause on one of the dusty leaves laddering up a goldenrod's stem, wings closed up like two hands held palms together; it untouched itself to go winking and blinking, now here, now there, echoing itself over the empty, wind-stirred prairie.

While he waited for the Lord to button the top button of His work smock, give a hitch to His 'Boss of the Road' pants, and call for a whirlwind, Saint Sammy shaded his eyes with his hand and looked out over the prairie. It was there, just south of the correction line, that the heavens would be opened up, where he could see Ab Candy's buildings squat on the horizon. Sorrow and sighing would come to Ab Candy today.

He plucked the yellow head off a flower at his feet, crushed it, and stared down at the gummy threads stringing from the ball of his thumb. The grasses tossed around him, their sibilance lost in the rising voice of the wind. High above him and all around him as he squatted in the fence corner, he could hear it utterly lost and utterly wild in its singing intensity. Calm and peace were in him now; the terror was gone as he watched the far cloud hung low on the horizon perceptibly spread its darkness up the sky. The Lord was on His way. He would smite Mr Candy hip and thigh and shin. Saint Sammy would hate to be Mr Candy, for there would be none to comfort him.

A tumbleweed went bounding past, caught itself in the strands of the fence, then, released, went rolling on its way. An unnatural dusk grew over the whole prairie as the wind rose, licking up the topsoil in its course across the land, filling the air with the spread darkness of dust, singing fierce and lost and lonely, rising and rising again, shearing high and higher still, singing vibrance in a void, forever and forever wild.

As far as Saint Sammy could see, around him now the long grasses lay flat to the prairie earth, like ears along the back of a frightened jack rabbit. He could feel the wind solid and real against his chest as the steady push of a giant hand. It plastered his beard around his cheek, stung his face with dust, snatched at his very breath, and filled him with a ringing awareness of himself.

And from the darkness all around, scarcely distinguishable from the throating wind, came the voice of the Lord:—

'Sammy, Sammy, this is her and I say ontuh you that she is a dandy, for I have tried her out! Moreover I have tried her out! I have blowed over Tourigny's henhouse; I have uprooted Tincher's windbreak, took the back door off of the schoolhouse, turned over the girls' toilet, three racks, six grain wagons; I have blowed down the power line in four places. I have wrecked Magnus Petersen's windmill! In two hours did I cook her up, and moreover I say ontuh you in two hours shall she die down! And when she hath died down, go you ontuh Ab Candy's where he languishes, and you shall hear the gnashing of teeth which are Ab Candy's and he shall be confounded! Thus saith the Lord God of hosts, enter intuh thy pianah box and hide for the fear of the Lord! Count your labels, Sammy, count them one by one!'

5

And in the dark depths of his home, Saint Sammy did the Lord's bidding, going over and over his collected underwear labels by the light of a flickering lantern. And when the light of the lantern had become weak and the light of day had become strong again, Saint Sammy lifted the sacking and went out.

The wind was discreet in the grasses again; just the loose blow dirt, piled slightly higher and sharply rippled as the sand of creek beds is engraved by the water's current, showed that the Lord's wind has passed. A silence lay over everything. A gopher squeaked hesitatingly, questioningly. A suave-winged hawk slipped his shadow over the face of the prairie, and a jack rabbit, startled, ears ridiculously erect, went off past the fence in an idiotic bounce.

Saint Sammy started for Mr Candy's, his shoulder high, his arm swinging wide, his walk punctuated as though he had a spring under one heel; the wiry prairie grass brushed against and clung to his pant legs; looping grasshoppers sprang sailing ahead of him and disappeared, to lift again in brief, clicketing flight. Here and there the yellow petals of black-eyed Susans hung about, their chocolate domes pointing up. Once Saint Sammy picked a nodding flax flower and stared long at the striplings in its shallow blue throat.

He crossed the road before Mr Candy's farm.

Mr Candy was standing where his barn had been.

Saint Sammy halted. He stared with Mr Candy at the utter, kindling-wood ruin of what had been the barn. No stick stood. In the strewn wreckage not even the foundation outline was discernible. The barn might have been put through a threshing machine and exhaled through the blower. Certainly, the Lord's vengeance had been enough to give a badger the heartburn.

There was awe in the old and quavering voice of Saint Sammy as it lifted in the stillness of Mr Candy's farmyard.

'The Lord hath blew! He hath blew down the barn of the fundamental Baptist that hath sinned in his sight! Like He said, sorra an' sighin' hath come to Ab Candy!'

Mr Candy turned to Saint Sammy; he looked into Saint Sammy's eyes, water blue, mildly wild with a fey look which said that he was childlike, senile, or gently insane. He looked at the squeezed intensity of the old man's face, and he thought of the two sections of flax he had planted; he thought of the years of rust and drought and hail and the many wheat plagues; he thought of the thirst of flax, and he wondered at the cost of pine for church pews. He said:—

'You kin stay.'

Saint Sammy's arms lifted as in a benediction.

'I looked an' I beheld! The heavens was opened up, an' there was a whirlwind a-comin' out-a the west, liftin' like a trumpet spinnin' on her end, an' there was fire inside of her, an' light like a sunset was all around about her! Plumb out-a the midst-a her come the voice-a the Lord sayin', "Sammy, Sammy git up off of thy knees, for I am going to speak ontuh you! The prairie shall be glad, an' she shall blossom like the rose! She shall blossom abundantly! The eyes-a the blind shall see, an' the ears-a the deef shall hear! The lame is gonna leap like the jack rabbit, an' the water shall spout ontuh the prairie, an' the sloughs shall be full—plumb full!"'

Saint Sammy's arms came down.

'Amen!' said Mr Candy.

THE MOVE

Gabrielle Roy

I have perhaps never envied anyone as much as a girl I knew when I was about eleven years old and of whom today I remember not much more than the name, Florence. Her father was a mover. I don't think this was his trade. He was a handyman, I imagine, engaging in various odd jobs; at the time of the seasonal movings—and it seems to me that people changed their lodgings often in those days—he moved the household effects of people of small means who lived near us and even quite far away, in the suburbs and distant quarters of Winnipeg. No doubt, his huge cart and his horses, which he had not wanted to dispose of when he came from the country to the city, had made him a mover.

On Saturdays Florence accompanied her father on his journeys, which, because of the slow pace of the horses, often took the entire day. I envied her to the point of having no more than one fixed idea: Why was my father not also a mover? What finer trade could one practice?

I don't know what moving signified to me in those days. Certainly I could not have had any clear idea what it was like. I had been born and had grown up in the fine, comfortable house in which we were still living and which, in all probability, we would never leave. Such fixity seemed frightfully monotonous to me that summer. Actually we were never really away from that large house. If we were going to the country for a while, even if we were only to be absent for a day, the problem immediately arose: Yes, but who will look after the house?

To take one's furniture and belongings, to abandon a place, close a door behind one forever, say good-by to a neighborhood, this was an adventure of which I knew nothing; and it was probably the sheer force of my efforts to picture it to myself that made it seem so daring, heroic, and exalted in my eyes.

'Aren't we ever going to move?' I used to ask Maman.

'I certainly hope not,' she would say. 'By the grace of God and the long patience of your father, we are solidly established at last. I only hope it is forever.'

She told me that to her no sight in the world could be more heartbreaking, more poignant even, than a house moving.

'For a while,' she said, 'it's as if you were related to the nomads, those poor souls who slip along the surface of existence, putting their roots down nowhere. You no longer have a roof over your head. Yes indeed, for a few hours at least, it's as if you were drifting on the stream of life.'

Poor Mother! Her objections and comparisons only strengthened my strange hankering. To drift on the stream of life! To be like the nomads! To wander through the world! There was nothing in any of this that did not seem to me complete felicity.

Since I myself could not move, I wished to be present at someone else's moving and see what it was all about. Summer came. My unreasonable desire grew. Even now I cannot speak of it lightly, much less so with derision. Certain of our desires, as if they knew about us before we do ourselves, do not deserve to be mocked.

Each Saturday morning I used to go and wander around Florence's house. Her father—a big dirty-blond man in blue work clothes, always grumbling a little or even, perhaps, swearing—would be busy getting the impressive cart out of the barn. When the horses were harnessed and provided with nose bags of oats, the father and his little daughter would climb onto the high seat; the father would take the reins in his hands; they would both, it seemed to me, look at me then with slight pity, a vague commiseration. I would feel forsaken, of an inferior species of humans unworthy of high adventure.

The father woud shout something to the horses. The cart would shake. I would watch them set out in that cool little morning haze that seems to promise such delightful emotions to come. I would wave my hand at them, even though they never looked back at me. 'Have a good trip,' I would call. I would feel so unhappy at being left behind that I would nurse my regret all day and with it an aching curiosity. What would they see today? Where were they at this moment? What was offering itself to their travelers' eyes? It was no use my knowing that they could go only a limited distance in any event. I would imagine the two of them seeing things that no one else in the world could see. From the top of the cart, I thought, how transformed the world must appear.

At last my desire to go with them was so strong and so constant that I decided to ask my mother for permission—although I was almost certain I would never obtain it. She held my new friends in rather poor esteem and, though she tolerated my hanging continually about them, smelling their odor of horses, adventure, and dust, I knew in my heart of hearts that the mere idea that I might wish to accompany them would fill her with indignation.

At my first words, indeed, she silenced me.

'Are you mad? To wander about the city in a moving wagon! Just picture yourself,' she said, 'in the midst of furniture and boxes and piled-up mattresses all day, and with who knows what people! What can you imagine would be pleasant about that?'

How strange it was. Even the idea, for instance, of being surrounded by heaped-up chairs, chests with empty drawers, unhooked pictures—the very novelty of all this stimulated my desire.

'Never speak of that whim to me again,' said my mother. 'The answer is no and no it will remain.'

Next day I went over to see Florence, to feed my nostalgic envy of their existence on the few words she might say to me.

'Where did you go yesterday? Who did you move?'

'Oh, I'm not sure,' Florence said, chewing gum—she was always either chewing gum or sucking a candy. 'We went over to Fort Rouge, I think, to get some folks and move them way to hell and gone over by East Kildonan.'

These were the names of quite ordinary suburbs. Why was it that at moments such as these they seemed to hold the slightly poignant attraction of those parts of the world that are remote, mysterious, and difficult to reach?

'What did you see?' I asked.

Florence shifted her gum from one cheek to the other, looking at me with slightly foolish eyes. She was not an imaginative child. No doubt, to her and her father the latter's work seemed banal, dirty, and tiring, and nothing more similar to one household move than another household move. Later I discovered that if Florence accompanied her father every Saturday, it was only because her mother went out cleaning that day and there was no one to look after the little girl at home. So her father took her along.

Both father and daughter began to consider me a trifle mad to endow their life with so much glamour.

I had asked the big pale-blond man countless times if he wouldn't take me too. He always looked at me for a moment as at some sort of curiosity—a child who perhaps wasn't completely normal—and said, 'If your mother gives you permission . . . ' and spat on the ground, hitched up his huge trousers with a movement of his hips, then went off to feed his horses or grease the wheels of his cart.

The end of the moving season was approaching. In the blazing heat of summer no one moved except people who were being evicted or who had to move closer to a new job, rare cases. If I don't soon manage to see what moving is like, I thought, I'll have to wait till next summer. And who knows? Next summer I may no longer have such a taste for it.

The notion that my desire might not always mean so much to me, instead of cheering me, filled me with anxiety. I began to realize that even our desires are not eternally faithful to us, that they wear out, perhaps die, or are replaced by others, and this precariousness of their lives made them seem more touching to me, more friendly. I thought that if we do not satisfy them they must go away somewhere and perish of boredom and lassitude.

Observing that I was still taken up with my 'whim,' Maman perhaps thought she might distract me from it by telling me once more the charming stories of her own childhood. She chose, oddly enough, to tell me again about the long journey of her family across the prairie by covered wagon. The truth must have been that she herself relived this thrilling voyage into the unknown again and again and that, by recounting it to me, she perhaps drained away some of that heartbreaking nostalgia that our life deposits in us, whatever it may be.

So here she was telling me again how, crowded together in the wagon —for Grandmother had brought some of her furniture, her spinning wheel certainly, and innumerable bundles—pressed closely in together, they had journeyed across the immense country.

'The prairie at that time, she said, seemed even more immense than it does today, for there were no villages to speak of along the trail and only a few houses. To see even one, away far off in the distance, was an adventure in itself.'

'And what did you feel?' I asked her.

'I was attracted,' Maman admitted, bowing her head slightly, as if there were something a bit wrong, or at least strange, about this. 'Attracted by the space, the great bare sky, the way the tiniest tree was visible in this solitude for miles. I was very much attracted.'

'So you were happy?'

'Happy? Yes, I think so. Happy without knowing why. Happy as you are, when you are young—or even not so young—simply because you are in motion, because life is changing and will continue to change and everything is being renewed. It's curious,' she told me. 'Such things must run in families, for I wonder whether there have ever been such born travelers as all of us.'

And she promised me that later on I too would know what it is to set forth, to be always seeking from life a possible beginning over—and that perhaps I might even become weary of it.

That night the intensity of my desire wakened me from sleep. I imagined myself in my mother's place, a child lying, as she had described it, on the floor of the wagon, watching the prairie stars—the most luminous stars in either hemisphere, it is said—as they journeyed over her head.

That, I thought, I shall never know; it is a life that is gone beyond recall and lost—and the mere fact that there were ways of life that were over, extinct in the past, and that we could not recover them in our day, filled me with the same nostalgic longing for the lost years as I had felt for my own perishable desires. But, for lack of anything better, there was the possible journey with our neighbors.

I knew—I guessed, rather—that, though we owe obedience to our parents, we owe it also to certain of our desires, those that are strangest, piercing, and too vast.

I remained awake. Tomorrow—this very day, rather—was a Saturday, moving day. I had resolved to go with the Pichettes.

Dawn appeared. Had I ever really seen it until now? I noticed that before the sky becomes clean and shining, it takes on an indecisive color, like badly washed laundry.

Now, the desire that was pushing me so violently, to the point of revolt, had no longer anything happy or even tempting about it. It was more like an order. Anguish weighed upon my heart. I wasn't even free now to say to myself, 'Sleep. Forget all that.' I had to go.

Is it the same anguish that has wakened me so many times in my life, wakens me still at dawn with the awareness of an imminent departure, sad sometimes, sometimes joyful, but almost always toward an unknown destination? Is it always the same departure that is involved?

When I judged the morning to be sufficiently advanced, I got up and combed my hair. Curiously enough, for this trip in a cart, I chose to put on my prettiest dress. 'Might as well be hung for a sheep as a lamb,' I said to myself, and left the house without a sound.

I arrived soon at the mover's. He was yawning on the threshold of the barn, stretching his arms in the early sun. He considered me suspiciously.

'Have you got permission?'

I swallowed my saliva rapidly. I nodded.

A little later Florence appeared, looking bad-tempered and sleepy.

She hitched herself up onto the seat beside us.

'Giddup!' cried the man.

And we set out in that cool morning hour that had promised me the transformation of the world and everything in it—and undoubtedly of myself.

And at first the journey kept its promise. We were passing through a city of sonorous and empty streets, over which we rolled with a great noise. All the houses seemed to be still asleep, bathed in a curious and peaceful atmosphere of withdrawal. I had never seen our little town wearing this absent, gentle air of remoteness.

The great rising sun bleached and purified it, I felt. I seemed to be traveling through an absolutely unknown city, remote and still to be explored. And yet I was astonished to recognize, as if vaguely, buildings, church spires, and street crossings that I must have seen somewhere before. But how could this be, since I had this morning left the world I had known and was entering into a new one?

Soon streetcars and a few automobiles began to move about. The sight of them looming upon the horizon and coming toward us gave me a vivid sense of the shifting of epochs.

What had these streetcars and automobiles come to do in our time, which was that of the cart? I asked myself with pleasure. When we reached Winnipeg and became involved in already heavy traffic, my sense of strangeness was so great that I believed I must be dreaming and clapped my hands.

Even at that time a horse-drawn cart must have been rare in the center of the city. So, at our side, everything was moving quickly and easily. We, with our cumbrous and reflective gait, passed like a slow, majestic film. I am the past, I am times gone by, I said to myself with fervor.

People stopped to watch us pass. I looked at them in turn, as if from far away. What did we have in common with this modern, noisy, agitated city? Increasingly, high in the cart, I became a survivor from times past. I had to restrain myself from beginning to salute the crowds, the streets, and the city, as if they were lucky to see us sweeping by.

For I had a tendency to divide into two people, actor and witness. From time to time I was the crowd that watched the passage of this astonishing cart from the past. Then I was the personage who considered from on high these modern times at her feet.

Meanwhile the difficulty of driving his somewhat nervous horses through all this noise and traffic was making the mover, whom I would have expected to be calmer and more composed, increasingly edgy. He complained and even swore noisily at almost everything we encountered. This began to embarrass me. I felt that his bad temper was spoiling all the pleasure and the sense of gentle incongruity that the poor people of the present era might have obtained from our appearance in their midst. I should have very much liked to disassociate myself from him. But how could I, jammed in beside him as I was?

Finally, we took to small, quieter streets. I saw then that we were going toward Fort Garry.

'Is that the way we're going?'

'Yes,' replied Monsieur Pichette ungraciously. 'That's the way.'

The heat was becoming overpowering. Without any shelter, wedged between the big bulky man and Florence, who made no effort to leave me a comfortable place, I was beginning to suffer greatly. At last, after several hours, we were almost in the country.

The houses were still ranked along narrow streets, but now these were short and beyond them the prairie could be seen like a great recumbent land—a land so widespread that doubtless one would never be able to see either its end or its beginning. My heart began once more to beat hard.

There begins the land of the prairies, I said to myself. There begins the infinite prairie of Canada.

'Are we going to go onto the real prairie?' I asked. 'Or are we still really inside the city limits?'

'You are certainly the most inquisitive little girl I've ever seen in my life,' grumbled Monsieur Pichette, and he told me nothing at all.

Now the roads were only of dirt, which the wind lifted in dusty whirlwinds. The houses spaced themselves out, became smaller and smaller. Finally they were no more than badly constructed shacks, put together out of various odds and ends—a bit of tin, a few planks, some painted, some raw—and they all seemed to have been raised during the night only to be demolished the next day. Yet, unfinished as they were, the little houses still seemed old. Before one of them we stopped.

The people had begun to pile up their belongings, in the house or outside it, in cardboard cartons or merely thrown pell-mell into bedcovers with the corners knotted to form rough bundles. But they were not very far along, according to Monsieur Pichette, who flew into a rage the moment we arrived.

'I only charge five dollars to move people,' he said, 'and they aren't even ready when I get here.'

We all began to transport the household effects from the shack to the cart. I joined in, carrying numerous small objects that fell to my hand—saucepans with unmatching covers, a pot, a chipped water jug. I was trying, I think, to distract myself, to keep, if at all possible, the little happiness I had left. For I was beginning to realize that the adventure was taking a sordid turn. In this poor, exhausted-looking woman with her hair plastered to her face, and in her husband—a man as lacking in amiability as Monsieur Pichette—I was discovering people who were doomed to a life of which I knew nothing, terribly gray and, it seemed to me, without exit. So I tried to help them as much as I could and took it upon myself to carry some rather large objects on my own. At last I was told to sit still because I was getting in everyone's way.

I went to rejoin Florence, who was sitting a short distance away on a little wooden fence.

'Is it always like this?' I asked.

'Yes, like this—or worse.'

'It's possible to be worse?'

'Much worse. These people,' she said, 'have beds, and dressers. . . .'

She refused to enlighten me further.

'I'm hungry,' she decided and she ran to unpack a little lunch box, took out some bread and butter and an apple and proceeded to eat under my nose.

'Didn't you bring anything to eat?' she asked.

'No.'

'You should have,' she said, and continued to bite hungrily into her bread, without offering me a scrap.

I watched the men bring out some soiled mattresses, which they carried at arm's length. New mattresses are not too distressing a sight; but once they have become the slightest bit worn or dirty I doubt that any household object is more repugnant. Then the men carried out an old torn sofa on their shoulders, some bedposts and springs. I tried to whip up my enthusiasm, to revive a few flames of it, at least. And it was then, I think, that I had a consoling idea: we had come to remove these people from this wretched life; we were going to take them now to something better; we were going to find them a fine, clean house.

A little dog circled around us, whimpering, starving, perhaps anxious. For his sake more than my own maybe, I would have liked to obtain a few bits of Florence's lunch.

'Won't you give him a little bit?' I asked.

Florence hastily devoured a large mouthful.

'Let him try and get it,' she said.

The cart was full now and, on the ground beside it, almost as many old things still waited to be stowed away.

I began to suffer for the horses, which would have all this to pull.

The house was completely emptied, except for bits of broken dishes and some absolutely worthless rags. The woman was the last to come out. This was the moment I had imagined as dramatic, almost historic, undoubtedly marked by some memorable gesture or word. But this poor creature, so weary and dust-covered, had apparently no regret at crossing her threshold, at leaving behind her two, three, or perhaps four years of her life.

'Come, we'll have to hurry,' she said simply, 'if we want to be in our new place before night.'

She climbed onto the seat of the cart with one of the younger children, whom she took on her knees. The others went off with her father, to go a little way on foot, then by streetcar, to be ahead of us, they said, at the place where we were going.

Florence and I had to stand among the furniture piled up behind.

The enormous cart now looked like some sort of monster, with tubs and pails bouncing about on both sides, upturned chairs, huge clumsy packages bulging in all directions.

The horses pulled vigorously. We set out. Then the little dog began to run along behind us, whimpering so loudly in fear and despair that I cried, imagining that no one had thought of him, 'We've forgotten the little dog. Stop. Wait for the little dog.'

In the face of everyone's indifference, I asked the woman, whose name was Mrs Smith, 'Isn't he yours?'

'Yes, he's ours, I suppose,' she replied.

'He's coming. Wait for him,' I begged.

'Don't you think we're loaded up enough already?' the mover snapped dryly, and he whipped his horses.

For a long moment more the little dog ran along behind us.

He wasn't made for running, this little dog. His legs were too short and bowed. But he did his best. Ah yes! He did his best.

Is he going to try to follow us across the whole city? I thought with distress. Awkward, distracted, and upset as he was, he would surely be crushed by an automobile or a streetcar. I don't know which I dreaded most: to see him turn back alone toward the deserted house or try to cross the city, come what might. We were already turning onto a street that was furrowed with tracks. A streetcar was approaching in the distance; several cars passed us, honking.

Mrs Smith leaned down from the seat of the cart and shouted at the little dog, 'Go on home.'

Then she repeated, more loudly, 'Go on home, stupid.'

So he had a sort of name, even though cruel, yet he was being abandoned.

Overcome with astonishment, the little dog stopped, hesitated a moment, then lay down on the ground, his eyes turned toward us, watching us disappear and whimpering with fright on the edge of the big city.

And a little later I was pleased, as you will understand, that I did not need to look at him any longer.

I have always thought that the human heart is a little like the ocean, subject to tides, that joy rises in it in a steady flow, singing of waves, good fortune, and bliss; but afterward, when the high sea withdraws, it leaves an utter desolation in our sight. So it was with me that day.

We had gone back across almost the whole enormous city—less enormous perhaps than scattered, strangely, widely spread out. The eagerness of the day diminished. I even think the sun was about to disappear. Our monster cart plunged, like some worn-out beast, toward the inconvenient, rambling neighborhoods that lay at the exact opposite end of the city to the one from which we had come.

Florence was whiling away the time by opening the drawers of an old chest and thrusting her hand into the muddle inside—the exact embodiment, it seemed to me, of this day—bits of faded ribbon; old postcards on whose backs someone had one day written: Splendid weather, Best love and kisses; a quill from a hat; electricity bills; gas reminders; a small child's shoe. The disagreeable little girl gathered up handfuls of these things, examined them, read, laughed. At one point, sensing my disapproval, she looked up, saw me watching her rummage, and thumbed her nose in spite.

The day declined further. Once more we were in sad little streets, without trees, so much like the one from which we had taken the Smiths that it seemed to me we had made all this journey for nothing and were going to end up finally at the same shack from which I had hoped to remove them.

At the end of each of these little streets the infinite prairie once more appeared but now almost dark, barely tinted, on the rim of the horizon, with angry red—the pensive, melancholy prairie of my childhood.

At last we had arrived.

Against that red horizon a small lonely house stood out black, quite far from its neighbors—a small house without foundations, set upon the ground. It did not seem old but it was already full of the odor and, no doubt, the rags and tatters of the people who had left it a short time ago. However, they had not left a single light bulb in place.

In the semidarkness Mrs Smith began to search through her bundles, lamenting that she was sure she had tucked two or three carefully away but no longer remembered where. Her husband, who had arrived a short time before us, distressed by the dimness and the clumsiness of his wife, began to accuse her of carelessness. The children were hungry; they started to cry with fretful frightened voices, in an importunate tone that reminded me of the whimpering of the little dog. The parents distributed a few slaps, a little haphazardly, it seemed to me. Finally Mrs Smith found a light bulb. A small glow shone forth timidly, as if ashamed at having to illuminate such a sad beginning.

One of the children, tortured by some strange preference, began to implore, 'Let's go home. This isn't our home. Oh let's go back home!'

Mrs Smith had come across a sack of flour, a frying pan and some eggs while she was searching for light bulbs and now she courageously set to work preparing a meal for her family. It was this, I think, that saddened me most: this poor woman, in the midst of complete disorder and almost in the dark, beginning to make pancakes. She offered some to me. I ate a little, for I was very hungry. At that moment I believe she was sorry she had abandoned the little dog. This was the one small break in the terrible ending of this day.

Meanwhile Monsieur Pichette, in a grumbling anxiety to be finished, had completely emptied the cart. As soon as everything was dumped on the ground in front of the door, he came and said to Mr Smith, 'That's five dollars.'

'But you have to help me carry it all in,' said Mr Smith.

'Not on your life. I've done all I have to.'

Poor Mr Smith fumbled in his pocket and took out five dollars in bills and small change, which he handed to the mover.

The latter counted the money in the weak glimmer that came from the house and said, 'That's it. We're quits.'

In this glimmer from the house I noticed that our poor horses were also very tired. They blinked their eyes with a lost expression, the result of too many house movings, no doubt. Perhaps horses would prefer to make the same trip over and over again—in this way they would not feel too estranged from their customary ways. But, always setting out on new routes, toward an unknown destination, they must feel disconcerted and dejected. I had time, by hurrying, to fetch them each a handful of tender grass at the end of the street where the prairie began.

What would we have had to say to each other on our way back? Nothing, certainly, and so we said nothing. Night had fallen, black, sad, and impenetrable, when we finally reached the old stable, which had once seemed to me to contain more magic and charm than even the cave of Aladdin.

The mover nevertheless reached out his hand to help me down from the cart. He was one of those people—at least I thought so then—who, after being surly and detestable all day, try at the last moment to make amends with a pleasant word for the bad impression they have created. But it was too late, much too late.

'You're not too tired?' he asked, I believe.

I shook my head and after a quick good night, an unwilling thank you, I fled. I ran toward my home, the sidewalk resounding in the silence under my steps.

I don't believe I thought of rejoicing at what I was returning to—a life that, modest as it was, was still a thousand miles away from that of the Pichettes and the Smiths. And I had not yet realized that this whole shabby, dull, and pitiless side of life that the move had revealed to me today would further increase my frenzy to escape.

I was thinking only of my mother's anxiety, of my longing to find her again and be pardoned by her—and perhaps pardon her in turn for some great mysterious wrong whose point I did not understand.

She was in such a state of nervous tension, as a matter of fact—although neighbors had told her I had gone off early with the Pichettes—that when she saw me it was her exasperation that got the upper hand.

She even raised her hand to strike me. I did not think of avoiding punishment. I may even have wanted it. But at that moment a surge of disillusionment came over me—that terrible distress of the heart after it has been inflated like a balloon.

I looked at my mother and cried, 'Oh why have you said a hundred times that from the seat of the covered wagon on the prairie in the old days the world seemed renewed, different, and so beautiful?'

She looked at me in astonishment.

'Ah, so that's it!' she said.

And at once, to my profound surprise, she drew me toward her and cradled me in her arms.

'You too then!' she said. 'You too will have the family disease, departure sickness. What a calamity!'

Then, hiding my face against her breast, she began to croon me a sort of song, without melody and almost without words.

'Poor you,' she intoned. 'Ah, poor you! What is to become of you!'

THE NINETEEN THIRTIES ARE OVER

Miriam Waddington

The nineteen thirties
are over; we survived
the depression, the Sacco-
Vanzetti of childhood
saw Tom Mooney smiling
at us from photographs,
put a rose on the grave
of Eugene Debs, listened
to our father's stories
of the Winnipeg strike and
joined the study groups
of the OBU always keeping
one eye on the revolution.

Later we played records
with thorn needles, Josh
White's *Talking Union* and
Prokofief's *Lieutenant Kije,*
shuddered at the sound of
bells and all those wolves
whirling past us in snow
on the corner of Portage
and Main, but in my mind
summer never ended on the
shores of Gimli where we
looked across to an Icelandic
paradise we could never see
the other side of; and I
dreamed of Mexico and shining
birds who beckoned to me
from the gold-braided lianas
of my own wonder.

These days I step out
from the frame of my wind-
battered house into Toronto
city; somewhere I still
celebrate sunlight, touch
the rose on the grave of
Eugene Debs but I walk
carefully in this land
of sooty snow; I pass the
rich houses and double
garages and I am not really
this middle-aged professor
but someone from
Winnipeg whose bones ache
with the broken revolutions
of Europe, and even now
I am standing on the heaving
ploughed-up field
of my father's old war.

WILLOW SONG

Merna Summers

When I was eight years old I had a favourite place and a favourite person. My favourite place was the old Hadley farm, a house where nobody lived. It was the only empty house I'd ever seen—abandoned farm houses were not so common then as they were to become later—and I liked to hear my footsteps in its hollow rooms, to take note by changes of wallpaper colours the places where pictures had once hung, to calculate by depth of painted borders the size of congoleum rugs long since removed. In one bedroom, a room I considered mine, there was an airy yellow paper on the walls. In an inner corner the paper had peeled back. What was revealed was first a pink paper decorated with blue flowers, and then a dull beige paper decorated with brown and grey flowers.

I explored the leavings of the Hadleys like an archaeologist, seeking meaning in the broken pickle crock I found in the bushes behind the house, the still-thriving rhubarb at the edge of what had once been their garden, the frayed and rotted lengths of rope that stirred in the wind between poles that had supported their children's swing. They were people I'd never seen, not even in photographs, but I felt I knew them better than I knew my own family, who in any case were a mass of contradictions.

Once, coming to the Hadley place in June, I saw that the tall green shrubs that lined the driveway were lilacs. Purple blossoms—thousands and thousands and thousands of them—had appeared on the bushes, overcoming the air with their sweetness. I walked among them in something like distress. All that blooming, and for whom? Not for me, for I had come to them only by chance. And yet if I hadn't happened along, there would have been no-one to see their glory. I wept for the lilacs and for Mrs Hadley who had planted them. I wanted to make it up to her that I was there and she was not. I tried to see with her eyes and smell with her nostrils.

But I didn't tell anyone nearer at hand about the lilacs. I didn't say, 'Come, see.' The Hadley place was mine. I never went there except alone. That was necessary.

The only person I wanted to show it to, in any case, was Mrs Hadley. No. Mr Hadley too. Mr Hadley and Mrs Hadley, one at a time. I saw myself walking along the drive with Mr Hadley. 'Lilacs break the heart,' he would say, and I would nod sadly. Then he would thank me for loving his lilacs when there was no-one else to do it. I saw myself helping Mrs Hadley make pickles, chopping cucumbers ever so carefully. Above all else I wanted to please the Hadleys, to devote myself utterly to serving them. Their house was my favourite place.

My favourite person? Well, beginning with the spring I was eight, my favourite person was my uncle, Billy Becker. Uncle Billy, who was nineteen the year I was eight, was my father's youngest brother, the youngest of a large family. Everyone adored him. It was the fact that he was unmarried and still living at home that made my grandparents' house my favourite place-to-stay.

By the time I was eight, I had an insider's knowledge of a good many houses. Both my mother and my father were members of large families, and in both families it was the custom for children to spend school holidays on the road, as it were, visiting with uncles, aunts and grandparents. We didn't see this visiting as any special treat. We 'packed our turkey,' as the family saying was, as happily, but as casually, as children in other families might search out a rope to skip.

Older children in our two families—my mother's and my father's—might be sent out when help was needed: when an aunt was under the weather or an uncle hard-pressed with field work. But if younger children were also kept on the move—and we were—it must simply have been a family inclination to share each other's children.

'It'll give us a rest,' parents said as their children left them, and no doubt it did. If it imposed a corresponding week or ten days of unrest on the uncles, aunts or grandparents who took us off their hands, I was never aware of it. Perhaps the older members of the families didn't think about our visits one way or the other, any more than we did ourselves. Fathers plowed, mothers cooked and gardened, children circulated.

Visiting a Becker house was a very different experience from visiting a Stinson house. My father was a Becker. So was I. And so, I thought, was my mother. It was my mother's family who were Stinsons.

In Becker houses, children were made much of. 'Hello, Sunshine,' my Uncle Billy would greet me, picking me up and lifting me up to his own eye level. 'How's my girl today?'

In my father's family, people were always asking me things like that. 'Whose girl are you, Barbara?' they would ask, or, 'Are you my girl?' In my mother's family, no one was anybody's girl.

I wasn't very old before I realized that the two families expected very different sorts of things from me. In my mother's family, after I'd put in a long and tiring day of trying to behave for company, nobody ever said, 'You were a good girl.' You were expected to be good, and no nonsense about it.

With my father's family, on the other hand, goodness was regarded as an accomplishment. 'You should have *seen* her!' they would cry. It was almost as if you'd brought off a miracle.

The two families were different in just about every way there is to be different. They had a different idea of celebration. A Becker wedding was a feast. There was roast beef and roast chicken and raisin pie and people. The people sat in a hall and passed heavy bowls and platters around long tables.

To the Stinsons, there was something painful about all that plenty. At their weddings, the tables were shorter and so was the food. People sat around individual card tables nibbling at what my father called 'Stinson sandwiches,' multi-layered concoctions held together by unlikely fillings.

'You don't go to a wedding to *eat,*' my grandmother Stinson said firmly.

On the other hand, Stinson houses had a quiet comfort undreamed of by Beckers. Sunday dinner was a reassuring ritual, with a good deal of fussing about the quality of the Yorkshires, and as much ceremony in the service as my aunts could muster. None of them had complete sets of silver or bone china, but each aunt had a pattern she was collecting. Each also had some special sugar shell or pickle fork or berry spoon that had come, in some unexplained way, 'from England.' Once my grandmother Stinson showed me two gold-lined silver spoons in a velvet case. They were to be mine when I was old enough, she said. I looked forward to having them without impatience.

To me, attending church was one of the great pleasures of visiting a Stinson house, for my mother and father followed the Becker practice of staying away. The Stinsons worshipped God in the Church of England. 'Naturally,' I want to say about this, for all their predilections were English. On trips to the city, Stinsons stocked up on Ridgeway's tea and Peak Frean biscuits and ginger beer. When they felt that alcohol was called for, they drank sherry. Only my grandparents had ever actually seen England, but all my aunts gloried in tea cosies and toast racks and tea strainers. They went in for candlewick crochet and cutwork embroidery. They decorated their walls with pictures of country cottages surrounded by lupins, or brown-toned prints of decomposing abbeys. They wore sweaters that looked as if they'd been boiled, and they called their washcloths 'flannels.'

When it came to being English, they were, as my father said, 'terrible as an army with banners.' But what really irritated him was their unvoiced assumption that the rest of the world, if it had had any say in the matter, would have chosen to share their origins. Englishness was a trump card, and trump takes Ace.

Once, driven past prudence by some English smugness of my grandmother's, my father felt called upon to remind her that it was the Jews, not the English, who were God's chosen people.

'Be fair, Stanley,' he claimed she said. 'There weren't any English people around when He was making the choice.'

It's because of my Stinson aunts that I still find it hard to believe that not all Englishwomen are fanatically clean housekeepers. Becker housekeeping was catch-as-catch-can. 'Nobody's house is clean all the time,' my Becker aunts told each other, but they were wrong. Stinson houses were. In a Stinson house, even the slop pail never smelled bad.

I liked that, but I liked the haphazard Becker houses too. The Stinsons had a passion for things that matched—matching forks, matching chairs, Blue Boy and Pink Lady in matching frames. In Becker houses the only things that ever matched were the five-pound coffee jars that were used to store rolled oats and brown sugar.

'If you want to have nice things you've got to take care of them,' my grandmother Stinson said. My grandmother Becker might show you how to play the Jew's harp or mouth organ, or join you in teaching the dog to jump over the broom handle, but she never talked Dutch cleanser or furniture polish. She had no time for that.

When I was very young I was totally confused by the differences in the two families. Then, in church one day with a Stinson aunt, I heard the text: 'I am come that they might have life, and that they might have it more abundantly.' I saw then that the differences in their two ways of life were probably divinely ordained. The Stinsons, who went to church, had abundantly furnished houses. The Beckers, no church-goers, had no such abundance of things.

There were other differences that I expected to have made clear to me in time. Why was it, for instance, that Stinsons reproved you for drawing attention to yourself, while Beckers applauded the same sort of behaviour?

My mother contended that my father's family paid more attention to me than was good for me. If that was true, my Uncle Billy Becker must have been the worst for me of them all.

When I stayed with my grandparents I rode beside Uncle Billy all day on the stoneboat, and he pointed out and identified kinds of birds, kinds of stones, kinds of clouds. At night he took me for rides on his bicycle. Our first bicycle ride together, I gripped the handlebars nervously and, with no clear idea of their purpose, succeeded in steering us into the ditch. As we picked ourselves up, I didn't know whether to laugh or cry.

'Never mind, Sunshine,' Uncle Billy said. 'You've just had your first spill off a bicycle.' He made it sound like an event, something I ought to remember.

If Billy had a gift for living, and he did, it centred around his extraordinary sense of occasion. He understood that everyone longs to have life present him with some occasions worth remembering. If an old farmer sold out and moved to town, if a young couple were married and shivareed, if a local girl topped the province in her grade nine exams, it might be someone else who did the work of putting on a party, but it would be Uncle Billy who made it different from all other parties. He might write a funny poem, or paint a banner that said 'Welcome Home, Mr Forsyth,' or organize a chorus to commemorate the event in song. Billy wasn't one to do things by halves.

The Stinsons, planning a bridal shower or a christening tea, worried about doing things right. Billy worried about giving people something to remember.

Billy also had a taste for practical jokes, some of which I now think could not have brought delight to anyone, but I'm sure nobody then ever censured him for it. Billy made people feel as if something was happening in their lives, and anyone who can do that is forgiven a lot.

He was as quick of temper as he was of generous impulse, but if you liked him, you forgot the first and remembered the second. Most people liked him. It would have been hard not to; he was so full of enthusiasms. Billy wanted to do everything there was. He wanted to be able to identify the stars, to call the flowers by their names, to collect rock samples. He wanted to re-cane chairs, to build stone wishing wells, to take up taxidermy. When my grandmother discovered that Billy was enrolled in three correspondence courses at once, 'You're biting off more than you can chew,' she warned him.

'Too many people worry about that,' Billy said. 'The thing to do is take as big a bite as you can, and then chew like crazy.'

My grandmother had no answer for that. Like all Beckers, she was no meagre biter herself.

The spring I was eight the schools were closed by a scarlet fever epidemic and I was spending the unexpected holiday with Grandpa and Grandma Becker. With me was my brother, Vernon, who was five.

Billy's enthusiasm that spring was for egg-mounting. Not egg-*collecting*, or at least not especially egg collecting. He'd been collecting birds' eggs for years. He had the big ones stored in tissue-filled shoe boxes and the small ones stored, one to a box, in the little wooden containers in which cousin Lotta got her vials of insulin. These boxes were of smooth white wood and were beautifully built with dovetailed corners and slide-in lids. They'd suited Billy's purpose very well as long as his purpose was storage. Now he'd decided that the time had come to put his collection on display, and he had begun to build cases he intended to hang on the wall.

Billy didn't have many tools to work with. It was wonderful to see what he could do with a fret saw and a keyhole saw and a bag of finishing nails. When I got there, he had only one showcase finished, the one that was to hold his hawk eggs. These eggs, compared to the ones in the insulin boxes, were large. Each had its own four little walls to enclose it, and its own name neatly lettered on a white card beneath it.

'Billy's got about every egg there is,' my grandmother said, but even I knew that wasn't true. He had left empty spaces in the case for hawk eggs he didn't have yet but hoped to get.

Looking over his shoulder one night, 'What's a pigeon hawk, Uncle Billy?' I asked. I was reading the name lettered beneath one of the empty compartments.

'A hawk that eats pigeons,' he said. 'It's not just an ordinary hawk when you come right down to it. It's a kind of falcon. And it lays its eggs in a magpie's nest.'

'Are they rare?' I asked. I knew that being rare made an egg special.

'Anything's rare if you haven't got it,' Billy said.

My grandmother was standing at the cupboard baking a Dutch apple cake. Vernon was sitting on the floor, sliding the lid of an empty insulin box in and out.

'I know where I could get a pigeon hawk's egg,' Billy said. He lettered another white card before he answered my unspoken question. 'The trouble is, it's in a nest on a branch that wouldn't hold my weight.'

My grandmother turned away from the cupboard, instantly alert. 'I don't want you talking the children into climbing any trees, Billy,' she said. 'I mean that.'

And to us, 'You're not to go after that egg, mind,' she said. 'I don't care what Billy offers you to do it.'

'Now, Ma,' Billy said, grinning. 'You know I wouldn't do a thing like that.'

'You!' my grandmother said. 'You! I'm surprised you haven't sweet-talked the hawk into bringing you the egg himself.' She didn't sound cross. If Uncle Billy was the kind of boy no-one could resist, I saw that she liked him that way.

'I mean it just the same,' she said again, and went back to her baking.

After a while Billy took me on his knee and began to tell me about the eggs that made up his collection. His voice when he spoke to me seemed to pay me honour. It made me feel as if I amounted to more than I'd supposed. I was intensely aware of Billy's arm around my shoulder, his fingers on my bare arm, as he talked.

It seemed as if each egg had its own story. Collecting birds' eggs, I saw, was no cut-and-dried business, but a chancey pursuit filled with hazards. Listening, I loved Uncle Billy for the dangers he had passed through.

The next morning Billy took Vernon and me with him out to the field to haul in some bundles left behind by the threshers. The hayrack was empty as we set out, and wheat kernels skipped on the bare floorboards like drops of water on a hot frying pan. We had to wrap ourselves around the rack front to keep from doing the same.

'The hawk's nest is in a big Balm of Gilead down in the valley,' Billy said when we stopped for a gate at the top of a hill.

'Grandma said we weren't supposed to go after it,' Vernon said. He was that kind of kid when he was five.

'And nobody asked you to, did they kid?' Uncle Billy said.

The next day Vernon went to town with my grandparents. I stayed home to cook Uncle Billy's dinner. As I was slicing cold potatoes into the frying pan, 'Vernon's afraid to climb that tree,' I announced. 'He's scared of falling.'

'But you're not scared, are you Sunshine?' Uncle Billy said.

'I climb trees all the time,' I said, which was a lie. 'I'll bet I could climb that big old Balm like nothing.' I was expecting Billy would refuse to let me try.

'You probably could,' he said. 'Tree-climbing's only dangerous if you're scared.'

I put the lid on the potatoes and got out the sealer of meat my grandmother had left for us.

'If you were a different kind of girl,' Billy said, 'I'd offer you a quarter to climb that tree.' He went to the basin in the corner, poured some water into it, and began to wash up. 'But unless I miss my guess,' he said, 'you're the kind of girl, if she did it at all, would do it for love, not money.'

I was pleased at how well my uncle Billy understood me.

Would I climb the tree? Would I, in years to come, be able to hear Uncle Billy tell people, 'I'd never have been able to complete my collection without the help of my niece, Barbara Becker'?

'Where is the nest exactly?' I asked.

'I'll show you this afternoon,' Uncle Billy said.

Billy had a drawstring bag fitted out with a padded case that he used to keep eggs from breaking while he was collecting them. We took it with us as we set out on our walk down to the valley.

The day was glorious. The spring hills were yellow with buffalo bean, the soddy clearings bristled with buckbrush, and reefs of silver willow zig-zagged down the side of rain-washed gullies. Overhead, big cumulus clouds were hightailing it across the sky toward Saskatchewan.

We entered the horse pasture by a rich-soiled hollow. I saw that there'd been a sprinkle of rain the night before, and the ground had covered with puffballs. Below us was the valley of the Wandering River. It had been a wet spring, and the river had overrun its banks and flooded the bottom lands. Close by the river's willow-hung edges, two white horses stood knee deep in their pasture. Blue above and blue below and, as far as we could see, the blue of hills behind the river.

I stood in my high pasture, princess among the puffballs, and went from seeing the valley to *becoming* it. The hills were mine and the river was mine and so were the white horses.

The pigeon hawk had chosen for her brooding a magpie's nest in the marshy lowlands where my grandfather's hay lands reached the Wandering River. Here grew cow parsnip and Heal-All, Indian pipe and smartweed. The trees were red willow and poplar and Balm of Gilead.

Even if Billy hadn't known where the nest was, we would have had no difficulty finding it, for, as we came near, the two parent birds flew up protesting loudly against our intrusion and trying to drive us away. They were small birds, not much bigger than jays, but I knew they were fierce. I couldn't see their curved talons and falcon beaks, but I knew they were there. They circled above the nesting tree, their wings beating rapidly.

'They won't attack me, will they?' I asked.

'I don't think so,' Uncle Billy said. 'I never yet met the hawk would tangle with a man.'

The tree, valley big, was rough of bark and shiny of leaf. Wisps of spring cotton still clung to its branches. Cotton lifted from the ground when we moved. The ground was pungent and sticky with the cast-off husks of the tree's leafing out. They stuck to our shoes like dates.

'I could boost you up to the first branch,' Uncle Billy said. 'You'd have to shinny up by yourself from there.'

I looked up. The nest, a ramshackle dome of broken sticks, was black against the sky. It was out on a limb, all right, and it was pretty high up.

'I'm not sure if I should let you do it,' Uncle Billy said.

'But I *want* to,' I said. The evening before, sitting on his knee, I'd understood the expression, 'She's soft on him.' I had felt soft all over, soft and without any will of my own. But I had a will now.

'I'll get you the egg,' I said. 'I can climb this easy.'

Billy was wearing a ball jacket, gold satin with maroon cotton banding at the neck and bottom. He gave it to me to protect my arms. It was still warm from his body when I put it on. I zipped it up and took the egg bag from him and hung it around my neck. Then I began to climb.

What was it like, pulling myself up that tree? I don't really remember. Later, when I was on the ground again, I saw that the inside of my knees had been scraped raw by the rough bark. I didn't feel it as it was happening. Nor do I know how my arms and legs managed to pull me from foothold to foothold. I wasn't a tomboy, and I didn't have the strength of the habitual tree-climber. To climb so tall a tree should have been impossible for me. Yet I did it, without feeling pain or even—once I'd begun—fear.

I reached the limb that held the nest and inched my way outward. Then I saw what I hadn't realized before: that it wasn't possible to rise above it and look in. The nest was tall, perhaps three feet in depth. I didn't know how to proceed. Nor could I call down to Uncle Billy. One eight-year-old girl might balance on this limb, but not one eight-year-old girl plus her voice.

Billy, watching from below, realized my problem. 'There should be holes in the side,' he called. 'Try to stick your arm in that way.'

I felt around, found an opening, and nudged my way in. What I found there seemed to be a nest within a nest, a hard mud kernel in the middle of the pile of deadwood. By groping, I found the eggs, still warm from their parents' bodies, and I took one. It was quite a trick to keep the hold on one hand easy, so as not to break the egg, while the other hand and the rest of the body were hanging on for dear life, but somehow I did it. Then, either at the nest or at the branch's fork with the main tree, I managed to get the egg into the padding in the bag. I hung the bag backwards around my neck and began to come down.

As soon as I got to the bottom Uncle Billy opened the bag. 'Boy, oh Boy!' he said. 'You got it here all in one piece. I don't know how you did it, but you did it.'

The egg was reddish brown with dark brown markings. I touched it. Then I lifted it to my face. It smelled warm.

I looked at Uncle Billy and we both smiled. I was through with pickle crocks and peeling wallpaper. It was living stuff I was dealing in now.

'Does the egg belong to you?' I asked him. What I wanted him to say was that it belonged to us both: him and me together.

'I guess so,' he said. 'Sure. I don't know as the hawk would want it back with our smell on it.'

I wanted to keep my climb a secret, not out of fear of punishment, but because it would be better that way. But Billy said that Grandma would have to be told.

'Don't worry, Sunshine,' he said. 'Your grandma's bark is worse than her bite.'

He was right about that anyway. My grandmother had quite a lot to say as she put salve on my legs, but what most of it added up to was that it was no use to cry over spilled milk; what was done couldn't be undone, and forgive and forget was her motto. I thought once more how different she was from the Stinsons. They didn't either forgive or forget. What would they have said to me under similar circumstances? To Billy? A broken promise was a serious thing with them, and when anyone failed to live up to their standards, they remembered it. The offender was in their bad books for good.

I was glad that my grandmother Becker was forgiving, for her house that spring was the best of all possible places to be. Every night I helped Billy with his egg-mounting. I was an initiate now, a partner. Touching a finger to an egg I would feel myself in the presence of fast-beating hearts and feathery down. Nest-building was locked in those eggs, and homing flight at day's end, and bird song.

I didn't realize then that a collected life is a doomed life. To me the eggs were merely in a period of waiting. When the time was right, they would get on with their becoming.

Billy was important to me, but I was important to him too. 'Billy thinks that Barbara's "just it," I heard my grandmother tell someone one day. I knew that Billy didn't feel the same way about Vernon, but that was all right with me too.

One night, when I was coming down the stairs with a bottle of India ink to write labels for Billy, I heard his voice from the kitchen, quick with anger.

'Look what you made me do,' Billy said.

I came into the room and saw him facing Vernon. Vernon was cowering, uncertain whether to cry or call Grandma or run away.

'I didn't do anything,' Vernon said.

'You were standing too close to my elbow,' Billy said. 'How do you expect me to get anything done with a kid pushing up against me all the time?'

There was a small, buff-coloured egg lying broken at their feet. Vernon bent down and tried to pick up the pieces of shell.

'Was it an important one, Uncle Billy?' I asked. What I meant was: was it a kind hard to come by?

'It could have been for all he cares,' Billy said.

I could tell by his voice that I was included in his anger, but I forgave him.

'Now clear out, both of you, before I lose my temper,' he said.

Vernon held it against Billy that he had hollered at us. I was ashamed of my brother. You had to take things into account with Billy. What he said Tuesday, meaning it, he no longer meant on Wednesday. You were expected to know that and consider it unsaid.

'Don't be an old woman, Vernon,' Billy said when the third day came and Vernon was still sulking. Billy and I did not like boys who were old women.

After Vernon and I went back to our own house, life seemed very humdrum to me. It wasn't just novelty I craved, I think, but meaning as well. I had always had a hankering for a religious life. It persisted, even though I knew that, as a Becker, I ought to be above all that. Beckers saw religion as something other people went in for, something not in very good taste. Beckers even took it as an insult when anyone sent them a religious Christmas card.

Just the same, I envied children who, at bedtime, were asked, 'Did you say your prayers?' instead of 'Did you wash your feet?' My need to worship, wherever it came from, did not come from without. Perhaps every human being feels it, whether or not there is anybody there.

One day, flipping through an old National Geographic, I came across a picture that moved me profoundly. It was of a lone hawk, riding the air on motionless wings. I knew enough about birds to be pretty sure that the hawk was an osprey, but I pretended to myself that it was a pigeon hawk. I cut it out and found a frame for it. Then I got out my fountain pen and on the cardboard backing wrote an inscription.

'To my favourite girl with all my love,' I wrote. I signed it, 'Uncle Billy.'

I put the picture in the frame and hung it on my bedroom wall, over a piece of furniture that we called a chiffonier.

All that summer I picked little bouquets and placed them in front of it. When fall came and the garden froze, I took to moving the hawk's picture from over the chiffonier to the dressing table and back again. I wanted to come into the room thinking of something else and have it surprise me.

Curiously, when Uncle Billy started to go around with Emily Patmore, what I felt was not jealousy but rather a deep delight. Emily was dark-haired and beautiful. It was as if she'd been specially selected to serve in my stead. *I* might have to go to school and gather eggs and carry in nightwood, but Emily—if she married Billy—could be with him all day, every day.

During the months they were going out together, when I washed dishes, I was not Barbara washing dishes for Mama, but Emily washing dishes for Billy. If on Saturday I helped Mama make pies, the hands that sliced the apples or rolled the piecrust were not my own hands, nor were the pies constructed to fill any ordinary hunger.

About a month before their wedding, I came home from school one day to find Billy and Emily in the living room. They'd been making the rounds of the relatives, and they were talking about their wedding plans.

Catching sight of me, 'Hey, why don't we dress the kid up and let her pass the cake or something?' Billy said. And so I did that.

In our family not even newly weds held themselves aloof from the visits of circulating children. At least Billy and Emily didn't. They asked me to come and stay with them a couple of months after the wedding.

'How's my girl?' Billy asked the old question when my father delivered me to their door. He had a different way of saying it than the other uncles, a way that made it seem like he was saying a good deal more.

I loved Billy and Emily's house. Everything in it might have been planned with me in mind. Some rooms have a quality of light that sets them apart from other rooms. My room in the Hadley house had had it; so did the room that was prepared for me here. There was a pale yellow paper on the walls, and dotted sheer curtains at the windows. The dresser drawers smelled of Camay soap.

Some nights Uncle Wallace and Aunt Margaret walked over; they only lived a half mile away. Then we would all gather around the radio and listen to *The Great Gildersleeve* or *Fibber McGee and Molly*.

The nights the three of us were alone together were made of different stuff altogether. 'Go and get your hair brush,' Billy would say to Emily, and she would get it. Then she would sit down on the floor in front of him and he would brush her hair, slowly and without words. When I went to bed, I couldn't sleep. I would lie there aching with the wonder of it. Would I ever be grown up?

By the time the next summer came, I was old enough to be expected to be of some use in the world. I had my own jobs to do at home, and I had the confidence that comes from never having failed at anything important. When I heard that Emily wasn't well, that one of the older girls would have to go over to take care of her, I hoped that I might be the one to be chosen.

My mother, when she told me that I had been, didn't say what was the matter with Emily. There had been a flu going around, and I supposed she had it. Perhaps my mother even hinted that that was the problem.

Emily vomited all the time. I held her head and them emptied the basin. She wasn't supposed to leave her bed except to use the chamber pot, so I took over the rest of the house as well. It was easy to forget that I was only ten, easy for me and maybe even easy for Billy, who was twenty-one, and Emily, who was a year younger.

Emily usually felt a little brighter in the evenings. Billy and I would go in and sit by her bedside, and Billy would tell us about the new chicken house he had started to build: how he was going to use sunlight and proper ventilation to prevent poultry disease, how he had designed the roosts for easy cleaning, how a chicken house so well-lit and draught-free would affect the egg production of any flock fortunate enough to be under its roof. Billy wasn't going to have barred rocks or leghorns like everyone else, but a breed new to Willow Bunch called Rhode Island Reds. We gathered that they were the most wonderful hens that ever pecked or scratched.

Billy had spent a great deal of time on his plans, and his farm work had got rather behindhand as a result. He ran from one thing to another, harrowing a few rounds on his summerfallow, seeding an acre or two of brome grass, weeding a row of Emily's garden. And of course every day he had to milk cows and separate milk.

I cooked Billy's meals and cleaned Billy's house and tried to help him with the garden and separating. Billy harrowed and hammered. Emily vomited. She wasn't as pretty as she had been before, and there was a sour smell in her room that no amount of cleaning and airing ever quite removed.

One morning, when I'd got the fire going in the cook stove and was starting to cook breakfast, Billy came in looking worried.

'Your Aunt Emily's not feeling very good today,' he said. 'I want you to keep a close eye on her and call me right away if anything goes wrong.'

I didn't know what I was watching for, but I hovered over her all morning. She looked about the same to me. Billy was a little late coming in at noon—he had been putting together a gable vent and had forgotten about the time—and he went at once to Emily's room.

'You okay?' he asked from the door.

Emily smiled weakly. 'If you can call this okay,' she said. She had vomited three times that morning.

'You sure you don't want to go to the hospital?' he asked. 'I could phone and tell them I'm bringing you in.' There wasn't a telephone in Billy and Emily's house. They used Uncle Wallace's.

'The doctor said it wouldn't make much difference one way or the other,' Emily said. 'He said it would be touch and go either way.' She had a swallow of water from a glass by her bed. 'I don't know if there's anything he could do,' she said. 'He sounded as if he thought the sooner I got it over with the better.' She sounded tired and uncertain, as if she wanted someone else to make the decision for her.

Billy thought the decision had been made. He didn't want her to go to the hospital, and so he supposed that she didn't want to go.

'What you need is a good nap,' he said. 'A nap and then a nice cup of tea.'

His prescription may or may not have reassured Emily. It reassured me. 'Don't you worry about a thing, Uncle Billy,' I told him. 'I'll take care of her.'

'Billy, I'm scared.' It was Emily who said it, but Billy who looked it. His face, just for a moment, was desperate.

Then, 'What kind of talk is that?' he demanded. 'You're going to be just fine.' He talked a little more, persuading himself.

'I'm leaving you in good hands,' he said. Then, I suppose to give Emily courage, he extracted a promise from me. 'You won't leave the house even for a minute, will you Sunshine?' he asked.

I promised that I would not.

'Just call if you need me,' Billy told me as he went back to his work. 'I'll be right here.'

I washed the dinner dishes and set the kitchen to rights. Then I went to see if Emily needed anything.

Usually I helped Emily out of bed when she needed to use the chamber pot, left her alone, and then came back to help her in again. After the first few days I had got used to seeing her in her nightgown, and she had got used to being seen. But when I went in that afternoon I saw that she had already been up. She was sitting on the edge of the bed, a blanket wrapped around her so that her nightgown was almost hidden. She was pale, and there were beads of perspiration on her upper lip.

'Are you cold?' I asked, because of the blanket. 'Would you like me to close the window?'

'The window!' she said. 'The window!

'For the love of God, Barbara, I'm bleeding to death.'

I realized then that there was a new smell in the sick room. Warm blood. It lay in a pool on the floor near her bed where, I supposed, Emily had vomited it. I had heard of people vomiting blood before. All of them had died.

'What shall I do?' I asked.

'Call your Uncle Billy,' she said. Then she lay down, still wrapped in her blanket. 'I want my mother,' I heard her say as I ran out of the house.

In the yard, 'Uncle Billy,' I called. 'Uncle Billy.'

But he wasn't there. There was no answer, not from the chicken house, nor from the summerfallow, nor from the field of brome. I ran first toward one and then toward another, all the time calling.

I couldn't leave Aunt Emily. I had promised I would stay with her. But if I didn't get help she would die.

At last I gave up calling and began to run down the road toward Uncle Wallace's. It wasn't far, but it was too far for running. Aunt Margaret, at work in her garden, saw me coming and ran out to meet me.

'Aunt Emily is dying,' I told her.

'You hush that kind of talk,' Aunt Margaret said fiercely. 'Nobody's dying around here.' Then she went into the house to phone the doctor.

By the time she got through, I had regained my breath. We climbed into Uncle Wallace's car—Aunt Margaret knew how to drive—and we returned to Billy's house.

'The doctor will be here in half an hour,' Aunt Margaret told Emily briskly. 'Now how much blood have you lost?'

Emily indicated the pool on the floor. 'That's most of it, I think,' she said. 'But I'm still losing it.'

'Barbara, you get a mop and . . .' Aunt Margaret stopped herself. 'You shouldn't be in here at all,' she said. 'I'll clean it up before Billy comes in and sees it.'

I went out and sat in the kitchen. It didn't seem odd to me that I—who had held Emily's head over the basin and emptied her chamber pot—should be shooed away now. Some time or other I must have realized that her trouble was not the flu.

When Billy came in, 'Aunt Emily's not well,' I told him. Now that I knew where it came from, it was unthinkable to tell him about the blood. 'The doctor's coming. Aunt Margaret's with her.'

I suppose Billy knew what had happened. 'Damn it all, kid,' he said. 'Why didn't you call me?'

'I didn't know where you were,' I said.

'And you damn well didn't look very hard, did you?' he said. It took my brain a moment to register the words.

'I thought you were going to take care of her,' he said.

His voice was hot with accusation. I remember some of the things he said after that, though not the order he said them in. He accused me of not wanting Emily to get well. He called me useless. He said he'd only been away a moment and I hadn't half tried. But it wasn't what he said that hurt the most. It was that he spoke as if I, Barbara, scarcely existed. I might never have existed at all.

He didn't stop until Aunt Margaret came out and told him to get ahold of himself. 'You're upsetting Emily,' she said.

'Just get this kid out of my sight, that's all,' Billy said. 'If she's still here when I come back in I won't be responsible for what I do.'

Then he went out to the road to watch for the doctor. Aunt Margaret sent me home to her place across the fields.

'Billy was beside himself,' I heard Aunt Margaret tell my mother later.

'She'll get over it,' my mother said. In a way she was right. Nothing hurts forever. In any case, there are some kinds of hurts you can get only once, like smallpox.

After that, I stopped circulating among relatives on my school holidays. 'She's getting to be that age,' my mother explained when my relatives asked about it.

One day, pulled by an impulse I didn't try to analyze, I walked over to the old Hadley place again. I found it different. Pickle crock, peeling wallpaper, frayed swing ropes—all were still in place, but they'd lost their power to move me. There was no reason to go there any more.

I didn't want to see Billy and I found it surprisingly easy to avoid him. Girl cousins, at family parties, often congregated in a bedroom. I had always scorned these feminine huddles, but I joined them now. By this and other means I was able to keep a certain distance between us for nearly two years.

To an adult, a year or two is not time at all. Children, I think, have the truer perception of time. In the two years since I had been banished from Billy's house, Emily had got pregnant again and had had a baby. Vernon had started school and passed into grade two. Grandma Becker had started to lose her hearing. Nothing was as it had been.

As for me, different things gave me pleasure now. I pored over magazine articles on table-setting and interior decoration. I was learning twelve different ways to fold a table napkin. My grandmother Stinson was teaching me to do candlewick crochet, and I had picked my own patterns in Royal Albert and Community Plate.

The spring I was twelve the Beckers gathered at my grandparents' house to celebrate their fiftieth wedding anniversary. I knew I would see Billy, but I planned to keep the usual distance between us. Except for an accident of timing, I might have succeeded.

Uncle Wallace had brought a bottle of rum, and the men were down in the cellar having a drink. I was at the stove, filling bowls with vegetables. Just as I turned to carry a bowl of turnips to the table, the cellar door opened and there stood Billy, his face slightly flushed from the rum, not two feet away from me. We were face to face.

Perhaps Billy didn't know what to do about me any more than I knew what to do about him. Perhaps he thought if he made enough noise it would cover over all that had been, and put us on a new footing. Whatever the reason, his voice when he spoke was inordinately loud.

'Well, how's my girl?' he asked. He didn't wait for an answer.

'This little lady and I used to be pretty good friends, didn't we Sweetheart?' he said. 'How've you been, anyway?'

'Fine,' I said. It would have been unthinkable not to answer at all.

'We've missed you,' he said. 'You ought to come over and see us some time.'

Then a new thought struck him and his face lit up. 'There's a sparrow hawk nesting in a tree at the edge of my hay quarter,' he said.

He turned to the rest of them. 'That'll fetch her if anything will,' he said.

He probably thought it was the truth he spoke.

I said the bowl of turnips was hot: I'd have to put it on the table... and that was the end.

I felt old, a thousand years older than this boy with all his enthusiasms. There was no reason to tell him that the only hawk that would ever mean anything to me had been ripped up and consigned to the flames a long, long time ago.

THE LOONS

Margaret Laurence

Just below Manawaka, where the Wachakwa River ran brown and noisy over the pebbles, the scrub oak and grey-green willow and chokecherry bushes grew in a dense thicket. In a clearing at the centre of the thicket stood the Tonnerre family's shack. The basis of this dwelling was a small square cabin made of poplar poles and chinked with mud, which had been built by Jules Tonnerre some fifty years before, when he came back from Batoche with a bullet in his thigh, the year that Riel was hung and the voices of the Metis entered their long silence. Jules had only intended to stay the winter in the Wachakwa Valley, but the family was still there in the thirties, when I was a child. As the Tonnerres had increased, their settlement had been added to, until the clearing at the foot of the town hill was a chaos of lean-tos, wooden packing cases, warped lumber, discarded car tires, ramshackle chicken coops, tangled strands of barbed wire and rusty tin cans.

The Tonnerres were French halfbreeds, and among themselves they spoke a *patois* that was neither Cree nor French. Their English was broken and full of obscenities. They did not belong among the Cree of the Galloping Mountain reservation, further north, and they did not belong among the Scots-Irish and Ukrainians of Manawaka, either. They were, as my Grandmother MacLeod would have put it, neither flesh, fowl, nor good salt herring. When their men were not working at odd jobs or as section hands on the C.P.R., they lived on relief. In the summers, one of the Tonnerre youngsters, with a face that seemed totally unfamiliar with laughter, would knock at the doors of the town's brick houses and offer for sale a lard-pail full of bruised wild strawberries, and if he got as much as a quarter he would grab the coin and run before the customer had time to change her mind. Sometimes old Jules, or his son Lazarus, would get mixed up in a Saturday-night brawl, and would hit out at whoever was nearest, or howl drunkenly among the offended shoppers on Main Street, and then the Mountie would put them for the night in the barred cell underneath the Court House, and the next morning they would be quiet again.

Piquette Tonnerre, the daughter of Lazarus, was in my class at school. She was older than I, but she had failed several grades, perhaps because her attendance had always been sporadic and her interest in schoolwork negligible. Part of the reason she had missed a lot of school was that she had had tuberculosis of the bone, and had once spent many months in hospital. I knew this because my father was the doctor who had looked after her. Her sickness was almost the only thing I knew about her, however. Otherwise, she existed for me only as a vaguely embarrassing presence, with her hoarse voice and her clumsy limping walk and her grimy cotton dresses that were always miles too long. I was neither friendly nor unfriendly towards her. She dwelt and moved somewhere within my scope of vision, but I did not actually notice her very much until that peculiar summer when I was eleven.

'I don' t know what to do about that kid,' my father said at dinner one evening. 'Piquette Tonnerre, I mean. The damn bone's flared up again. I've had her in hospital for quite a while now, and it's under control all right, but I hate like the dickens to send her home again.'

'Couldn't you explain to her mother that she has to rest a lot?' my mother said.

'The mother's not there,' my father replied. 'She took off a few years back. Can't say I blame her. Piquette cooks for them, and she says Lazarus would never do anything for himself as long as she's there. Anyway, I don't think she'd take much care of herself, once she got back. She's only thirteen, after all. Beth, I was thinking—what about taking her up to Diamond Lake with us this summer? A couple of months rest would give that bone a much better chance.'

My mother looked stunned.

'But Ewen—what about Roddie and Vanessa?'

'She's not contagious,' my father said. 'And it would be company for Vanessa.'

'Oh dear,' my mother said in distress, 'I'll bet anything she has nits in her hair.'

'For Pete's sake,' my father said crossly, 'do you think Matron would let her stay in the hospital for all this time like that? Don't be silly, Beth.'

Grandmother MacLeod, her delicately featured face as rigid as a cameo, now brought her mauve-veined hands together as though she were about to begin a prayer.

'Ewen, if that half-breed youngster comes along to Diamond Lake, I'm not going,' she announced. 'I'll go to Morag's for the summer.'

I had trouble in stifling my urge to laugh, for my mother brightened visibly and quickly tried to hide it. If it came to a choice between Grandmother MacLeod and Piquette, Piquette would win hands down, nits or not.

'It might be quite nice for you, at that,' she mused. 'You haven't seen Morag for over a year, and you might enjoy being in the city for a while. Well, Ewen dear, you do what you think best. If you think it would do Piquette some good, then we'll be glad to have her, as long as she behaves herself.'

So it happened that several weeks later, when we all piled into my father's old Nash, surrounded by suitcases and boxes of provisions and toys for my ten-month-old brother, Piquette was with us and Grandmother MacLeod, miraculously, was not. My father would only be staying at the cottage for a couple of weeks, for he had to get back to his practice, but the rest of us would stay at Diamond Lake until the end of August.

Our cottage was not named, as many were, 'Dew Drop Inn' or 'Bide-a-Wee,' or 'Bonnie Doon.' The sign on the roadway bore in austere letters only our name, MacLeod. It was not a large cottage, but it was on the lakefront. You could look out the windows and see, through the filigree of the spruce trees, the water glistening greenly as the sun caught it. All around the cottage were ferns, and sharp-branched raspberry bushes, and moss that had grown over fallen tree trunks. If you looked carefully among the weeds and grass, you could find wild strawberry plants which were in white flower now and in another month would bear fruit, the fragrant globes hanging like miniature scarlet lanterns on the thin hairy stems. The two grey squirrels were still there, gossiping at us from the tall spruce beside the cottage, and by the end of the summer they would again be tame enough to take pieces of crust from my hands. The broad moose antlers that hung above the back door were a little more bleached and fissured after the winter, but otherwise everything was the same. I raced joyfully around my kingdom, greeting all the places I had not seen for a year. My brother, Roderick, who had not been born when we were here last summer, sat on the car rug in the sunshine and examined a brown spruce cone, meticulously turning it round and round in his small and curious hands. My mother and father toted the luggage from car to cottage, exclaiming over how well the place had wintered, no broken windows, thank goodness, no apparent damage from storm-felled branches or snow.

Only after I had finished looking around did I notice Piquette. She was sitting on the swing, her lame leg held stiffly out, and her other foot scuffing the ground as she swung slowly back and forth. Her long hair hung black and straight around her shoulders, and her broad coarse-featured face bore no expression—it was blank, as though she no longer dwelt within her own skull, as though she had gone elsewhere. I approached her very hesitantly.

'Want to come and play?'

Piquette looked at me with a sudden flash of scorn.

'I ain't a kid,' she said.

Wounded, I stamped angrily away, swearing I would not speak to her for the rest of the summer. In the days that followed, however, Piquette began to interest me, and I began to want to interest her. My reasons did not appear bizarre to me. Unlikely as it may seem, I had only just realised that the Tonnerre family, whom I had always heard called half-breeds, were actually Indians, or as near as made no difference. My acquaintance with Indians was not extensive. I did not remember ever having seen a real Indian, and my new awareness that Piquette sprang from the people of Big Bear and Poundmaker, of Tecumseh, of the Iroquois who had eaten Father Brebeuf's heart—all this gave her an instant attraction in my eyes. I was a devoted reader of Pauline Johnson at this age, and sometimes would orate aloud and in an exalted voice, *West Wind, blow from your prairie nest; Blow from the mountains, blow from the west*—and so on. It seemed to me that Piquette must be in some way a daughter of the forest, a kind of junior prophetess of the wilds, who might impart to me, if I took the right approach, some of the secrets which she undoubtedly knew—where the whippoorwill made her nest, how the coyote reared her young, or whatever it was that it said in Hiawatha.

I set about gaining Piquette's trust. She was not allowed to go swimming, with her bad leg, but I managed to lure her down to the beach—or rather, she came because there was nothing else to do. The water was always icy, for the lake was fed by springs, but I swam like a dog, thrashing my arms and legs around at such speed and with such an output of energy that I never grew cold. Finally, when I had had enough, I came out and sat beside Piquette on the sand. When she saw me approaching, her hand squashed flat the sand castle she had been building, and she looked at me sullenly, without speaking.

'Do you like this place?' I asked, after a while, intending to lead on from there into the question of forest lore.

Piquette shrugged. 'It's okay. Good as anywhere.'

'I love it,' I said. 'We come here every summer.'

'So what?' Her voice was distant, and I glanced at her uncertainly, wondering what I could have said wrong.

'Do you want to come for a walk?' I asked her. 'We wouldn't need to go far. If you walk just around the point there, you come to a bay where great big reeds grow in the water, and all kinds of fish hang around there. Want to? Come on.'

She shook her head.

'Your dad said I ain't supposed to do no more walking than I got to.'

I tried another line.

'I bet you know a lot about the woods and all that, eh?' I began respectfully.

Piquette looked at me from her large dark unsmiling eyes.

'I don't know what in hell you're talkin' about,' she replied. 'You nuts or somethin'? If you mean where my old man, and me, and all them live, you better shut up, by Jesus, you hear?'

I was startled and my feelings were hurt, but I had a kind of dogged perseverance. I ignored her rebuff.

'You know something, Piquette? There's loons here, on this lake. You can see their nests just up the shore there, behind those logs. At night, you can hear them even from the cottage, but it's better to listen from the beach. My dad says we should listen and try to remember how they sound, because in a few years when more cottages are built at Diamond Lake and more people come in, the loons will go away.'

Piquette was picking up stones and snail shells and then dropping them again.

'Who gives a good goddamn?' she said.

It became increasingly obvious that, as an Indian, Piquette was a dead loss. That evening I went out by myself, scrambling through the bushes that overhung the steep path, my feet slipping on the fallen spruce needles that covered the ground. When I reached the shore, I walked along the firm damp sand to the small pier that my father had built, and sat down there. I heard someone else crashing through the undergrowth and the bracken, and for a moment I thought Piquette had changed her mind, but it turned out to be my father. He sat beside me on the pier and we waited, without speaking.

At night the lake was like black glass with a streak of amber which was the path of the moon. All around, the spruce trees grew tall and close-set, branches blackly sharp against the sky, which was lightened by a cold flickering of stars. Then the loons began their calling. They rose like phantom birds from the nests on the shore, and flew out onto the dark still surface of the water.

No one can ever describe that ululating sound, the crying of the loons, and no one who has heard it can ever forget it. Plaintive, and yet with a quality of chilling mockery, those voices belonged to a world separated by aeons from our neat world of summer cottages and the lighted lamps of home.

'They must have sounded just like that,' my father remarked, 'before any person ever set foot here.'

Then he laughed. 'You could say the same, of course, about sparrows, or chipmunks, but somehow it only strikes you that way with the loons.'

'I know,' I said.

Neither of us suspected that this would be the last time we would ever sit here together on the shore, listening. We stayed for perhaps half an hour, and then we went back to the cottage. My mother was reading beside the fireplace. Piquette was looking at the burning birch log, and not doing anything.

'You should have come along,' I said, although in fact I was glad she had not.

'Not me,' Piquette said. 'You wouldn' catch me walkin' way down there jus' for a bunch of squawkin' birds.'

Piquette and I remained ill at ease with one another. I felt I had somehow failed my father, but I did not know what was the matter, nor why she would not or could not respond when I suggested exploring the woods or playing house. I thought it was probably her slow and difficult walking that held her back. She stayed most of the time in the cottage with my mother, helping her with the dishes or with Roddie, but hardly ever talking. Then the Duncans arrived at their cottage, and I spent my days with Mavis, who was my best friend. I could not reach Piquette at all, and I soon lost interest in trying. But all that summer she remained as both a reproach and a mystery to me.

That winter my father died of pneumonia, after less than a week's illness. For some time I saw nothing around me, being completely immersed in my own pain and my mother's. When I looked outward once more, I scarcely noticed that Piquette Tonnerre was no longer at school. I do not remember seeing her at all until four years later, one Saturday night when Mavis and I were having Cokes in the Regal Café. The jukebox was booming like tuneful thunder, and beside it, leaning lightly on its chrome and its rainbow glass, was a girl.

Piquette must have been seventeen then, although she looked about twenty. I stared at her, astounded that anyone could have changed so much. Her face, so stolid and expressionless before, was animated now with a gaiety that was almost violent. She laughed and talked very loudly with the boys around her. Her lipstick was bright carmine, and her hair was cut short and frizzily permed. She had not been pretty as a child, and she was not pretty now, for her features were still heavy and blunt. But her dark and slightly slanted eyes were beautiful, and her skin-tight skirt and orange sweater displayed to enviable advantage a soft and slender body.

She saw me, and walked over. She teetered a little, but it was not due to her once-tubercular leg, for her limp was almost gone.

'Hi, Vanessa.' Her voice still had the same hoarseness. 'Long time no see, eh?'

'Hi,' I said. 'Where've you been keeping yourself, Piquette?'

'Oh, I been around,' she said. 'I been away almost two years now. Been all over the place—Winnipeg, Regina, Saskatoon. Jesus, what I could tell you! I come back this summer, but I ain't stayin'. You kids goin' to the dance?'

'No,' I said abruptly, for this was a sore point with me. I was fifteen, and thought I was old enough to go to the Saturday-night dances at the Flamingo. My mother, however, thought otherwise.

'Y'oughta come,' Piquette said. 'I never miss one. It's just about the on'y thing in this jerkwater town that's any fun. Boy, you couldn' catch me stayin' here. I don' give a shit about this place. It stinks.'

She sat down beside me, and I caught the harsh over-sweetness of her perfume.

'Listen, you wanna know something, Vanessa?' she confided, her voice only slightly blurred. 'Your dad was the only person in Manawaka that ever done anything good to me.'

I nodded speechlessly. I was certain she was speaking the truth. I knew a little more than I had that summer at Diamond Lake, but I could not reach her now any more than I had then. I was ashamed, ashamed of my own timidity, the frightened tendency to look the other way. Yet I felt no real warmth towards her—I only felt that I ought to, because of that distant summer and because my father had hoped she would be company for me, or perhaps that I would be for her, but it had not happened that way. At this moment, meeting her again, I had to admit that she repelled and embarrassed me, and I could not help despising the self-pity in her voice. I wished she would go away. I did not want to see her. I did not know what to say to her. It seemed that we had nothing to say to one another.

'I'll tell you something else,' Piquette went on. 'All the old bitches an' biddies in this town will sure be surprised. I'm gettin' married this fall—my boyfriend, he's an English fella, works in the stockyards in the city there, a very tall guy, got blond wavy hair. Gee, is he ever handsome. Got this real classy name. Alvin Gerald Cummings—some handle, eh? They call him Al.'

For the merest instant, then, I saw her. I really did see her, for the first and only time in all the years we had both lived in the same town. Her defiant face, momentarily, became unguarded and unmasked, and in her eyes there was a terrifying hope.

'Gee, Piquette—' I burst out awkwardly, 'that's swell. That's really wonderful. Congratulations—good luck—I hope you'll be happy—'

As I mouthed the conventional phrases, I could only guess how great her need must have been, that she had been forced to seek the very things she so bitterly rejected.

When I was eighteen, I left Manawaka and went away to college. At the end of my first year, I came back home for the summer. I spent the first few days in talking non-stop with my mother, as we exchanged all the news that somehow had not found its way into letters—what had happened in my life and what had happened here in Manawaka while I was away. My mother searched her memory for events that concerned people I knew.

'Did I ever write you about Piquette Tonnerre, Vanessa?' she asked one morning.

'No, I don't think so,' I replied. 'Last I heard of her, she was going to marry some guy in the city. Is she still there?'

My mother looked perturbed, and it was a moment before she spoke, as though she did not know how to express what she had to tell and wished she did not need to try.

'She's dead,' she said at last. Then, as I stared at her, 'Oh, Vanessa, when it happened, I couldn't help thinking of her as she was that summer—so sullen and gauche and badly dressed. I couldn't help wondering if we could have done something more at that time—but what could we do? She used to be around in the cottage there with me all day, and honestly, it was all I could do to get a word out of her. She didn't even talk to your father very much, although I think she liked him, in her way.'

'What happened?' I asked.

'Either her husband left her, or she left him,' my mother said, 'I don't know which. Anyway, she came back here with two youngsters, both only babies—they must have been born very close together. She kept house, I guess, for Lazarus and her brothers, down in the valley there, in the old Tonnerre place. I used to see her on the street sometimes, but she never spoke to me. She'd put on an awful lot of weight, and she looked a mess, to tell you the truth, a real slattern, dressed any old how. She was up in court a couple of times—drunk and disorderly, of course. One Saturday night last winter, during the coldest weather, Piquette was alone in the shack with the children. The Tonnerres made home brew all the time, so I've heard, and Lazarus said later she'd been drinking most of the day when he and the boys went out that evening. They had an old woodstove there—you know the kind, with exposed pipes. The shack caught fire. Piquette didn't get out, and neither did the children.'

I did not say anything. As so often with Piquette, there did not seem to be anything to say. There was a kind of silence around the image in my mind of the fire and the snow, and I wished I could put from my memory the look that I had seen once in Piquette's eyes.

I went up to Diamond Lake for a few days that summer, with Mavis and her family. The MacLeod cottage had been sold after my father's death, and I did not even go to look at it, not wanting to witness my long-ago kingdom possessed now by strangers. But one evening I went down to the shore by myself.

The small pier which my father had built was gone, and in its place there was a large and solid pier built by the government, for Galloping Mountain was now a national park, and Diamond Lake had been re-named Lake Wapakata, for it was felt that an Indian name would have a greater appeal to tourists. The one store had become several dozen, and the settlement had all the attributes of a flourishing resort—hotels, a dance-hall, cafés with neon signs, the penetrating odours of potato chips and hot dogs.

I sat on the government pier and looked out across the water. At night the lake at least was the same as it had always been, darkly shining and bearing within its black glass the streak of amber that was the path of the moon. There was no wind that evening, and everything was quiet all around me. It seemed too quiet, and then I realized that the loons were no longer here. I listened for some time, to make sure, but never once did I hear that long-drawn call, half mocking and half plaintive, spearing through the stillness across the lake.

I did not know what had happened to the birds. Perhaps they had gone away to some far place of belonging. Perhaps they had been unable to find such a place, and had simply died out, having ceased to care any longer whether they lived or not.

I remembered how Piquette had scorned to come along, when my father and I sat there and listened to the lake birds. It seemed to me now that in some unconscious and totally unrecognised way, Piquette might have been the only one, after all, who had heard the crying of the loons.

ELEGY FOR WONG TOY

Robert Kroetsch

Charlie   you are dead now
but I dare to speak because
in China the living speak
to their kindred   dead.
And you are one of my fathers.

Your iron bachelorhood perplexed
our horny youth: we were born
to the snow of a prairie town
to the empty streets of our
longing.   You built a railway
to get there.

You were your own enduring   winter.
You were your abacus, your Chinaman's

eyes.   You were the long reach up
to the top of that bright showcase
where   for a few pennies
we bought a whole childhood.

Only a Christmas calendar
told us your name:
Wong Toy, prop., Canada Cafe:
above the thin pad of months,
under the almost naked girl
in the white leather boots
who was never allowed to undress
in the rows of God-filled houses

which you were never
invited to enter.

Charlie, I new my first touch
of Ellen Kiefer's young breasts
in the second booth from the back
                    in your cafe.
It was the night of a hockey game.
You were out in the kitchen
making sandwiches and coffee.

You were your own enduring
winter.   You were our spring
and we   like meadowlarks
hearing the sun   boom
under the flat horizon
cracked the still dawn alive
with one ferocious   song.

So Charlie   this is a thank you
poem.   You are twenty years
dead.   I hope they buried you
sitting upright in your grave
the way you sat   pot-bellied
behind your jawbreakers
and your licorice plugs,
behind your tins of Ogden's fine cut,
your treasury of cigars,

and the heart-shaped box of chocolates
that no one ever took home.

AUNT MATILDA

George Ryga

The house was silent, dark and lonely as I neared the front door. But familiar odours reached me as I came closer, and they were comforting—there was the scent of rotting wood, washed with lye and beef-fat soap. This was Aunt Matilda—she smelled that way herself. Over to one side of the yard, I picked out the outline of the water-pump over the well—which again conjured childhood visions of an old man deep in thought. And the old laundry tub still hung grey against the dark, weather-beaten siding of the house.

I tried the door and found it locked. I knocked, gently at first, but there was no reply. I knocked again, louder, until my knuckles ached.

'Aunt Matilda? Are you in? It's me, Snit. I've come home. Let me in!'

Have you ever known a sleepless night—a night so silent you could hear the footsteps of a spider through it? I strained, and heard a sound, deep and far away in the house.

Then suddenly the door creaked open, and I smelled a sour, fevered face close to me.

'Snit! What do you want with me? Why did you come back? Get out! Go away and leave a poor woman in peace. I don't want to ever see you again—nobody wants to see you! Now go!' Her voice was so fierce it sounded like a burst of compressed air.

'Aunt Matilda—it's all right! I know you're all by yourself, and I won't bother ya none. I've just come visiting. Let me in—everything will be all right again!'

But she didn't move.

'Nothing will ever be right again, Snit. Never again! I can't hold you back with my hands. You've grown some. But you're not wanted here any more by me or the folks hereabouts.' Her voice sounded tired and distant now. Then she walked back into the house, leaving the door open.

I hesitated a moment, then followed her in.

Only three years had gone by, but the face staring at me across the pine table in the light of the kerosene lamp had aged by ten times those three years. It was frightening—saddening. Her eyes were dead and tired, like those of a dog peering into a sudden bright light after coming in from the dark outdoors. Her hair, too, had turned a yellow-grey and hung over her shoulders and face in sticky strands. The brown-flecked skin of her face and neck was crinkled and dry, like a piece of ancient chamois cloth which had been rolled into a ball when wet and allowed to mildew. She wore a dark, nondescript outer coat, which showed signs of having been worked and slept in, and which had ragged ends on the sleeves and along the bottom. Yet she seemed in place in that kitchen, where the stove had food cooked onto it and the walls were soiled and cracked.

Aunt Matilda's hands trembled violently as she pushed a cup of tea across the table to me. They were such thin hands, with the sinews showing through the parched, fallen skin.

'Don't stare at me like that! I can still count to one hundred,' she said, and grinned.

Her teeth were long, thin and badly decayed. Then, for no reason at all, her eyes lit up quickly, and I bent my head down. I was home, and things I had forgotten and learned not to fear began flooding my memory.

'I know you can, Aunt Matilda. Is the land in crop this summer?'

She glanced at me suspiciously and her tiny, tragicomic mouth set firmly. She lifted her cup to her lips without answering. But she was splashing her tea, her hands were trembling that violently now. I watched the hot liquid trickle down her wrist and underneath the ragged sleeve of her coat.

I had been taken away from my mother and my Aunt Matilda. At the 'home' it was rumoured I had been taken because of insanity in my family. Yet when I asked Mrs McGilvray any questions about it, she just stared at me and gave no reply. So I used to lie awake at nights, thinking—thinking about my father and the frogs. It didn't make much sense. And still it did—for when I tried hard to recall my father, and my home and the hills where I had lived, I would remember the frogs as well.

My father was afraid of frogs—he was afraid of many things. There was a slough of stagnant water on the boundary line with the farm north of us. In the spring and early summer frogs croaked all night through, and Father sat up with the light on and his eyes wild with fear. He walked about the kitchen a lot of those nights, with his hands cupped over his ears and keeping us awake with his pacing and muttering. Not that it bothered me much, for I got used to this, just as I got used to going to bed on a hungry stomach.

He had been a quiet man, with a little sprig of brown moustache under his nose. Every Sunday morning, he trimmed his moustache with scissors, and if my aunt or mother saw him and laughed at his vanity, he would get so embarrassed as to leave the house and sit in the yard until they apologized and called him in.

He was so shy—so completely helpless. He always sat on the bench nearest the door in church. If he walked along the road and met a neighbour coming towards him, he would be the first to step out of the road, and with his head bent low in confusion, wait until the neighbour walked by. He always owed money to Tom Whittles at the store—everybody did. My father would not go near the store, for he felt Whittles would pick on him—which he did—and humiliate him. So my aunt did our buying, and infrequently, when she felt like going out, my mother.

There was the Hallowe'en night when all hell broke loose in the countryside. My aunt didn't allow me to go out, so I lay in bed and planned what I would do to her when I got big and strong enough. I'd starve her and beat her, that's what I would do.

Outside, the kids were setting up a lot of noise, yelling 'Monkey Mandolin! Monkey Mandolin—come out and play!'

This was me they were calling for; but inside the kitchen my father and mother were arguing. He was supposed to go to the barn to finish his chores with the cattle and horses, but he felt all the shouting was against him, and he was afraid of getting stoned or hit by a kid.

'You damned coward!' I heard my mother shout at him.

'Leave him alone, Nellie—you're as foolish as he is,' my aunt said in a quiet voice, but Mother kept right on.

'All right—I'll get the boy to protect you!

'Snit!' she called. 'Get up and take your father to the barn. He's scared of the dark!'

I got up and went into the kitchen, avoiding my aunt's eye. Then I took my father by the hand and led him outside. He was crying, or it sounded like it, for his head was down and I couldn't see his face. I walked to the barn with him, and the kids didn't do anything, for I was set to lace the dickens out of anyone who picked on my pa.

He wasn't a good farmer, but he kept us well fed and dressed as the next man. But he was wasteful in a lot of ways. He had a horse he doted on—a bay stud which he fed all year round on oat and barley chop, which was bad, for other folk only used these choice feeds when they worked their horses. In the winter, the animals had to fend for themselves by pawing away snow and eating what they could find beneath.

My father used to harness the bay to the stoneboat and go out into the field to load stones and haul them against the fence until the field was clear of rock for one season. Each year it was the same, for each summer you plowed up as many stones as you had picked off the land the year before. Sometimes I would run out to help him. If he didn't see me coming, I'd find him talking to the horse as he worked. He also talked to the horse as he dressed him down for the night in the barn. I got quite a kick out of standing outside the barn door in the moonlight, listening to him apologize to the horse for working him so hard, and promising him all sorts of pleasant things 'soon'—when times got better.

'He's just a kid—a kid who grew a moustache,' my aunt would say to my mother when they thought I wasn't listening.

'Oh, God!' my mother would sigh bitterly. 'Why don't you take him, if you feel so soft for him?'

Aunt Matilda would laugh in a high, terrible way.

'It's too late, Nellie! You shoulda thought of that fifteen years ago!'

Without any warning, the bay stud got colic and died. My father buried him on the hillside where he had led him to die. When he returned to the house, he sat down at the kitchen window and stared and stared into the yard. I remember how he held his chin in his hand, his fingers reaching up and hooked over his lower lip until his teeth became dry and dull in his face. When Aunt Matilda came into the house and saw him, she scolded him for sitting around, and asked him to go with her into the garden and help out with hoeing potatoes.

He wouldn't move, even when night came.

A couple of days of this, and we were all pretty worried about him. Mother and my aunt tried everything, but he just sat there and stared into the yard.

'Leave him alone, Matilda,' my mother said with a hard laugh. 'Just wait until he wants to eat, and we'll see if he gets anything for behaving like that—trying to scare us!'

Saying that didn't help, for Pa didn't seem to miss his meals. He wouldn't even look at the tea Aunt Matilda made and held under his nose.

Mother went to bed, where she remained, coughing and moaning all day. In the evening, she rose and approached Father.

'If only Mother was alive—she'd know how to deal with you!' she shouted, stamping her foot.

Father looked up, dropping his hand away from his chin. For the first time I could remember, his voice was strong, and he looked hard into the face of my mother.

'I been thinking, Nellie,' he said. 'We did something awful wrong. All the fires in hell won't burn it out of you or me. . . . '

I never heard him finish what he was saying. Mother closed her eyes tight and pressed her hands against the sides of her head. Then, quick as a cat, she let go and jumped at me. She grabbed me by the arm and jerked me to my feet and away from the table, which surprised me, with her being so sick and all. She steered me to the door and ordered me out.

Aunt Matilda followed and led me down the road towards the church. She put her arm over my shoulder as we walked, and in a soft voice which was as sad as it was gentle, told me not to listen to what folks said, because folks like us were given to doing peculiar things sometimes, and talking like people with the fever of drink upon them. We walked a long way that evening, and I felt very close to my aunt. I took the hand she held over my shoulder, and squeezed it with both of mine.

When we came back, Mother had gone to bed, and I was surprised to hear my pa whistling cheerfully. He was sitting in front of the kitchen stove now, oiling up the old rifle he used for scaring owls in the scrub. Then he put a shell in the gun, and holding it over his arm, walked to me and Aunt Matilda. He patted me on the head and went out.

'Where you going?' my aunt asked, almost in a whisper. But Father was gone.

Like a person in a dream, my aunt moved to the kitchen table, where she sat down. Then she stared into the lamplight, her face twitching something awful. I spoke to her, but she didn't hear me, so I went to bed.

Mother and she went to look for him in the morning. They found him with his face in the frog pond. They kept me home when they buried him, so I never did see what he looked like with the back of his head blown off...

I will never forget how it hurt to have my first tooth pulled. But the death of my father did not leave any disturbing pain with me. His life had given me no particular joy or sadness; and like the ghost he was, he neither took anything away nor left anything with me.

'I'm only glad he came to his senses long enough to end it this way. Who would have taken care of him in a few more years?' Mother said to Aunt Matilda over supper one evening. My aunt glanced at me, then opened her lips to say something. But I never heard her thoughts, for she nodded her head and remained silent.

Aunt Matilda worked the fields alone after this, for Mother was not a woman of the land. She hated the soil—the hot, dry summers, and the cold, windy winters which kept folks around the kitchen stove for warmth, months on end. The harder Aunt Matilda worked, the less she spoke. I never helped, for she didn't ask me, and I did not volunteer, choosing instead to spend my time drifting around the neighbourhood and waiting for the next day, in hopes it would bring some exciting, interesting change.

It was the summer following my father's death that Mother confined herself to bed as an invalid, and I lost interest even in her.

Some four miles distant to the east of us was a ravine which cradled a stream during the spring, when water ran off the hills from winter snow. The life of the stream was short. Two weeks after break-up the land was dry, and with no run-off to replenish it, the water in the stream-bed disappeared. Across this ravine, on a flat, windy bit of land, stood an old log schoolhouse which had been put up by some Norwegian settlers long before my time. Years ago, the stories have it, these people gave up trying to make a living off the dead soil of the hills, and emigrated back to the land of their ancestors. But the school was kept open.

I went to this school for one year—just long enough to pick up the alphabet and a raging hatred of the long-armed teacher, Miss Bowen, who always picked her ears with a hairpin while contemplating my punishment for coming late each morning. Not that it was all my fault. I had never been brought up to tell time—one day didn't crowd another, so hours were insignificant. Besides, we didn't have a clock in our house.

I dropped out of school earlier than other children of our parts. Some of them went two years.

There was an inspector of schools who lived in town. Each fall, he drove out to our community calling on each of the farms here. He argued and shouted at our folk to send the kids to school, or he'd make trouble. But our people were suspicious of him and said they wouldn't. In a very official way he would then write down the names of all who resisted learning, and then before he left he threatened he'd see what he could do about it. He always said that, and nobody paid him any mind until he came around the next year. My aunt and mother didn't argue; they just walked away from him. But others argued and told him why they wouldn't send us to learn.

'We don't raise kids for school in these parts!' folks would shout at him.

'A kid don't need to learn t'read and write for to be able to grow potatoes and oats! Give a kid a bit of school, and he stops obeying his elders and betters. Next thing, they run off—an' who's gonna take care of us when we get old?'

Maybe the school inspector was impressed by this argument, for he never did make trouble among us.

If there was such a thing as a meeting-place for our folk, then I would say it was the church. Here everybody congregated on a Sunday, and there was much singing, shouting and 'hallelujahs'—all sweaty and hot, with their hands pounding the backs of the benches in front, and the floor creaking under pounding feet. Reverend Nigel Crowe was the preacher in our church. He lived in town and came out to preach his sermon, often arriving a day earlier so he could stay over with Tom Whittles at the store. They were good friends—even resembled each other in appearance.

Reverend Crowe was as bald as a stone on top and heavy around the stomach. He had large, bushy grey brows that twitched and jumped when he got worked up during his sermon about any sort of sin.

'Why were the children of Israel punished?' he would thunder, his brows bouncing. 'They was sinnin'!' A churchful of feet would slam and hands would clap together.

'Why are we punished with the vengeance of drought?'

'We is sinnin', *sinnin'*, SINNIN'!' The voice of the congregation rose in a chant, and fifty frightened, gleaming faces leaned forward and stared at Reverend Crowe.

Quite often, the reverend got so fired up with his own preaching, he'd step down from the pulpit and walk right among his congregation, asking the same questions and getting the same answers.

'Where does the Almighty send the sinners?'

'To hell!' the congregation would shout back, a quaver of fear in their collective voice.

'And what happens in hell?'

'We burn—we burn!' A moan now, and scarey enough to give a kid the creeps.

After the sermon and the singing, Reverend Crowe would walk with Tom Whittles over to the store. Many of the folks were still excited by the church service, and would follow, hoping somehow that the minister would say more to comfort or fever them up. Tom Whittles wanted folks to follow, for it meant he'd be able to sell stuff in the store. So he'd argue mildly with Reverend Crowe as they walked. And close at his heels the country folk followed, listening hard.

Tom Whittles was a religious man. He resembled the minister in his baldness and fatness, although he lacked Reverend Crowe's shaggy brows and his voice was thinner. But he kept a Bible on his store counter at all times, right next to the weigh scales. He'd finger the Bible as he poured peanuts to sell to kids, cheating like the devil by pouring the nuts on the further end of the scale tray to make more weight. I discovered this trick long before I knew how it was accomplished. On a balanced small seesaw I placed a half-pound tin of tobacco against a half pound of peanuts I got from Aunt Matilda. The tobacco easily overbalanced the peanuts. Tom Whittles sold a lot of peanuts in his store, and I often wondered why Reverend Crowe didn't mention this sort of cheating in a sermon. Maybe he didn't know about it.

Yet, as I have said, Whittles was a religious, industrious man. Besides running his store, he knew how to build chimneys in houses. So he had more money than anybody else, and being alone without a family, he lived and dressed better than even Reverend Crowe. But he had a streak of hard meanness in him. One incident has remained fresh in my memory, because somehow what happened has a bearing, I feel, on all the events which followed.

Shortly after Stanley Muller died, Aunt Matilda had a way of suddenly getting mad at everyone and everything about her. She'd flare up and sound off on things which didn't concern her, and it used to upset my mother if it happened in a public place. This day was a Sunday, and I recall how Aunt Matilda fidgeted and twisted in her seat in church during the sermon, her face hot and her eyes dark and bothered. Folks sitting on the other side of her turned and stared at her, for she made small sounds under her breath while everybody was trying to hear Reverend Crowe.

After the sermon, Reverend Crowe moved down through the church to the back door, where Tom Whittles stood waiting to shake his hand. Folks rose and crowded outside. As always, Tom Whittles and the minister began walking to the store, followed by the usual crowd of people from the congregation. Before we were even out the church gate, Whittles was questioning the minister on Scripture, and Reverend Crowe was replying in a firm, strong voice.

'What's he saying?' Aunt Matilda was crowding forward to be alongside the two men.

'What's got into you, Mat?' Mother caught my aunt's arm and tried to hold her back.

'I just want to know what they're saying. I don't think either of them know what they're talking about!' my aunt said sharply. Mother looked at her hard.

'Be quiet and don't go making a fool of yourself!' she warned.

Aunt Matilda pressed on, however, and was among the first to get in when Whittles unlocked his store. By the time we came in, she was leaning on the counter, watching the storekeeper and Reverend Crowe, who were both behind the plank partition.

'I see what you mean, Reverend Nigel,' Whittles was drawling, as he opened a bag of money to put into his change drawer. 'Anyway, that was a right good sermon you gave this morning, and may the Lord hear it and take kindness upon us and you for it!'

'Thank you, brother Tom,' Reverend Crowe replied, straightening his shoulders, for even though they spoke to each other by first names, the minister showed no intense warmth to the storekeeper while the store was full of people. He was still the preacher, just stepped down from his pulpit.

'Amen,' someone in the back of the store echoed. One of the women asked about the price of lard at that moment.

Then, out of the blue, Aunt Matilda stopped all conversation.

'There is no God!' she exclaimed, her lips trembling and her eyes bright and sharp. Mother pushed in beside her and told her to mind what she was saying. Aunt Matilda pushed her away with an elbow.

Both Tom Whittles and Reverend Crowe turned pale with surprise. As for the rest of the crowd, you could hear a pin fall in that shop. The woman with the lard still held the package high over her head, and her arm froze there.

Whittles was the first to regain his senses. Looking over the heads of the folk in the store, he cleared his throat. Then he fixed a mean stare on my aunt.

'What did you say, you black-faced harlot?' he almost shouted, his voice high and thin. The preacher's brows began twitching with nervousness.

'There is no God!' Aunt Matilda spat out the blasphemy for the second time, and there were gasps of horror around us. But my aunt paid no mind. Looking straight in the eye of the storekeeper, she said in a dangerous voice, 'You call me that name again, and I'll scratch your damned eyes out, Whittles!'

She looked like she could do it, too.

Whittles got scared then, and backed nearer to the minister. But at the same time the folk around us began to chide and scold Aunt Matilda; and when the noise picked up, Mother got me and my aunt each by an arm, and steered us outside.

Mother did a powerful lot of coughing as we walked home that morning. She kept saying to Aunt Matilda that she had gone and fixed us all up proper with her big mouth and thoughtless ways. Then she said she knew what folks were thinking, and it was well enough to leave things as they stood.

At that point, Aunt Matilda stopped and turned to Mother. As she spoke, she kicked road dust to one side with her foot.

'If there is a God why don't He take pity on us and give us what the heart wants most? Why don't He give us some rain and a garden of flowers—just once? Why? Because there ain't no hell for us who live in this hell here—and as for the other place, it's all a nice story and nothing more!'

Which was talk way over my head, so I walked on by myself without listening to what Mother had to say in reply. They argued all the way home.

Next Sunday, folks avoided us at church meeting, and whispered and pointed in our direction when they thought we weren't looking. For the first time in my life, I felt hot and choked up among all these people and all the secret things they thought. When Reverend Crowe started in singing and waving his hand to get everybody in the congregation singing with him, I said to Mother I wanted a pee, and sneaked outside.

The church ground was small, and by the time I got out, there were about six other kids standing around and trying to get some action going. They were pushing against one another, and one kid was grinding on the toes of a smaller guy with his heel, trying to get the kid to fight. When they saw me, they all made a circle around me like I was something strange and new.

'Fee! Fee! Fee! Yore aunt's a bad-un, and she ain't got no right staying around here in a Chrishun community!' It was Mickey Rogers who said that. Mick was a kid who lived one farm north of us, and whom I could lick hands down any time. I started for him, and the circle broke and scattered. When they were at a safe distance, they all shouted like a bunch of magpies.

'Go home, ya little bugger, and take yer aunt with you, if ya know what's good fer her!'

'We'll get ya, Mandolin!'

Mick got out the gate and on the road, so I gave up chasing him and started walking back into the church.

'Yah! Yah!' he shouted, with his dirty hands cupped over his mouth. 'They'll take ya away to a little bastard home! Yuh'll see—They're makin' a paper on ya! Ya'll see! The Mandolins are bad-uns!'

'The Mandolins are buggers!' the other kids started to singsong, and I was glad to get back into church and over to my aunt and mother.

FROM *Hungry Hills*

THERE IS NO ONE HERE EXCEPT US COMEDIANS

Eli Mandel

1
In what we call dreams I see
a fairground of wheels inside wheels
where I am turned into nobody
nobody's son nobody's daughter

and orphanages
where children
drag toward iron gates yellow dolls
and huge rolling balls
made in the shape of towering fathers

2
I pray nightly for release
I ask of a door shaped like a bat
to fly away with me
I want to be in a wheatfield
stupid as grain yellowing in the sun
I want to be something like a bird,
part reptile, able to stare blankly
for minutes
        at jade trees
        at jewelled grass
        the crystal city

whispering blasphemy
I want to walk over the doors of the city
my bird feet tinkling at keyholes

I want you to know I am innocent
I want you to open the last door
into the field of orphan wheat
the orient grain the green golden corn

UKRAINIAN CHURCH

Miriam Waddington

Little father your
rhythmic black robe
against white snow
improvises you
a black note
on a white keyboard

let me follow
into your churchbarn
through the gate
to the onion domes
where your carrot
harvest burns
a fire of candles

let me follow
in the cool light
as you move through
God's storehouse
as you put the bins
in order as you set
each grain in place

let me follow
as your voice
moves through the
familiar liturgy
to the low caves
of Gregorian chant
and let me hear
little father

how you pray
for all your geese
for the cow fertile
at Easter, and the
foundations of new
houses to be strong
and firmly set

and let me hear
how you beseech
for all your people
a clear road, an
open gate and
a new snowfall
fresh, dazzling
white as birchbark

REQUIEM FOR BIBUL

Jack Ludwig

Once upon a time—if we counted time not by calendars but by assimilated history and scientific change I'd be tempted to say four or five thousand years ago: before total war and all-out war, before death camps, Nagasaki, before fusion and fission, jets, moon shots, aeronauts, Luniks in orbit, before antibiotics, polio vaccine, open-heart surgery, before TV, carburetors and other wonders of automation, before dead-faced hoods on motorcycles, dead-faced beatniks on maldecycles—once upon *that* kind of time lived a boy and his horse.

The year was 1939. This is no pastoral tale. The boy and the horse are both dead.

Twenty years late, counting time by the calendar, I write you of this boy Bibul and his horse Malkeh, of Bibul's ambition and his sad sad end. In time-sorrowed perspective I record for you the imprint Bibul left on my mind and feeling—his tic-like blink, his coal-black hair in bangs over his forehead, his emerycloth shaver's shadow, his ink-stained mouth, his immutable clothes that wouldn't conform to style or the seasons: always black denim Relief-style pants whitened by wear and washing, always a brown pebbled cardigan coiled at the wrists and elbows with unravelled wool, always a leather cap with bent visor, split seams, matching the colour and texture of Bibul's hair. An old ruined Malkeh, scorned before lamented, making her daily round under Bibul's urging, dragging his creak of a fruit-peddler's wagon through Winnipeg's 'island' slum north of the Canadian Pacific Railway Yards.

Bibul peddled while my time burned: in 1939 all of us high-school boys owlish with sixteen- and seventeen-year-old speculation, almost missed seeing this Bibul foxy with world-weary finagling. We were out to save the world, Bibul a buck. Hip-deep in reality, trying to beat tricky suppliers, weasely competitors, haggling customers, Bibul couldn't believe in us vaguesters. Peddling had forced him to see, hear, and judge everything. By his practical measure we were simply unreal. We'd speculate: Bibul would respond with *yeh-yeh*—the Yiddish double affirmative that makes a negative. He didn't have to say a word, or raise sceptical eyebrow, or even frown with that tic. His smell alone argued a reality out of reach of our politely neutral Lux, Lifebuoy, Vitalis middle-class sweetness: 'effluvium Bibul' we called that mixture of squashed berries, bad turnips, dank pineapple crates, straw, chickens, sad old horsey Malkeh. Bibul had a grand gesture to sweep away our irrelevance, a sudden movement of the hand like a farmwife's throwing feed to chickens, his nose sniffing disgust, his sour mouth giving out a squelching sound, 'aaaa.' Sometimes he sounded like a goat, other times a baby lamb—just 'aaaa,' but enough to murder our pushy pretentions.

We were a roomful of competitive sharks—math sharks, physics sharks, English, Latin, history sharks, secretly, often openly, sure we surpassed our teachers in brain and knowhow. Joyfully arrogant we shook off the restricting label high-school student, considering ourselves pros—mathematicians, scientists, writers, artists. In our own minds we had already graduated from the University, had passed through Toronto or Oxford, were entangled in public controversies with great names in our respective fields, ending right but humble, modestly triumphant. But where was Bibul in this league? As loud as we pros hollered Bibul heard nothing. He only yawned, slouched, even snoozed, gave out with that killing *yeh-yeh*, poked his greyish nose into his peddler's notebook red with reality's ooze of tomato.

'Bibul,' we'd say in the break between classes, 'do semantics mean nothing to your knucklehead? An intellectual revolution's coming. You've got to stand up and be counted. What'll it be? Are you *for* Count Korzybski or against him?'

'Aaaa,' aaed Bibul, and his chicken-feeding motion sent us back to ivory towers.

'You' nuddin' bud gids,' he'd say haughtily whenever we disturbed his audit of fruit-and-vegetable reality, 'a 'ell of a lod you guys know aboud live.'

Though we jeered and mocked, treated him like a clown, he was one of us, so how could we disown him? Kings of St John's High, lording it from our third-floor eminence over the giants and dwarfs living the underground life in the school's basement ascreech with whirling lathes and milling machines, or those second-floor, salt-of-the-earth commercial students dedicated to bookkeeping, typing, the sensible life, we of course wanted to pass our nobility on to Bibul. We ran the yearbook and could have established him there—but on the 'island' English ran a poor second to Ukrainian, Polish, German, or in his case, Hebrew. We could have made him captain of the debating team, but peddling wrecked that: wrought up he stammered, angry he slobbered, no way to win arguments. Being a businessman, like his breed he had no time for politics; being tone-deaf he was a flop at glee-club try-outs. At sports he was dreadful. He couldn't swim a stroke, or skate, was flubbyknuckled at baseball, slashing pigeon-toed at soccer, truly kamikaze going over a hurdle. And women? He had no time for them in his practical life: his old mare Malkeh and the ladies who haggled with him were the only females Bibul knew.

In recognition of his memo-book involvement we made Bibul our room treasurer.

After classes we theoreticians sprawled on the school green and took pleasure from long-limbed, heavy-thighed, large-breasted girls thwarting an educator's pious wish that the serge tunic neutralize the female form. Bibul was never with us. At the closing bell he'd run off to his horse and wagon, set to run the gauntlet of his customers (*shnorrers*, pigs he called them); and early on a morning, when we theoreticians-turned-lover, weary after a long night of girl-gaming, sat in Street Railways waiting houses knocking ourselves out over noisy reading of Panurge's adventure with the Lady of Paris, Bibul, up and dressed since 4:00 a.m., struggled at the Fruit Row for bruised fruit and battered vegetables in competition with wizened peddlers and their muscular sons. At nine, bleary-eyed all, theoretician and practical man rose to greet the morn with a mournful *O Canada*.

Lost in abstraction, and me, I thought little of Bibul in those days. He was a clown. A mark. A butt. The peddling was part of the sad desperate struggle for money every family in the depression knew. Bibul was the eldest of four children, his widowed ma supporting them on what she could make out of a tiny grocery store, doing the best she could, the dear lady, known throughout the 'island' as 'The Golden Thumb' and the 'Adder,' the latter reference ambiguous, meaning either snakes or computation, Bibul's ma being famous for a mathematical theorem that said 5 + 6 = 12 or 13, whichever was higher.

Not till the year of our graduation did I discover why Bibul peddled with such dedication, why he rode out like a teen-age Don Quixote to do battle with those abusive, haggling, thieving *shnorrers*.

And what a riding-out that was! His paintless wagon listed like a sinking ship, sounded like resinless fiddles in the hands of apes, each wheel a circle successfully squared. Bibul sat on a tatter of leatherette bulging at the ends like a horsehair creampuff; over his wilted greens and culled fruit Bibul's faultless-in-his-favour scales made judgement, this battered tin scoop more dented than a tin B-B target. And what was more fitting than a nag like Malkeh to drag that crumbling wagon on its progress?

As grim as Don Quixote's Rosinante would look next to elegant Pegasus, that's how Malkeh would have looked next to Rosinante: she was U-shaped in side view, as if permanently crippled by the world's fattest knight lugging the world's heaviest armour. She sagged like a collapsed sofa with stuffing hanging low. She was bare as buffed mohair, her shoulders tanned from the rub of reins, her colour an unbelievable combination of rust, maroon, purple, bronze, found elsewhere only in ancient sun-drenched velvets. Her tail was a Gibson Girl's worn discarded feather boa, its fly-discouraging movements ritualistic, perfunctory, more to let flies know that Malkeh wasn't dead than that she was alive. Her legs, like a badly carpentered table, were of assorted lengths, which made Malkeh move by shuffling off like a pair of aged soft-shoe dancers in final farewell. Her hooves were fringed with fuzzy hairs like a frayed fiddle-bow abandoned to rain and sun, her horseshoes dime-thin, rusty as the metal hinges on her wagon's tail-gate. To encourage Malkeh to see Bibul covered her almost-blind eyes with a pair of snappy black racing-horse blinkers trimmed with shiny silver rivets, a touch to her décor like a monocle in the eye of a Bowery bum.

Out of compassion, out of loyalty to this wreck of a horse, Bibul let his wagon go to ruin: wood could be camouflaged with paint or varnish but where was covering to hide or revive said old mortal Malkeh?

One day I came to school early, and saw her.

She was the horse version of 'The Dying Gaul.' On Bibul's 'island' Malkeh suffered no invidious comparisons, but on a main thoroughfare like St John's High's Salter Street Malkeh was exposed to the cruelty of horse hierarchy, and her submarginal subproletariat hide was bared. High-stepping, glossy-flanked, curried and combed T. Eaton Company horses, middle-class cousins of aristocratic thoroughbreds seen only on race tracks, veered their rumps sharply as they passed, hooves steelringing, traces white as snow. Their tails were prinked out with red ribbon, their wagons chariots sparkling in red, white, gold against blue-blackness that could mean only good taste. These bourgeois horses had the true bourgeois comforts—warm blankets, stables with hay wall-to-wall, feedbags that offered privacy and nourishment. Their drivers looked like seacaptains, neat contrast to a slop like Bibul. And their commercial feed was gastronomical compared with the bad lettuce, wilted carrot tops, shrivelled beets Bibul shoved at Malkeh in a ripped old postman's pouch.

Malkeh took their snubs without flinching. It was part of the class struggle. What hurt was the heavy powerful working-class Percherons and their stinking garbage scows, when *they* avoided kinship with Malkeh, acting like a guest at a high-toned party ignoring a waiter who's a close relative.

Pity old Malkeh's vengeful heart: the only pleasure she got from her enforced station on Salter Street came from knowing flies used her as an aerodrome from which to launch vicious attacks on the elegant department-store horses passing.

I saw her. The Principal too saw her, slouched with resignation, a 'Don't' in an SPCA exhibit, her right foreleg flatteringly fettered by a cracked curling stone to give Malkeh the impression she had the vim and youth to turn runaway horse. Malkeh died a long time ago, but years before she did the Principal had her one visit gnomically memorialized and graven in metal: early next morning, where Malkeh had stood, this marker went up: 'No Parking At Any Time.'

Bibul never again brought her to school.

Which is not to say that life on the 'island' was without its grim side: what accounted for an almost-blind horse wearing blinkers? *Shnorrers!* Those women with bare feet stuck hurriedly into their husbands' outsize felt slippers, their hair uncombed, faces unmade, women in nightgowns at four on a sunshiny afternoon, hands clenching pennies and silver Bibul had to charm away from them with hard-sell and soft-soap. Singly they waited, in concert plotted, en masse moved in on him. Their purpose was simple—*get much, pay little.* To the victor went Bibul's spoiled spoils.

'Giddy ahb, Malgeh,' Bibul would holler from his high seat on the wagon, and his cry sounded to a *schnorrer*'s ears like a warring clarion.

Into the lists Malkeh dragged the keening wagon, onto the 'island' in ruins like a mediaeval town (Canadian history is short but our buildings add spice by getting older faster). Foundationless hovels kids might have built out of assorted-sized decks of cards sagged, leaned at crazy-house angles to astound Pisa. Gates tipsy as Malkeh's wagon swung on one hinge from a last lost post; dry, cracking wood fences leaned in surrender towards the ground, begging like old men in sight of a grave to be allowed to fall the rest of the way; windows were tarpaper-patched, like pirates' eyes, ominous as the blackness left in the streets by uninsured fires.

Behind every window or screen opaque with dust, behind every door splintered from kids' kicking waited the *shnorrers,* trying to make Bibul anxious, make him sweat a little, a cinch for persistent hagglers.

'Ebbles, ebbles, den boundz f'a quadder,' Bibul shouted.

Crafty with stealth the *shnorrers* didn't bite.

Unflustered, unfooled, Bibul took advantage of the phony war, biting off the only three unspotted cherries in his entire stock while Malkeh dragged the exposed tin rims of the wagonwheels into the frost heaves and back-lane crevices. That cramped stinking back lane was mutually agreeable as a Compleat Battlefield—for Bibul because the solid pall of chicken droppings and horse dung was fine camouflage for the imperfections Time and Decay wrought his produce, for the *shnorrers* because the narrow quarters made tampering with the scale easier, detection harder, filching a hot possibility.

'Whoa beg, whoa der Malgeh,' Bibul ordered, oblivious of the spying women.

There, among rusted bedsprings hung up like huge harps, torn mattresses resembling giant wads of steel wool, in a boneyard of Model T's, Malkeh and the wagon rested. Dogs scooted in darts of nervous yapping, cats hissed down from rust-streaked corrugated rooftops, pigeons wheeled high above Bibul's untroubled head, returning to perch on overhanging eaves like fans anxious to get close to a scene of scuffle.

The *shnorrers* tried to read Bibul's face: the text was that Sphinx-like tic of a blink. Stalling he mad entries into that memo-book, peeled an orange, scratched himself with casual but maddening thoroughness.

The *shnorrers'* united front crumbled. A foot slipped out from behind a door. Then a head.

'Wha' you gonna cheat me on t'day, Bibul?' rasped out of an impatient throat.

The war was on! Horseflies, the depression having made pickings so sparse they dropped their high standards and declared Malkeh a host, left the depressing fare of uncovered garbage cans (each lid long ago commandeered to be target in the minor-league jousts of the *shnorrers'* unknightly kids), and, hiding behind the *shnorrers* sneaking up to do Bibul battle, launched assault on old Malkeh's flat weak flanks.

The siege began, swiftly, deftly: a red-haired old woman flipped two-cent oranges into the one-cent bins, her other hand pointed up at the sky to make Bibul raise his eyes and predict weather.

Her accomplice brought Bibul back to reality, picking the bargains up before they'd even stopped rolling.

'Boyaboy Bibul, you god good tings in y' usually stinkin' stock, look here, Mrs Gilfix, at such oranges.'

Bibul's tic-like blink snapped like a camera shutter on their mischief.

'Give over here dem oniges,' he reproved them, '*yoisher*, show a liddle resdraind,' and the sad old innocents watched the two-cent numbers fall back into the two-cent bins.

On the other side of the wagon a pair of raspberry hands crushed away at lettuce greens.

'How much off f'damaged goods?' the criminal hollered, wiping lettuce juice off on her gaping nightgown.

But the red-haired old woman hadn't given up on oranges.

'Black head means black heart, robber,' she cried out, 'Perls d'fruit man who has a white head and eight kids and supports two unmarried sisters in Russia, from *him* I get fresher cheaper by two coppers—ha come, ha? Ha come?'

'My oniges are Sundgizd, Blue Gooze,' Bibul, a sucker for brand names, came back huffily, 'Berls' oniges grow on ebble drees.'

One man's quarrel is another woman's smoke screen. The *shnorrers* moved in, squeezing the fruit, poking, tapping, complaining with shrieks and curses that sent the pigeon-hearted pigeons high off their perches. Like a bucket brigade the ladies passed fruit up and down the length of the wagon, each nose an inspector, those with teeth taking their duties more seriously, tasters whose opinions Bibul could live without.

'*Schnorrers* dad youz are,' he hollered, holding up a nipped apple, a chewed-up orange, 'you god no gare vor my brovids?'

'Look how he's independent,' mocked the red-haired one, lunging fruitless after a fistful of cherries, 'look how he holds hisself big! His fadder's a doctor, maybe? Or the mayor?'

Bibul was a lone guard defending his fortress from desperate pillagers; ubiquitous as Churchill, many-handed as Shiva, he had to be compassionate as Schweitzer. Though *I* didn't know what Bibul's dedication to peddling was all about, the *schnorrers* did: Bibul was saving up to become a Rabbi. Bibul immersed himself in the practical, pedestrian, material life because of a Great Cause—the Yeshiva in New York, eventual immersion in a spiritual life dedicated to comfort suffering mankind.

How the *shnorrers* used that Great Cause in their war with Bibul! It was all double: in sincerity they poured out their hearts to him—an educated boy, soon to be a Rabbi, maybe he'd understand *their* side—the husband who had taken off and never come back, the bad-hearted rich relatives, the ungrateful kids, the treacherous friends, root, trunk, branch of a Jewish Seven Deadly Sins. They dizzied him with complicated stories, unsettled his strong stomach with demonstrations of human frailty—missing teeth, crossed eyes, wens, tumours, needed operations.

As a bonus to sincerity they hoped the tales would divert Bibul long enough for their aprons to fill with filched fruit.

Crying real tears Bibul would free an apricot from a fist already stained with cherry.

'A religious you call yourself?' the caught thief howled. 'God should strike me dead if I stole ever in my life one thing!'

Glancing up at the sky she moved closer to the other ladies: who knew what kind of pull with God a boy-studying-to-be-a-Rabbi had?

'Bibul, sveethard,' cooed one Mrs Itzcher, blemished but bleached, 'give off ten cents a dozen by oranges and Tillie'll show plenty appreciation.'

Bibul used his chickenfeed gesture to ward off temptation.

The *shnorrers* prayed God to give Bibul good enough ears to hear their laments but to compensate with a little dimming of the eyes so he wouldn't catch them stealing. When they lost they cursed in tones loud enough to be heard above the world's fishwifery in action.

No wonder Bibul considered us sharks irrelevant. After those *shnorrers* poured it on what was left to be said?

'My brudder's second wibe's kid wid da hump in back, Rabbi Bibul, has already her third miscarriage.'

In the midst of haggle they rained down proofs of suffering and absurdity—banged heads, cut knees, singed eyelashes, hands caught in wringers, slippery floors, broken steps, toppling ladders. The compensation they asked was meagre. Pity, a buy on a busted watermelon.

When we sharks, hot for culture, cool for Schoenberg, long on judgements, short on facts, turned our abstract expressions Bibul's way how else could he respond but with that 'aaaa'? What did our books and ideas have to compete with a *schnorrer*'s lament? Now when I think of that 'aaaa' I translate it 'When I was a child I spake as a child . . .' (may Bibul forgive me for quoting Saint Paul); 'aaaa' said 'vanity of vanities; all is vanity'; in explanation of the term for Mammon so that the rest would be with Abraham, Isaac, and Jacob; 'aaaa' said 'To everything there is a season, and a time to every purpose under the heaven.'

On St John's High School's Graduation Day Bibul was already at least half a Rabbi. The cardigan was gone, so too the denims and the black leather cap. He wore a fancy blue serge suit so new it still smelled of smoke. His sideburns were growing religiously into side curls, his emery-cloth shadow was now a beardlike reality. But it was Bibul's eyes I remember, excited, gay, snapping under that tic. He looked incredibly happy.

'Bibul,' I said seriously, 'you look beautiful in that suit!'

'Damorra, Joe,' he said low and secretive, 'damorra I go d'Noo Yorick an' d'Yeshiva.'

I talked to him without clowning. He told me what he wanted, explained the peddling.

'Bibul,' I said as we were walking out to our waiting parents, 'doesn't the idea of a city the size of New York scare you? You'll be strange. Winnipeg's a village—'

'Wadz t'be asgared?' Bibul said with that wave of his hand. 'Beoble iz beoble. I zeen all ginds aready.'

He told me he'd sold Malkeh to Perls the peddler. His mother walked proudly towards Bibul as we reached the street.

'Bibul,' I shouted as parents came between us, 'you'll be a terrific Rabbi! Good luck!'

He gave that chickenfeed flourish, but with new style, and with modesty.

'Aaaa,' I heard above the shouting congratulations of parents, the last time I heard or saw Bibul.

That fall we sharks entered the University, and Canada the war. Winnipeg was transformed, full of aircrew trainees from places I knew about before only through postage stamps, men with yellow skins, red, brown, black, Maori tribesmen from New Zealand, bushmen from Australia, strange-sounding South Africans, carved-faced Indians thronging the streets and beer parlours. But far off in New York, Bibul, who had known war with the *shnorrers*, paid little attention to this latest struggle. He studied Torah and Talmud. He made his spending money selling fruit to Lower East Side *shnorrers* at the Essex Street Market.

Bibul's old Winnipeg customers haggled half-heartedly with old man Perls and old horse Malkeh, the one mercifully deaf, the other nearly blind. The depression seemed over: money came easier.

Once in a long while I checked in at Bibul's mother's store and, gleaning news of Bibul, let her weigh me up a light pound of corned beef. She wore her hair Buster Brown, carried a huge buxom body on little feet in grey-white tennis shoes.

She shoved a letter at me.

'Look how a educated boy writes?' she said, pugnaciously proud. 'Who but a Rabbi could understand such words?'

She pulled it back before I could answer.

'See him only, just look,' she pushed a picture at my eyes.

Bibul huddled against a bare Williamsburg wall grinning the same grin as the three other Bibuls in the picture, all of them bearded and wild as Russians, in black beaver hats bought with money they had earned tutoring the Americanized grandchildren of rich Chassidim.

'Some boy, my Bibul,' his mother called to me as I was leaving.

Winter passed and the war grew grimmer. Spring was beautiful, the war more dreadful. Summer was hot, particularly in New York where Bibul divided his time between the Yeshiva and Essex Street's *shnorrers*. For days the temperature was in the high nineties. Bibul had never known such heat. He couldn't study, sleep, sell. In desperation he took himself one evening to the 'Y,' forgetting in the heat that he'd never learned to swim.

An attendant, going off duty, warned Bibul away, told him not to enter the pool. Who can be blind to Bibul's response?

'Aaaa,' and that gesture.

He drowned.

His *shnorrers* on the 'island,' being told, wept and lamented. We sharks, even in the midst of war's casualties, were moved and stricken. Bibul was the first of us to die.

I cannot find Bibul's like in Winnipeg today.

Somebody waved a T-square wand over the old 'island,' bringing it the ninety-degree angle unknown in Bibul's far-off day. Progress pretends Bibul's 'island' never really existed: the lanes are paved, the rot-wood of wall and fence has been sloshed over with paint. A few sneaky signs of the old world are around: a clothesline pole, exhausted from long years of soggy fleece-lined underwear to support, seems ready to give up the ghost; an outside staircase, impermanent as a hangman's scaffold, mocks the fire commission that asked for greater safety and got greater danger.

Malkeh is dead. The wagon is all bits and crumble.

Motorized peddlers in trucks like Brink's Cars zoom through the reformed 'island' late at night with the remnants of produce picked over by ringed and braceleted hands on the day route—River Heights, Silver Heights, Garden City, places of Togetherness, Betterness, Spotlessness, the polite answers Comfort has given to the sad old questions of Civilization.

'Apples, apples, two pounds for a quarter,' the peddlers call, but not too loudly, and the women once poor enough to be *shnorrers* (few are still alive), the women who have replaced the departed *shnorrers* in remodelled rebuilt houses, look over the fruit and vegetables (ironically like Bibul's old rejects and reduced-to-clears because of prior though elegant pawing), buy a little, haggle not at all, or withdraw with a snub at peddling, a bow in favour of the superior refrigeration of supermarkets.

Through the streets old Malkeh drew that creaking wagon urged on by leather-capped Bibul, chrome-trimmed cars speed in unending gaggle, their sport-capped, stylishly-hatted drivers in control of power the equivalent of four hundred un-Malkeh horses. The Mayor tells Winnipeggers to 'Think Big,' bid for the Pan-American Games, hang out more flags and buntings. Slums like Bibul's 'island' and the City Hall are fortunately doomed: Winnipeg is obviously a better place to live in.

Who doesn't welcome prosperity?

But the fact remains: I cannot find Bibul's like in Winnipeg today.

And that is why here and now, in this, his and my city, I write you this requiem for Bibul, for his face, for his Great Cause, his tic, his wave, his 'aaaa.' In love and the joy of remembering I sing you this Bibul and all that's past and passing but not to come.

When the City Hall is torn down they will build Winnipeg a new one; but where, O where shall we find more Bibuls?

FATHER

Dale Zieroth

Twice he took me in his hands and shook
me like a sheaf of wheat, the way a dog shakes
a snake, as if he meant to knock out my tongue
and grind it under his heel right there
on the kitchen floor. I never remembered
what he said or the warnings he gave; she
always told me afterwards, when he
had left and I had stopped my crying. I
was eleven that year and for seven more years
I watched his friends laughing and him
with his great hands rising and falling
with every laugh, smashing down on his knees
and making the noise of a tree when it cracks
in winter. Together they drank chokecherry
wine and talked of the dead friends and the
old times when they were young, and because
I never thought of getting old, their
youth was the first I knew of dying.

Sunday before church he would trim
his fingernails with the hunting knife
his East German cousins had sent, the same
knife he used for castrating pigs and
skinning deer: things that had nothing
to do with Sunday. Communion once
a month, a shave every third day, a
good chew of snuff, these were things
that helped a man to stand in the sun for
eight hours a day, to sweat through each
cold hail storm without a word, to freeze
fingers and feet to cut wood in winter, to do

the work that bent his back a little more
each day down toward the ground.

Last Christmas, for the first time, he
gave presents, unwrapped and bought
with pension money. He drinks mostly coffee
now, sleeping late and shaving every day.
Even the hands have changed: white, soft,
unused hands. Still he seems content
to be this old, to be sleeping in the middle
of the afternoon with his mouth open as if there
is no further need for secrets, as if he is
no longer afraid to call his children fools
for finding different answers, different lives.

HUNTING

W. D. Valgardson

In his prime, Sonny Brum had been 280 pounds of muscle that angled sharply from broad, straight shoulders to a narrow waist, but years of sitting around a display room drinking coffee and eating jelly busters as he waited for customers had thickened him. The muscle had diminished but his appetite had not and a heavy roll of flesh sagged over his belt. His head was square, his skin swarthy and his nose, which was large and hooked, had been broken so many times that it was permanently bent to the left. A white scar curved like a third eyebrow in the middle of his forehead. When he walked, he did so with a hesitating limp.

If he had been older, he could have been a casualty of some foreign war, one of those who put on blue blazers and lay wreaths once a year, but he was not. His facial scars had been gathered in the vicious struggles of semi-pro football and his knee-cap had been smashed during the first game he played for the Winnipeg Blue Bombers. Although his first game as a pro had been his last, he had, on the wall of his office, a 24-by-18-inch photograph of himself in uniform with the rest of the team and he always carried a wallet-size duplicate along with his birth certificate and his driver's licence.

Although it was only seven o'clock, he had been awake since five. First, he lay in bed and worried. Then, when he couldn't stand to be inactive any longer, he dressed and paced through the cold rooms of the house. Because it was Sunday and there was no hunting, he was afraid that Buzz Anderson and Roger Charleston, having nothing to keep them entertained, would want to return home. Not having got their deer right away had made them discontented. Even though they hadn't complained, he could tell that it wouldn't take much for them to decide to leave. Since he was unable to think of anything else to keep them happy, he had decided to take them to the bootlegger's.

They had meant to use the entire house but they couldn't get the furnace to work so they had moved three cots into the kitchen and were heating the room with a catalytic heater.

Sonny swung open the kitchen door and let it bang closed behind him. Roger sat up and dug the knuckles of his index fingers into his eyes. He kicked himself free of his blankets and swung his feet over the edge of the cot. His legs, like the rest of him, were pale and flat looking. All he had on were jockey shorts as he sauntered over to the counter and bent down to peer outside.

'We're going to get some snow,' he said.

The sky was dull grey and the distant sun was small and pale. On the horizon there was a ridge of pewter cloud.

'Good,' Sonny replied. 'That'll make tracking easier. You wound a deer and he'll leave a trail nobody can miss. Blood on the snow's the best thing you can have.'

Roger stood on one leg, then the other, to pull on his pants. 'We've got to see them before we shoot them.' His voice carried a hint of irritation. He tucked in his shirt, then went back to standing on one leg to pull on his white coveralls.

'Hey, Buzz, what do you want for breakfast?' Sonny lit the Coleman stove and put on the coffee-pot.

Buzz groaned and sat up. He had on an orange toque and a matching scarf. He was constantly afraid of catching a cold or getting laryngitis and not being able to host his morning radio show for housewives. 'Bacon, eggs, coffee, whisky,' he said. 'In that order.' With a sigh, he dropped back onto the bed.

The kitchen smelled stale. The house was solid and large, with five bedrooms upstairs, four rooms downstairs and a full basement, but it had been empty for so long that the front yard was overgrown with young poplars.

After breakfast, when Sonny led the way outside, the air was sharp. The Russian thistle, touched by frost, drooped blackly. In the muted light the branches of the trees were stark and brittle looking. Huddled together on the porch, the three of them studied the dark edge of the forest that gaped toward them, then turned to study the yellows and browns of the fields that staggered toward the horizon.

'See there!' Sonny called out, punching his large red fist in the air. His two companions squinted and strained to see what had excited him, but there was nothing except the trees and weeds.

Keeping his left leg stiff, he awkwardly descended the stairs and with his massive arms moving before him in a breast stroke, swept the saplings out of his way. The other two followed him uncertainly. He snapped off the stem of a poplar and held it out for their inspection. The top had been bitten off and the tender outer bark nibbled away.

'Look at that,' he said. 'There were deer in here last night. Tomorrow morning we can get up early and shoot one or two from the doorway.'

Buzz and Roger's interest had risen sharply and, for the moment, Sonny's worry eased. Their goodwill was crucial to him. After recuperating from a series of operations on his knee, he had become a salesman with a Ford dealership next to the stadium. He hated every minute of his fifteen years of working for someone else but by saving every cent possible, and buying and selling used cars out of his backyard, he finally managed to gather enough for a down payment on a dealership. At the same time, he moved his wife and daughter into a new house in a good neighbourhood. Then, a series of small reverses combined with too little capital squeezed him into a position where he had to have more money or lose his business.

During his two years in his new neighbourhood, he had assiduously cultivated his neighbours in the hope of turning them into customers. Now, pressed for cash, and unable to obtain further credit, he had invited Roger and Buzz on a hunting trip.

Neither of them had been deer hunting before but both had said they would like to go hunting. That, and the fact that they both had steered customers his way in return for a bottle of whisky or a pair of football tickets, made him choose them. As well, he knew from a credit check he had had run on them, that they had a fair amount of money salted away. What he intended to do was wait until they both had a deer and a few drinks and then offer to make them silent partners. He already had the papers made up.

Buzz quit studying the chewed stems and started for the car. His low, gentle voice drew women to his program in large numbers but he never allowed himself to be photographed if he could help it. He was barely five feet tall and his face—round and smooth, with slightly bulging eyes, a small, nearly bridgeless nose, red hair and freckles—made him look like a mildly retarded child.

They set off in Buzz's car, a maroon Cadillac he had bought for $200. It wasn't much to look at. The left rear door was caved in, its window held together with a black spider-web of electrician's tape. The fenders were so rusted that their edges resembled brown lace, but the motor ran well and the tires still had half a penny's width of rubber. Its major fault was that the steering was so loose that Buzz had a hard time keeping it under control.

The area they were driving through had, at one time, been the bottom of a lake. Now, a series of gravel ridges marked the successive shorelines. In the hollows, swamp grass that was the same pale brown as a red squirrel's ruff rose as high as the car windows and willow clustered in dark, impenetrable thickets. The crests were crowded with scrub oak, hazel and black poplar.

It was on the crest of a ridge that they saw a buck standing in a hazel thicket.

'Lookit that!' Roger hollered, startling Buzz so badly that he jammed on the brakes. Sonny was sitting in the back. The sudden stop nearly pitched him into the front seat.

'Look at that rack,' Buzz sighed, thinking of the family room in his basement. 'He's got seven points.'

'I told you,' Sonny said jubilantly. 'I told you the way it was.'

'We don't have our rifles,' Roger reminded them. He had a long tubular face and the minute he was unhappy he looked like an undertaker. He pressed as close as possible to the windshield.

'I put my .22 into the trunk, remember,' Sonny answered. 'Give me the keys.'

Buzz handed him the keys and Sonny slipped outside. Without taking his eyes off the buck, he crept to the rear of the car. Easing the trunk up slowly, he reached past the spare wheel and lifted out a rifle wound in burlap. He unwrapped it, raised it to his shoulder and squeezed the trigger. There was a sharp click.

Cursing under his breath, he tip-toed along the driver's side of the car. 'Bullets,' he whispered urgently. 'I left them in the glove compartment.'

The buck was so close that Sonny could have hit it with a rock. It stood at an angle to them, shoulder-deep in brush, its head turned sideways. The curving antlers looked polished.

'Here,' Buzz said, shoving the box out of the window upside down. As Sonny snatched the box, the lid popped open and the cartridges cascaded to the ground. Sonny stood stupefied, then flung the empty box aside and scooped up a handful of cartridges and gravel. Before he could get a bullet into the chamber, the buck trotted across the road and disappeared with a bound.

Sonny fumbled a moment longer, then bitterly snapped, 'Son-of-a-bitch!' He restrained an impulse to smash the car window.

As Roger and Buzz joined him, Sonny handed Roger the rifle. Then he and Buzz picked up the spilled cartridges.

'I couldn't get a bullet into the gun,' Sonny explained defensively. The incident had shaken him. The buck seemed symbolic. Everything, his house, his business, his independence, seemed ready to slip away while he stood and watched helplessly.

'It was Sunday anyway,' Buzz replied.

'Mounties,' Roger warned. A black car had topped the adjacent ridge and was racing toward them. As Buzz and Sonny ran to the side of the road, Roger stood stupefied, then, as his long legs scissored beneath him, carrying him to safety, he flung the rifle into the bush.

Seconds later, a black Ford rocketed past, spraying them with gravel. The driver was an old woman with a green, wide-brimmed hat jammed over her ears.

With a sigh of relief, Buzz sat on a tree stump. Dramatically, he felt his heart. 'You shouldn't do that, Roger. If my sponsors ever found out that I had been arrested for hunting illegally. . . .' He left the rest unsaid.

'Where's my rifle?' Sonny asked.

Wordlessly, Roger scurried into the bush and began flailing about like a wounded duck. When he found the rifle, he waved it over his head.

To be certain the rifle was not damaged, Sonny loaded it, then fired three times. A hundred feet away, on the edge of the road, gravel flew into the air and a tin can jumped and spun on its rim before falling back. With a grunt of satisfaction, he rewrapped the rifle and stuffed it under the front seat.

Buzz brought back the can. It was pitted with rust but the edges of the bullet holes were bright and shiny. Where a hollow-nosed slug had entered, the hole was smaller than the end of a little finger. Where it exited, the hole was larger than a nickel and the edges were bent back like the sepals of a rose after the petals have fallen.

As they drove, they passed some farmhouses that, except for the television aerials on the roofs, looked abandoned. Frequently, they saw people working among the roadside bushes. Buzz slowed down.

'What are they doing?' he asked.

'Collecting hazelnuts,' Sonny answered. 'They husk them and sell them to the wholesale in Winnipeg.'

A man and woman were working close to the road. Each held a gunny sack. The man wore rubber boots, overalls, a brown jacket and cap. The woman wore a red *babushka*, a brown jacket and a faded dress with men's pants underneath. Two boys, dressed exactly like their father, emerged to stare at the car. Like their parents, they might have been part of the weathered landscape. From a short distance, they were nearly indistinguishable from the trees.

Buzz pulled away. 'They can't get much for their work.'

'They don't.' Sonny was glad they were moving again. The sight of the children had been like a thrust of pain. He had been like that once. Suddenly, he could feel the weight of the scoop shovel. The stink of manure clogged his nostrils and the car seemed filled with the restless shifting of cattle.

Every morning from the time he was eight he had shovelled out the barn. In the evenings and on weekends, he hauled or pitched hay or cut wood or staggered behind the stone boat, drunk with tiredness, as he attempted the hopeless task of trying to clear the fields of their yearly crop of stone.

'What keeps people here?' Roger asked.

'Stupidity. They don't know nothing and they don't want to know nothing.'

On either side, the ditches were clogged with bulrushes. Behind the ditches were hay fields, then thin lines of trees marking the edges of the fields and more trees.

'Slow down,' Sonny said. 'It should be along here.' He was puzzled, apologetic. He had Buzz turn at the next crossroads but, after 200 yards, the road trailed away to a grassy path.

A farmhouse with the wreckage of three cars littering its front yard appeared on their right. Someone had tarpapered the outside walls and tacked on laths and chicken wire but had never put on stucco. Tattered plastic from the previous winter clung to the window-frames. The yard was adrift with chickens.

Sonny could hear the steady one-stroke beat of a small engine as he braved a black mongrel that rushed up to bare his teeth and glare malevolently from pus-stained eyes.

Behind the house, a rawboned woman in a grey shapeless dress that came to her ankles was washing clothes in a gasoline washing machine. She looked no friendlier than her dog but, when Sonny motioned to her, she moved close enough to hear what he had to say. Her face was haggard, her eyes sunken and suspicious and her hair was pinned in an untidy bun at the back of her neck. Sonny forced a smile while he tried to keep an eye on the dog, which constantly twisted out of sight.

'We've got lost. We're looking for Joe Luprypa's place,' he explained.

'Down the road one mile, then turn west.' Her teeth were rotted to brown stumps.

He hadn't recognized her face but he remembered her voice. He looked at her more carefully. In the lined, coarse skin there was nothing to guide him but then she said, thinking he hadn't understood. 'It's that way. See. Go down to the mile road.'

Annie, sprang into his mind.

He nodded and said, 'Thank you. Thank you,' as he backed away. Except for the voice, he was unable to see any resemblance between the girl who sat in front of him at school and the woman with the ravaged face and raw, rough hands folded across drooping breasts.

As Sonny opened the car door, the dog lunged for his ankle but he was ready and caught it in the ribs with his foot. Joe Luprypa's driveway was deeply rutted and only wide enough for one car. It twisted down a gentle slope through a meadow of uncut hay and disappeared into a dense grove of poplars. The trees stopped at the beginning of a marsh. The car, caught by the twin ruts, was locked as securely to its path as any train. As a joke, Buzz took both hands from the wheel and clasped them behind his head. As the car bumped and rocked along the grooves in the dark earth, the wheel seemed to take on a life of its own.

In the centre of the grove there was a large patch of rutted dirt. They bounced toward a small house covered in plastic panelling that was supposed to look like natural stone. At the back of the house there was a summer kitchen painted bright purple. Permanently marching across the brown grass of the side yard to their diamond mine were plywood cutouts of the seven dwarves. An elderly blue pickup was parked to one side.

'No-one's home,' Buzz said. He sounded relieved. He could listen for hours to someone else's escapades, but when he became involved in one his enthusiasm quickly cooled. 'We might as well go.' He studied the house apprehensively.

Sonny shoved open his door and stepped away from the car. 'They're just waiting to see who we are.'

The back door cracked open but they couldn't see who had opened it. Then the door was flung back and a short, fat man in charcoal-grey suit pants, a white shirt and a red flowered tie, waddled over, threw his arms around Sonny and beat him on the back. 'Sonny! Long time no see. I wouldn't have recognized you except for that nose. It's still travelling in a different direction.'

'We've come for a drink.' Sonny waved his arm in a half-circle. 'I thought there'd be no place to park.'

Joe was studying Buzz and Roger closely.

'It's okay,' Sonny reassured him. 'They're next-door neighbours. Roger's in medicine and Buzz is in communications. Have you anything to drink?'

Joe nodded. Each time he ducked his head, he accumulated three more chins. 'A little.' He waved them inside. 'Go in,' he urged. 'What do you want? Government or homebrew? My Brother, Alec, made the homebrew.'

'Homebrew,' Sonny replied. 'I haven't had any for years.'

The house smelled strongly of cabbage. Joe's wife, a dried-out woman with a disapproving look frozen to her face, cleared the table and set out three beer glasses.

The kitchen was smaller and shabbier than Sonny remembered it. It was painted bright yellow. Flowers and birds cut from magazines had been glued to the cupboards and shellacked. The windows were crammed with geraniums in red clay pots. Over the doorway to the living-room there was a plaster crucifix. The blood on it had been brightened with purple paint. From his place at the kitchen table, all Sonny could see of the living-room was a high-backed brown chesterfield layered with scalloped pink and orange doilies. Above the chesterfield in an ornate gilt frame was a paint-by-number picture of a collie.

Joe scraped his feet and locked the door behind him. 'We've just come from church,' he explained. He was carrying a 26-ounce bottle that was smeared with mud and grass. He held the bottle to the light and grimaced with distaste.

'We sterilize our bottles. But on the outside it's like this because of the mounties' dogs. I have to tie the bottles with a string and throw them into the marsh.' He made a pulling motion with his hands. 'Then I go fishing.'

He rinsed the bottle under the tap. 'Five dollars for this. 65 cents for tomato juice.' After he pocketed Sonny's $6, Joe handed over the bottle and punched holes in a can. The tomato juice and homebrew swirled together like oil and water.

The homebrew was as raw as the cheapest bourbon. Joe brought a glass to the table and half filled it with tomato juice but his wife said, 'No. His liver's bad. He's just home from the hospital,' when Sonny went to add liquor.

Joe laughed to cover his embarrassment. 'It must be great to be in the city. I heard you on radio once, in a football game. Since then I heard you're doing good at cars. It's a good business. Everybody needs cars.'

'It's a great business,' Sonny enthusiastically agreed. He watched Roger and Buzz. 'You can make a lot of money. Right now I'm ready to expand. Profits are going to be even bigger. For $10,000 I'd make someone a one-quarter partner.'

Joe shook his head. 'That's big money.'

'It's a good investment,' Sonny added. 'Anybody buys in and from then on they collect while I work. No headaches, no problems, just profits.'

Joe raised his glass at Roger. 'Doctors always make lots of money. Somebody's always sick. That's the deal for your retirement fund.'

Roger laughed off the suggestion. 'Not me,' he protested. 'I like to put it in a nice safe bank.'

'Me, too,' Buzz agreed. 'No risk.' He gently felt his throat. 'You never know when a delicate instrument might lose its tone.'

Quickly, Sonny asked, 'How's business for you, Joe?'

'Not good. The mounties are a problem.'

'The mounties were always a problem.'

Joe was downcast. He made rings on the table with the bottom of his glass. 'Not like now. On weekends, in good weather, they park at the end of my driveway and sit all day. Nobody dares come. Last time, the judge said no more fines. From now on, jail. I'm too old for that.'

As Joe complained, Sonny could see how much he had changed. It was not just the new lines on his face or this thinning hair. He looked worn. At one time he had been prosperous. On weekends, fifty, a hundred people came and he dispensed homebrew from a water pitcher. Then, Joe's was a place to get drunk, pick a fight or pick up a woman.

They drank steadily. At noon, Joe's wife made them roast-pork sandwiches with lots of salt and thick slices of Spanish onion. Sonny bought another bottle. By two o'clock, Roger and Buzz were very drunk. Their conversation had become so loud they were nearly shouting.

Sonny kept his glass full of tomato juice. He wanted to stay sober so that he could lead the conversation back to his dealership when the time was right. He tried to follow the conversation but couldn't because Annie kept forcing her way into his thoughts. Once he had had a crush on her. She had been pretty, with large dark eyes and a soft mouth. Now, his wife, with her trips to the health spa and the clothing stores and beauty parlour, looked like an adolescent compared to Annie. Poverty had done that. It could still do it to his wife and daughter. If he lost his dealership, the ballet, music and figure-skating lessons would be the first to go. Then the house. He was 41 and no-one would want him when they could get college kids fresh out of school.

The more he brooded about it, the worse his situation seemed. The others were so involved in their story-telling that they ignored him. Then Roger started to tell Joe about the deer. As Roger demonstrated how he got rid of the rifle, his glass slipped and crashed into the cupboard. Joe brought him a new one.

'Shooting a deer on Sunday.' Joe frowned. 'That's bad.'

Buzz laughed and slopped his drink down the front of his coveralls. 'Never mind. Sonny couldn't have hit it anyway.' He stumbled from his chair and began scrambling around in a circle as he imitated Sonny's attempts to pick up the cartridges. Roger and Joe were shouting with laughter. As he turned faster and faster, like a dog chasing its tail, he shouted, 'A deer. Bullets. Help. A deer.'

Sonny was offended. He could see the story being told back home. Angrily, he said, 'You think I can't hunt? Come on, I'll show you.' He grabbed the bottle by the neck and marched outside. 'I'll get a deer the way we used to.'

Buzz and Roger staggered after him. A heavy, wet snow was starting to fall. Buzz drove the car to the main road. Sonny crouched in the back with the rifle sticking out the window.

'I'll show you some shooting,' he said.

They swerved wildly on the slick clay. The first thing Sonny shot was a stop sign. They halted to inspect it.

'See that,' he said, jabbing at the hole with his finger. 'Roger couldn't do that.'

'Sure, I could. Give me that rifle.' Roger grabbed the barrel.

'You're in no condition.' Sonny held onto the butt.

'I said give it to me.' Roger's voice was belligerent. He jerked the rifle out of Sonny's hands.

The snow was beginning to fall so heavily that the countryside was blurred. They started up again and Buzz had even more difficulty controlling the car. Roger leaned so far out the car window that he looked like he was going to fall out.

'Turn left,' Sonny ordered. 'That's the best way. There's always deer there.'

The road was so slick that they were reduced to a crawl. The snow covered the back window and clogged the windshield wipers.

'Turn here,' Sonny directed. 'We'll try along here.'

They followed the road for over a mile, then Buzz said excitedly, 'A deer.'

Roger emptied the rifle as Buzz skidded to a stop.

'Did you see it?' Buzz asked. Both he and Roger started down the road. Both had difficulty keeping their balance and they walked with exaggerated care, their legs stiffly spread. With a yelp, Buzz slipped backwards and sat down in the mud. Sonny stayed in the car.

'Sonny!' Roger screamed in a high, frightened voice. 'Sonny!'

When Buzz and Sonny reached Roger, he was kneeling beside a middle-aged woman in a faded brown coat with a fur collar. A man's felt cap was tied under her chin and her face was lined and shrunken. It looked like a small, dark leaf. She was an average-sized woman but lying on the ground, her legs drawn up so that only the toes of her black rubbers showed, she seemed a grotesque dwarf. Tightly gripped in her left hand was a gunny sack.

Sonny shook Roger's shoulder. 'Do something. You're a doctor.'

'No, I'm not.' Roger replied. 'I'm an optometrist.'

The woman was lying on her side and a red stain was spreading over the snow at her back. The stain was as scarlet as lipstick.

'You shot her,' Buzz accused him.

'You said it was a deer.' Roger's voice trembled.

The woman's slack mouth tightened, then, as her lips drew back over her teeth, she gave a low, harsh cry.

'Maybe she isn't hurt bad,' Roger said.

Behind them, Buzz gagged and threw up. Roger began to cry. 'Lady,' he said, his face stricken. 'I didn't mean it.'

'You shot her,' Buzz repeated.

Sonny turned on him. 'Shut up,' he ordered. 'You said she was a deer.'

Snow was gathering along the woman's nose and in the folds of her coat. Except for her harsh breathing and the muted throbbing of the car's exhaust, there was no sound. They stayed absolutely still, watching the blood spread outward, becoming pink at its edge.

Just then, the woman's eyes, which had been nearly shut, opened wide and fixed fiercely upon them. Her body tensed and, for a moment, it seemed as if she would rise and strike them. Instead, her body was shaken with a violent convulsion and she rolled onto her back. After that, she was still.

'It was an accident,' Roger mumbled.

'Manslaughter,' Sonny replied harshly. 'You were both drunk.'

'We've got to get her out of here.' As Buzz spoke, he began to back away. Roger hesitated, then he rose. Together they rushed for the car. Buzz tried to open the front door on the passenger's side but his hands were trembling so violently he couldn't control them. Sonny yanked open the rear door and shoved Buzz, then Roger, inside.

The snow was falling heavily. The nearby woods were dark and endless. The air was filled with an impenetrable whiteness that isolated them in a landscape without familiar landmarks. There were no signs, not even the sun, by which to take their bearing.

'Joe,' Buzz said. 'He'll know.'

'Joe,' Sonny replied, 'won't know anything. He doesn't want to go to jail.' He put the car into gear.

In the back seat, Roger and Buzz stared through the windows but there was nothing except the endless whiteness. The world was blurred and indistinct and as dangerous as an unchartered coast in dense fog. Even the road was gradually disappearing.

'Where are we going?' Roger cried, his hands gripping the back seat. Buzz, his arms wrapped tightly around himself, sat hunched and mute.

Expertly, Sonny steered the car to the crest of the ridge. Roger repeated his plaintive question but Sonny, having already started them down the side of the ridge into the next hollow, was too busy to reply.

THE OIL

George Bowering

Sleepy old mind, I'm driving a car
across the prairie shivering under snow sky.
Old sky: I suddenly see with one rise of road
old buffalo fields,
there is nothing
but buffalo turds on the grass
from which we keep
the home fires burning.

Alberta
floats on a pool of natural gas
the Piegans knew nothing of
in their fright
in their flight
to the mountains.
We owe them that.

This straight line of highway
& ghost wheat elevators
everything here in straight lines
except the Indian fields,
they roll
we say, rolling hills,
but our things are

straight lines,
oil derricks, elevators, train tracks
the tracks of the white man
the colour of
no white man, but
dark as the earth
in its darkness,
down deep oozing things:
I mean oil.
Alberta's unnatural heritage
concocted of Catholic adoption agencies
& fundamentalist
crooked coffee-stained neckties
at the expense of Indian boys,
now Catholics with horses removed
from under them,
the Piegans crosst the Rockies
to British Columbia
where oil is more scarce
& people.
In the high trees they rise now.
with campfire smoke,
the smell of needles burning.

Buffalo shit smoke
burning in Alberta
by the road, highway 2 North.

Now a
Cadillac, I see a
nother Cadillac, & there
is the black straight road, &
a Cadillac,
two Cadillacs
on the road, racing, North,
the mountains to the left
blurred by a passing
Cadillac.

NETTLES

Anne Szumigalski

When I am old
I will totter along broken payments
the strings of my boots undone
smelling a bit strong like any
fat old woman who has forgotten
which day is Tuesday
(my bath night if you like)

stiff my clothes from old dirt
not sweat at my age mumbling
the cracked enamel mug

eleven cats playing
in my weedy yard drinking
my little ration of milk
with me   and withy withy
the cats circle around my house
at night singly filing
in and sleeping on the
saggy stained bed and the chair
and the crumby tabletop

One day they will find me dead
O dead dead
A stinking old bundle of
                                        dead

and in my hand
a peeled wand

and in my ear a cricket sitting
telling me stories and predictions

and the time of night

NIGHT JOURNEY AND DEPARTURE

R. E. Rashley

1. MEETING AT NIGHT

One remembers the road flowing from moulded corners
slowly emerging into runnels of sound.
One remembers the sense slowly converging,
folding its frayed antennae
into the soothing texture,
being nothing,
flowing along a tube into the night.

One remembers the eyes
flaring along the shadowed way,
unseen creatures of the wood
turning to stare
their intense baleful stare.

The shock of storm
crashing into attention,
wipers beating their fragile hands into the flood,
the rocking car,
the crawling—

The highway patrolman further along the route,
time running out with the dome light
churning its pulse of blood.
Impossible questions—
searching for symbols in the glove compartment,
holding up charts,
proofs—
Somehow one made responses,
spoke the expected words—

The road, again, pulling under and under
down the darkened chute.

One remembers
the town, the hotel, the night clerk emerging,
personal, speaking official words—
greeting.

The long drive home,
the talk,
the night air sweet in the side windows,
the stop to stretch legs at the roadside tables,
treading the earth,
the dark flowers of the leaves—

It was good, then, to be going,
and, if one could, one would gladly do it again,
but such things are a flowing.
Now it is all pulled under
what one remembers most is the earth smell
and the dark flowers of the leaves.

2. AIRPORT

The tantalizing, false, blue lights
blink as the great beast crosses
and, tamely, at heel, rolls in.
Things eaten at Edmonton
or further west disgorge.
It is time to part,
time for the words that cover, not conceal,
carefully tieing
nothings to inane nothings,
lieing—

A sudden bell shatters the quiet,
looses a clatter of indirections into the night
as if someone with a bright insensate laugh
lifted the top of the head and dropped in a handful of glass.

And the plane tears at the clutching grass
violent to be alone.
It is all right,
as the great thing grows toward flight,
to be saying with the mind,
'They are all gone into that world of light',
but the blood is crying plainly enough,
'The world is night'.

I AM A LAKE

Lorna Uher

i am a lake
patterned by your tracks
across the snow sifted
like white pollen on an
oval board

to cross me
you must flop on your belly
like a seal   drag your massive weight
up my legs   and across my chest
leaving a warm wide print
of your passing

if you insist
on walking
cracking jagged wounds
on my cold skin
with each thud of your heavy boots
i will open up   swallow you
hold you in my frozen mud
till spring

my fishes will lay
eggs in the cups of your eyelids
my lakebirds will nest in the hair
of your arms and your black thighs
the tongue of my water will ripple
your chest

after the thaw
as your feet send roots
through the softening mud
your fist will float to the surface
a tight white blossom
opening to the sun

SNAKEROOT

Gary Geddes

i
Along the dirt roads of summer,
black prairie mud oozing my toes,

sun-baked ridges of clay
crumbling, the childhood me

scrambles for Senega root,
in ditches, edges of pastures,

along the road allowance,
staggers home reeling from sun,

no more than an ounce of rare
weed in my pocket, craggy

pungent rattlesnake root, a
smell the nose remembers.

ii
The road to hell is paved. Along
its length snakes proliferate, wind

themselves about our lives, poison
the air we breathe. All night

the rattle of traffic, faces stare
from bloodshot windows. Somewhere

a root so potent it would cure
the sting of concrete and macadam,

hurt of steel, a burning in the lungs,
some magic elixir of leaves and sweet

grasses, essence of wildflowers, tiger
lily, gum of fresh, chewed wheat, free

to all takers, that will end the long
bitterness, mend the bruised heel.

OLE

Paul Hiebert

One may trace many influences which affected Sarah's work, influences great and small which touched her here and there; Ole, Rover, William Greenglow, Henry Welkin, Grandfather Thurnow, strong, masculine influences which affected her outlook, touching her mind, and leaving their light and sometimes their shadow upon her poetry. But to Ole, cheerful hard-working Ole, big of heart and feet, must go the honour of having been the first to put the young Sarah upon the path of poesy. It is significant, even symbolical, that just as years ago on the morning after Dominion Day, Ole himself was traced for miles across the alkali flats that lie north of Willows, so today one traces his splendid footprints across the dazzling pages of Saskatchewan literature.

Ole's other name is not known, or if it ever was known it has been forgotten. He answered simply to the name of Ole. When, on the rare occasions a more formal address became necessary as when the extra mail-order catalogue arrived, it became, Ole, c/o J. Binks. Professor Ambush has suggested that the name Ole may be a diminutive of Olafur or perhaps of Oleander, but no diminutive can possibly apply. He was above all a big man such as the West is fond of producing. His feet found their way with difficulty through the trousers of his store suit, his shoulders were of gnarled oak, and his two hands swung at his sides like slabs of teak. He was noted for his great strength. He could haul the stoneboat with its two full water barrels from the coulee to the house, and when, as sometimes happened, a horse would straddle the barbed wire fence, he would assist it from its predicament by lifting one end or another as the circumstances required. He had an equine playfulness and would toss Mathilda, even when eighteen and already large for her age, from the ground to the hayloft with great ease and to her infinite delight.

But if Ole's strength was great, his good nature and cheerfulness were even greater. No one is known ever to have offended Ole. His mind had that simplicity and directness and that acceptance of the world which one associates with his race and occupation. He and Rover were inseparable; Ole shared his lunches in the field with Rover, and the latter shared his fleas at night with Ole. Both had a deep and abiding affection for Sarah.

Neither Rover nor Ole actually wrote any poetry, at least none has come down to us unless we accept the terse verses, often fragmentary and sometimes illustrated, which Ole was fond of writing upon the granaries and other small buildings with a piece of coal. (Two of these boards, one of doubtful authenticity, are known to exist in private collections of Binksiana.) But where both Ole's and Rover's chief influence upon Sarah's poetic talent lay, was that it was they who first taught her the singing quality of verse. Rover's voice had a deep and throbbing cadence with which he tended to experiment in metrical forms especially on moonlight nights. Grandfather Thurnow's remark, that 'At least he cuts it up into stove lengths,' was at once a recognition of Rover's success and an appreciation of his talent. Ole's voice, on the other hand, was a high falsetto and tended to break. When it broke it took on a certain screeching quality, not altogether pleasant in itself, but particularly well adapted to the old Norse ballads and folksongs which he rendered with full pedal and with an abandon which aroused Sarah's boundless admiration. He translated these songs freely—almost too freely. But he planted the seeds of poesy in Sarah's heart, nor could Jacob Binks's frequent admonition to 'Shut up, you dam' squarehead!' prevent the seeds from sprouting.

Between Ole and Sarah there was a bond which was never broken. She leaned heavily on him throughout her life, both in the matter of chores and in the matter of inspiration; 'My staff and my stick, my Pole and my prop,' she says of him in a fragment of verse in which she reveals a rather hazy conception of the geography of northern Europe but acknowledges her debt. Ole was her slave and her dependable friend. It was he who first taught her the satisfaction of the occasional pipe, he taught her to swim in the dugout, he taught her all he knew about handling a calf, about farm machinery, and about Mathilda.

For Sarah, poetry was ever the expression of the soul, whether it was her own soul or somebody else's or simply that of Saskatchewan. In *The Hired Man on Saturday Night* she expresses Ole's soul and in its moment of greatest elation.

THE HIRED MAN ON SATURDAY NIGHT
A horse! A horse! Give me a horse,
To dash across the frozen north,
And wallow in the mire,
A noble barb with cloven hoof,
With brazen wings and blatant snoof,
And molten eyes of fire.

I'll carve a furlong through the snow,
And bring the bastard she-cat low,
And bind her to a tree,
That ding-bat dire, shall put her sire,
Out of the frying pan into the fire,
Where e'er she be.

With gathered rage of many an age,
I'll blot the boar from off the page,
And twist his face;
I'll smite the rooster in the snow,
And crafty Rover, dumb with woe,
Shall curse his race.

I'll tie a reef knot in the tail
Of Barney's bull—with tooth and nail
I'll fill his day with gloom;
The calf shall wail, the cow shall quail,
The horse shall totter and grow pale—
Give me room!

It would appear that on Ole's one free evening of the week he developed a sense of aloofness from farm animals which excluded even Rover. The poem does not approximate the high standard which Sarah usually sets for herself. However it has a swing and rhythm and Professor Marrowfat rates it very highly. He says, 'Sarah has hit it on the nose. I don't know much about farm animals, my line being literature. But I know just the feeling that Ole has. I have it myself almost every Saturday night.' Nevertheless, in the opinion of the Author, Sarah expresses the feeling more accurately in *Steeds*. Here the sense of elation is combined with the rush and sweep of horses. The occasion of this poem was the time when Ole returned from Willows on the late afternoon of election day, 1911. On that occasion he is alleged to have disappeared with two demijohns of linseed oil which he was transporting with his team from the Liberal to the Conservative Committee rooms. (The incident is recalled in the memoirs of the Hon. Grafton Tabernackel, at that time Administrator of the Farm Implement Oiling and Greasing Act.)

STEEDS

I have two dashing, prancing steeds,
Buttercup and Dairy Queen,
What for spirit, what for speed,
Matches this amazing team?
One is roan and one is plaid,
One a mare, and one a lad,
One a pacer, one a trotter,
One a son, and one a daughter:
When they're fastened side by side,
Yoked together in the traces,
Joyfully prepare to ride
O'er the big and open spaces;
Whoopee! Swift across the stubble,
Over boulders, banks and rubble,
Up the hill and down the glen,
Cross the county—back again,
Through the fence and greenhouse go,
Pumpkin garden—to and fro,
Pounding, puffing, like a dragon,
Kill the calf and smash the wagon,
Through the hayloft, dust and smother,
In one end and out the other—
Zowie! When their spirit's up!
Dairy Queen and Buttercup!

THE PRAIRIE: A STATE OF MIND

Henry Kreisel

Soon after I first arrived in Alberta, now over twenty years ago, there appeared in the *Edmonton Journal* a letter in which the writer, replying to some article which appeared sometime earlier, asserted with passionate conviction that the earth was flat. Now in itself that would have been quite unremarkable, the expression merely of some cranky and eccentric old man. Normally, then, one would not have been likely to pay very much attention to such a letter, and one would have passed it over with an amused smile. Nothing pleases us more than to be able to feel superior to pre-scientific man, secure behind the fortress of our own knowledge. I am no different in this respect from most other people. But there was something in the tone of that letter that would not allow me that kind of response. Far from feeling superior, I felt awed. Even as I write these lines, the emotion evoked in me by that letter that appeared in a newspaper more than twenty years ago comes back to me, tangible and palpable.

The tone of the letter was imperious. Surveying his vast domains, a giant with feet firmly rooted in the earth, a lord of the land asserted what his eyes saw, what his heart felt, and what his mind perceived. I cut the letter out and for some time carried it about with me in my wallet. I don't really know why I did that. I do know that in my travels round the prairie in those early years of my life in the Canadian west I looked at the great landscape through the eyes of that unknown man. At last I threw the clipping away, but the imagined figure of that giant remained to haunt my mind.

Years later I finally came to terms with that vision in a story that I called 'The Broken Globe'. This story deals with the clash between a father and his young son. The son, who is eventually to become a scientist, comes home from school one day and tells his father that the earth moves. The father, a Ukrainian settler, secure in something very like a medieval faith, asserts passionately that it does not and that his son is being tempted and corrupted by the devil. The story is told by a narrator, an academic who goes to visit the father, now an old man, to bring his greetings from his estranged scientist-son. At the end of the story, after the narrator has heard from the father about the conflict that alienated him from his son, the narrator rises to leave:

> Together we walked out of the house. When I was about to get into my car, he touched me lightly on the arm. I turned. His eyes surveyed the vast expanse of sky and land, stretching far into the distance, reddish clouds in the sky and blue shadows on the land. With a gesture of great dignity and power he lifted his arm and stood pointing into the distance, at the flat land and the low-hanging sky.

> 'Look,' he said, very slowly and very quietly, 'she is flat and she stands still.'
>
> It was impossible not to feel a kind of admiration for the old man. There was something heroic about him. I held out my hand and he took it. He looked at me steadily, then averted his eyes and said, 'Send greetings to my son.'
>
> I drove off quickly, but had to stop again in order to open the wooden gate. I looked back at the house, and saw him still standing there, still looking at his beloved land, a lonely, towering figure framed against the darkening evening sky.[1]

You will have noticed that the images I used to describe my imagined man seem extravagant—'a lord of the land,' 'a giant'. These were in fact the images that came to me and I should myself have regarded them as purely subjective, if I had not afterward in my reading encountered similar images in the work of other writers who write about the appearances of men on the prairie at certain times. Thus in Martha Ostenso's *Wild Geese* a young school teacher sees 'against the strange pearly distance . . . the giant figure of a man beside his horse,' and when he comes closer she recognizes Fusi Aronson, 'the great Icelander. . . . He was grand in his demeanor, and somehow lonely, as a towering mountain is lonely, or as a solitary oak on the prairie' (31).[2] On the very first page of *Settlers of the Marsh*, Philip Grove, describing two men 'fighting their way through the gathering dusk', calls one of them, Lars Nelson, 'a giant, of three years' standing in the country' (11).[3] And in his autobiography, *In Search of Myself*, Grove, recalling the origin of *Fruits of the Earth* and his first encounter with the figure who was to become Abe Spalding, describes the arresting and startling sight of a man plowing land generally thought to be unfit for farming. 'Outlined as he was against a tilted and spoked sunset in the western sky,' he writes, 'he looked like a giant. Never before had I seen, between farm and town, a human being in all my drives.' Grove goes on to tell how he stopped his horses and learned that this man had only that very afternoon arrived from Ontario, after a train journey of two thousand miles, had at once filed a claim for a homestead of a hundred and sixty acres, had unloaded his horses from the freight-car, and was now plowing his first field. And when Grove

[1] Henry Kreisel, 'The Broken Globe', in *The Best American Short Stories 1966*, edited by Martha Foley and David Burnett (Boston: Houghton Mifflin Co., 1966). p. 165.

[2] Martha Ostenso, *Wild Geese* (originally published 1925). References in parentheses are to the New Canadian Library edition, published by McClelland and Stewart, Toronto, 1961.

[3] Frederick Philip Grove, *Settlers of the Marsh*. References in parentheses are to the first edition, published by the Ryerson Press, Toronto, 1925.

expresses his surprise at the speed with which this newcomer set to work, the man replies, 'Nothing else to do' (259).[4]

I set the image of the giant in the landscape over against the more familiar one of man pitted against a vast and frequently hostile natural environment that tends to dwarf him, at the mercy of what Grove calls, in *Settlers of the Marsh,* 'a dumb shifting of forces' (152). Man, the giant-conqueror, and man, the insignificant dwarf always threatened by defeat, form the two polarities of the state of mind produced by the sheer physical fact of the prairie.

There are moments when the two images coalesce. So the observant Mrs Bentley, whose diary forms the substance of Sinclair Ross's novel *As for Me and My House,* records the response of a prairie congregation during the bleak and drought-haunted 1930s:

> The last hymn was staidly orthodox, but through it there seemed to mount something primitive, something that was less a response to Philip's sermon and scripture reading than to the grim futility of their own lives. Five years in succession now they've been blown out, dried out, hailed out, and it was as if in the face of so blind and uncaring a universe they were trying to assert themselves to insist upon their own meaning and importance. (19)[5]

All discussion of the literature produced in the Canadian west must of necessity begin with the impact of the landscape upon the mind. 'Only a great artist,' records Mrs Bentley, 'could ever paint the prairie, the vacancy and stillness of it, the bare essentials of a landscape, sky and earth' (59). W. O. Mitchell, in the opening sentences of *Who Has Seen the Wind*, speaks of the 'least common denominator of nature, the skeleton requirements simply, of land and sky' (3).[6] He goes on to describe the impact of the landscape on Brian O'Connal, a four-year-old boy, living in a little prairie town and venturing for the first time to the edge of town:

> He looked up to find that the street had stopped. Ahead lay the sudden emptiness of the prairie. For the first time in his four years of life he was alone on the prairie.
>
> He had seen it often, from the veranda of his uncle's farmhouse, or at the end of a long street, but till now he had never heard it. The hum of telephone wires along the road, the ring of hidden crickets, the stitching sound of

[4] Frederick Philip Grove, *In Search of Myself*. References in parentheses are to the first edition, published by the Macmillan Co. of Canada, Toronto, 1946.

[5] Sinclair Ross, *As for Me and My House* (originally published 1941). References in parentheses are to the New Canadian Library edition published by McClelland and Stewart, Toronto, 1957.

[6] W. O. Mitchell, *Who Has Seen the Wind* (originally published 1947). References in parentheses are to a new edition, published by Macmillan of Canada, Toronto, 1960.

> grasshoppers, the sudden relief of a meadow lark's song, were deliciously strange to him. . . .
>
> A gopher squeaked questioningly as Brian sat down upon a rock warm to the back of his thigh. . . . The gopher squeaked again, and he saw it a few yards away, sitting up, and watching him from his pulpit hole. A suave-winged hawk chose that moment to slip its shadow over the face of the prairie.
>
> And all about him was the wind now, a pervasive sighing through great emptiness, unhampered by the buildings of the town, warm and living against his face and in his hair. (11)

Only one other kind of landscape gives us the same skeleton requirements, the same vacancy and stillness, the same movement of wind through space—and that is the sea. So when Mrs Bentley records in her diary that 'there's a high, rocking wind that rattles the window and creaks the walls. It's strong and steady like a great tide after the winter pouring north again, and I have a queer, helpless sense of being lost miles out in the middle of it' (35), she might well be tossing in heavy seas, protected only by a small and fragile little bark. In Grove's *Over Prairie Trails,* that remarkable book of impressionistic essays describing seven trips that Grove made in 1917 and 1918 between Gladstone and Falmouth near the western shore of Lake Manitoba, the prairie as sea becomes one of the controlling patterns shaping the imagination of the observer. On one of these trips—in the dead of winter—Grove prepares his horse-drawn cutter as if it were a boat being readied for a fairly long and possibly dangerous journey:

> Not a bolt but I tested it with a wrench; and before the stores were closed, I bought myself enough canned goods to feed me for a week should through any untoward accident the need arise. I always carried a little alcohol stove, and with my tarpaulin I could convert my cutter within three minutes into a windproof tent. Cramped quarters, to be sure, but better than being given over to the wind at thirty below. (60-61)[7]

Soon the cutter, the horses, and the man meet the first test—very like a Conradian crew coming to grips with a storm at sea. A mountainous snowdrift bars the way. The horses, Dan and Peter, who become wonderful characters in their own right, panic. They plunge wildly, rear on their hind legs, pull apart, try to turn and retrace their steps. 'And meanwhile the cutter went sharply up at first, as if on the vast crest of a wave, then toppled over into a hole made by Dan, and altogether behaved like a

[7] Frederick Philip Grove, *Over Prairie Trails* (originally published 1922). References in parentheses are to the New Canadian Library edition, published by McClelland and Stewart, Toronto, 1957.

boat tossed on a stormy sea. Then order returned into the chaos. . . . I spoke to the horses in a soft, quiet, purring voice; and at last I pulled in' (69).

He becomes aware of the sun, cold and high in the sky, a relentless, inexorable force, and suddenly two Greek words come into his mind: Homer's *pontos airygetos*—the barren sea. A half hour later he understands why:

> This was indeed like nothing so much as like being out in rough waters and in a troubled sea, with nothing to brace the storm with but a wind-tossed nutshell of a one-man sailing craft. . . . When the snow reached its extreme depth, it gave you the feeling which a drowning man may have when fighting his desperate fight with the salty waves. But more impressive than that was the frequent outer resemblance. The waves of the ocean rise up and reach out and batter against the rocks and battlements of the shore, retreating again and ever returning to the assault. . . . And if such a high crest wave had suddenly been frozen into solidity, its outline would have mimicked to perfection many a one of the snow shapes that I saw around.(77)

And when, at the end of another journey, the narrator reaches home, he is like a sailor reaching harbor after a long voyage:

> there was the signal put out for me. A lamp in one of the windows of the school. . . . And in the most friendly and welcoming way it looked with its single eye across at the nocturnal guest.
>
> I could not see the cottage, but I knew that my little girl lay sleeping in her cosy bed, and that a young woman was sitting there in the dark, her face glued to the window-pane, to be ready with a lantern which burned in the kitchen whenever I might pull up between school and house. And there, no doubt, she had been sitting for a long while already; and there she was destined to sit during the winter that came, on Friday nights—full often for many and many an hour—full often till midnight—and sometimes longer. (18)

The prairie, like the sea, thus often produces an extraordinary sensation of confinement within a vast and seemingly unlimited space. The isolated farm-houses, the towns and settlements, even the great cities that eventually sprang up on the prairies, become islands in that land-sea, areas of relatively safe refuge from the great and lonely spaces. In *Wild Geese* Martha Ostenso describes a moment when the sensation of safety and of abandonment are felt to be evenly balanced:

> Fine wisps of rain lashed about the little house, and the wind whistled in the birch trees outside, bleak as a lost bird.

> These sounds defined the feelings of enclosed warmth and safety. . . . But they did also the opposed thing. They stirred the fear of loneliness, the ancient dread of abandonment in the wilderness in the profounder natures of these two who found shelter here. For an imponderable moment they sought beyond each other's eyes, sought for understanding, for communion under the vast terrestrial influence that bound them, an inevitable part and form of the earth, inseparable one from the other. (64)

At the same time the knowledge of the vast space outside brings to the surface anxieties that have their roots elsewhere and thus sharpens and crystallizes a state of mind. In *As for Me and My House* Mrs Bentley uses the prairie constantly as a mirror of her own fears, frustrations, and helplessness:

> It's an immense night out there, wheeling and windy. The lights on the street and in the houses are helpless against the black wetness, little unilluminating glints that might be painted on it. The town seemed huddled together, cowering on a high, tiny perch, afraid to move lest it topple into the wind. Close to the parsonage is the church, black even against the darkness, towering ominously up through the night and merging with it. There's a soft steady swish of rain on the roof, and a gurgle of eave troughs running over. Above, in the high cold night, the wind goes swinging past, indifferent, liplessly mournful. It frightens me, makes me feel lost, dropped on this little perch of town and abandoned. I wish Philip would waken. (5)

That, however, is not the only, perhaps not even the most significant response to the challenge of lonely and forbidden spaces. It is easy to see Mrs Bentley's reaction as prototypical of the state of mind induced by the prairie, but it would not be altogether accurate. It is one kind of response, but set over against it there is the response typified in Grove's *Settlers of the Marsh* by Niels Lindstedt, who, like a Conradian adventurer, a Lord Jim or a Stein, is driven to follow a dream. It expresses itself in 'a longing to leave and go to the very margin of civilization, there to clear a new place; and when it is cleared and people began to settle about it, to move on once more, again to the very edge of pioneerdom, to start it all over anew. . . . That way his enormous strength would still have a meaning' (180).

To conquer a piece of the continent, to put one's imprint upon virgin land, to say, 'Here I am, for that I came,' is as much a way of defining oneself, of proving one's existence, as is Descartes's *cogito, ergo sum*. That is surely why that man whom Grove saw plowing a field barely two hours after his arrival was driven to do it. He had to prove to himself that he was in some way master of his destiny, that he was fully alive, and that his strength had meaning. When he told Grove that he was doing what he was doing because there was nothing else to do, he was telling him the simple truth, but leaving a more complex truth unspoken, and probably even unperceived.

The conquest of territory is by definition a violent process. In the Canadian west, as elsewhere on this continent, it involved the displacement of the indigenous population by often scandalous means, and then the taming of the land itself. The displacement, the conquest of the Indians, and later the rising of the Métis under Louis Riel, are events significantly absent from the literature I am discussing. Occasionally Riel breaks into the consciousness of one or another of the characters, usually an old man or an old woman remembering troubled times; occasionally the figure of an Indian appears briefly, but is soon gone. No doubt that is how things appeared to the European settlers on the prairie; no doubt our writers did not really make themselves too familiar with the indigenous people of the prairie, seeing them either as noble savages or not seeing them at all, but it is likely that a conscious or subconscious process of suppression is also at work here.

The conquest of the land itself is by contrast a dominant theme, and the price paid for the conquest by the conqueror or the would-be conqueror is clearly and memorably established. The attempt to conquer the land is a huge gamble. Many lose, and there are everywhere mute emblems testifying to defeat. 'Once I passed the skeleton of a stable,' Grove records in *Over Prairie Trails,* 'the remnant of the buildings put up by a pioneer settler who had to give in after having wasted effort and substance and worn his knuckles to the bone. The wilderness uses human material up' (11). But into the attempted conquest, whether ultimately successful or not, men pour an awesome, concentrated passion. The breaking of the land becomes a kind of rape, a passionate seduction. The earth is at once a willing and unwilling mistress, accepting and rejecting her seducer, the cause of his frustration and fulfilment, and either way the shaper and controller of his mind, exacting servitude.

The most powerful statement of that condition in the literature of the Canadian west is, I think, to be found in Martha Ostenso's *Wild Geese,* the story of Caleb Gare, a tyrannical man who, himself enslaved to the land, in turn enslaves his whole family to serve his own obsession. Characteristically, Ostenso sees him as a gigantic figure. 'His tremendous shoulders and massive head, which loomed forward from the rest of his body like a rough projection of rock from the edge of a cliff,' she writes, 'gave him a towering appearance' (13). He is conceived in a way which makes it difficult to speak of him in conventional terms of human virtue or human vice, for he is conceived as 'a spiritual counterpart of the land, as harsh, as demanding, as tyrannical as the very soil from which he drew his existence' (33). He can only define himself in terms of the land,

and paradoxically it is the land and not his children that bears testimony to his potency and manhood. As he supervises his sons and daughters, grown up, but still only extensions of himself, working in the fields, he is gratified by the knowledge that what they are producing is the product of *his* land, the result of *his* industry, 'as undeniably his as his right hand, testifying to the outer world that Caleb Gare was a successful owner and user of the soil' (171). At night he frequently goes out with a lantern swinging low along the earth. No one knows where he does or why he goes, and no one dares to ask him, but his daughter Judith once remarks scornfully 'that it was to assure himself that his land was still all there' (18). Only the land can ultimately give him the assurance that he is alive: 'Before him glimmered the silver grey sheet of the flax—rich, beautiful, strong. All unto itself, complete, demanding everything, and in turn yielding everything—growth of the earth, the only thing on the earth worthy of respect, of homage' (126-27).

Being so possessed by the prairie, his mind and body as it were an extension of it, he cannot give himself to anyone else. Since he is incapable of loving another human being, he can receive no love in return. He marries his wife knowing that she has had a child born out of wedlock because this gives him the power of blackmail over her and, in a stern and puritan society, chains her forever to him and to his land. He knows that she once gave herself to another man in a way in which she can never give herself to him, but he cannot see that he chose her because he wanted someone who could not demand from him a love he is incapable of giving. Having committed his mind and his body to the land, greedily acquiring more and more, he can only use other human beings as instruments to help feed an appetite that can never be satisfied. His human feelings must therefore be suppressed, and the passion of his blood must remain forever frustrated, sublimated in his passion for the acquisition of more and more land. Man, the would-be conqueror, is thus also man, the supreme egoist, subordinating everything to the flow of a powerful ambition. 'Caleb Gare—he does not feel,' says Fusi Aronson, the Icelander. 'I shall kill him one day. But even that he will not feel' (31).

He does feel for his land. But the land is a fickle mistress, and he must live in perpetual fear, for he can never be sure that this mistress will remain faithful. She may, and indeed she does, with hail and fire destroy in minutes all that he has labored to build.

Caleb Gare's obsession may be extreme, and yet a measure of egocentricity, though more often found in less virulent form, is perhaps necessary if the huge task of taming a continent is to be successfully accomplished. At the same time the necessity of survival dictates cooperative undertakings. So it is not surprising that the prairie has produced the most right-wing as well as the most left-wing provincial governments in Canada. But whether conservative or radical, these governments have always been puritan in outlook, a true reflection of their constituencies.

The prairie settlements, insecure islands in that vast land-sea, have been austere, intensely puritan societies. Not that puritanism in Canada is confined to the prairie, of course, but on the prairie it has been more solidly entrenched that even in rural Ontario, and can be observed in something very like a distilled form.

It can be argued that in order to tame the land and begin the building, however tentatively, of something approaching a civilization, the men and women who settled on the prairie had to tame themselves, had to curb their passions and contain them within a tight neo-Calvinist framework. But it is not surprising that there should be sudden eruptions and that the passions, long suppressed, should burst violently into the open and threaten the framework that was meant to contain them. In the literature with which I am dealing this violence often takes the form of melodrama, and though this sudden eruption of violence sometimes seems contrived for the sake of a novel's plot, it is also clearly inherent in the life the novelists observed. It is natural that novelists should exploit the tensions which invariably arise when a rigid moral code attempts to set strict limits on the instinctual life, if not indeed to suppress it altogether. Thus illicit love affairs, conducted furtively, without much joy, quickly begun and quickly ended, and sometimes complicated by the birth of illegitimate children, can be used as a perhaps obvious but nevertheless effective center for a novel's structure, as for example in Stead's *Grain*, in Ostenso's *Wild Geese*, in Laurence's *A Jest of God*, in Ross's *As for Me and My House.*

It is because *As for Me and My House* contains the most uncompromising rendering of the puritan state of mind produced on the prairie that the novel has been accorded a central place in prairie literature. In the figure of Philip Bentley, a Presbyterian minister and artist *manqué*, we have—at least as he emerges from the diary of his wife—an embodiment of the puritan temperament, the product of his environment and much more a part of it than he would ever admit, angry not really because the communities in which he serves are puritan, but because they are not puritan enough, because they expect him to purvey a genteel kind of piety that will serve as a respectable front to hide a shallow morality. But his own emotions remain frozen within the puritan framework from which he cannot free his spirit. So he draws more and more into himself, becomes aloof and unknowable, not in the end so different from Caleb Gare, though in temperament and sensibility they seem at first glance to move in totally different worlds. Philip's wife is certain that 'there's some twisted, stumbling power locked up within him, so blind and helpless still it can't find outlet, so clenched with urgency it can't release itself' (80). His drawing and painting reflect an inner paralysis. He draws endless prairie scenes that mirror his own frustration—the false fronts on the stores, doors and windows that are crooked and pinched, a little schoolhouse standing lonely and defiant in a landscape that is like a desert, 'almost a lunar desert, with queer, fantastic pits and drifts of sand encroaching right to the doorstep' (80). Philip Bentley's emotional paralysis affects of course his relationship with his wife. Thus she describes in her diary how he lies beside her, his muscles rigid, and she presses closer to him, pretending to stir in her sleep, 'but when I put my hand on his arm there was a sharp little contraction against my touch, and after a minute I shifted again, and went back to my own pillow' (116).

Only once does the twisted power that's locked up within him find some kind of outlet—and then disastrously, when he seduces the young girl Judith who has come to help in the house during his wife's illness.

Prairie puritanism is one result of the conquest of the land, part of the price exacted for the conquest. Like the theme of the conquest of the land, the theme of the imprisoned spirit dominates serious prairie writing, and is connected with it. We find this theme developed not only in Ross's novel, where it is seen at its bleakest and most uncompromising, not only in Grove's and Ostenso's work, but also in more recent novels, such as Margaret Laurence's two novels, *The Stone Angel* and *A Jest of God*, and in George Ryga's *Ballad of a Stone Picker*, and, surprisingly perhaps, in W. O. Mitchell's *Who Has Seen the Wind*, which is conceived as a celebration and lyrical evocation of a prairie childhood. Brian O'Connal is initiated into the mysteries of God and nature, of life and death, but he is also brought face to face with the strange figure of the young Ben, a curious amalgam of noble savage and Wordsworthian child of nature. Again and again he appears, seemingly out of nowhere, soundlessly, the embodiment of a kind of free prairie spirit. His hair is 'bleached as the dead prairie grass itself' (12), his trousers are always torn, he never wears shoes. He has 'about as much moral conscience as the prairie wind that lifted over the edge of the prairie world to sing mortality to every living thing' (31). He does not play with other children, takes no part in organized school games. Though he can run 'with the swiftness of a prairie chicken,' and jump like an antelope, he refuses to have anything to do with athletic competitions. School itself is 'an intolerable incarceration for him, made bearable only by flights of freedom which totalled up to almost the same number as the days he attended' (147). The solid burghers of the town, strait-laced and proper, try desperately to tame him, for his wild spirit represents a danger to them. But they cannot control him any more than they can control the wind. Brian O'Connal is drawn to the young Ben, and though they rarely speak to each other, there grows up between them a strong bond, what Mitchell calls 'an extrasensory brothership' (89). The young Ben is Brian's double, the free spirit Brian would like to be, but dare not be. For Brian, one feels, will ultimately conform to the demands of his society and he will subdue the young Ben within himself.

Most of the works that I have dealt with were conceived and written more than a quarter of a century ago. There have been social and industrial changes on the prairie since then, and the tempo of these changes has been rapidly accelerating in the past ten years or so. Yet it is surprising that such novels as Adele Wiseman's *The Sacrifice* and John Marlyn's *Under the Ribs of Death*, published in the 1950s, and Margaret Laurence's *The Stone Angel* and *A Jest of God* and George Ryga's *Ballad of a Stone Picker*, published in the 1960s, should still adhere to the general pattern of the earlier works. The Winnipeg of Wiseman and Marlyn is the city of the 1920s and 1930s, a city of newly arrived immigrants, and the small towns of the Laurence and Ryga novels are clearly the small towns Ross and Ostenso knew.

For though much has changed in the west, much also still remains unchanged. Prairie puritanism is now somewhat beleaguered and shows signs of crumbling, but it remains a potent force still, and the vast land itself has not yet been finally subdued and altered. On a hot summer day it does not take long before, having left the paved streets of the great cities where hundreds of thousands of people now live, one can still see, outlined against the sky, the lonely, giant-appearing figures of men like Caleb Gare or the Ukrainian farmer in my story. And on a winter day one can turn off the great superhighways that now cross the prairies and drive along narrow, snow-covered roads, and there it still lies, the great, vast land-sea, and it is not difficult to imagine Philip Grove in his fragile cutter, speaking softly to Dan and Peter, his gentle, faithful horses, and preparing them to hurl themselves once more against that barren sea, those drifts of snow.

A child asked me if Paris were really more beautiful than Calgary. A university student spoke to me of the generosity of the city's millionaires—there are about a thousand of them—in the tone the young painters of the Middle Ages might have used of the Medici. One would have thought they had covered the city with museums and art galleries; questioned, he proved to be thinking particularly of MacMahon, who had underwritten the construction of a football stadium.

EUGÈNE CLOUTIER

MARGARET LAURENCE: A great many people write very autobiographical first novels. Well, your writing didn't begin in that way and neither did mine. I don't know whether one can really make any generalizations about this in terms of western Canada. I think that a great many people who grew up, as we both did, in the prairies, could hardly wait to get out. And it took a long time to see the value of that experience or to see it in some kind of perspective.

ROBERT KROETSCH: We didn't have the advantage that a young writer might have in an older area where there is a literature about his experience. I remember reading voraciously as a boy, and the fictional boys I read about were always doing things I couldn't begin to do, because we didn't have the big oak trees or whatever. And that sense of alienation made me feel that first I had to go see—I didn't really believe you could construct a world without huge wheatfields.

MARGARET LAURENCE: But this was one thing about growing up either on a farm or in a small town, the prairies anyway. It was both a stultifying experience and a very warm protective one too, because this was a place where no child could get lost: everybody knew who you were and who you belonged to. It was like a tribe, a clan, and I am sure this was your experience too. And as you said, the books that you read were not related to your experience. I remember—I must have been in my late teens, I suppose—when I read Sinclair Ross' novel, *As for Me and My House*, which was about a minister in a small prairie town; it hit me with tremendous force, because I realized for the first time that people could really write about my background.

From 'A Conversation with Margaret Laurence' by
ROBERT KROETSCH

THE FUTURE OF POETRY IN CANADA

Elizabeth Brewster

Some people say we live in a modern mechanized nation
where the only places that matter
are Toronto, Montreal, and maybe Vancouver;
but I myself prefer Goodridge, Alberta,
a town where electricity arrived in 1953,
the telephone in 1963.

In Goodridge, Alberta
the most important social events
have been the golden wedding anniversaries of the residents.
There have been a Garden Club, a Junior Grain Club, and a Credit Union,
and there have been farewell parties,
well attended in spite of the blizzards.

Weather is important in Goodridge.
People remember the time they threshed in the snow,
and the winter the temperature fell to seventy below.

They also remember the time
the teacher from White Rat School
piled eight children in his car
and drove them, as a treat,
all the way to Edmonton;
where they admired the Jubilee Auditorium
and the Parliament Buildings
and visited the CNR wash rooms
but were especially thrilled
going up and down in an elevator.

I hope at least one poet
in the next generation
comes from Goodridge, Alberta.

STREAK MOSAIC

Stephen Scobie

1

—Prairie? Did you say prairie?

—No, I said priority.

—Oh. Sorry.

—But I could say it for you, if you liked.

(And if I had, how would I have said it, then? Something flat, connected with grain. Something monotonous I slept through on the train. A word surrounding 'air'.)

—Say it.

—Prairie.

—That's not the way to say it.

—You say it.

—Prairie.

(Yes, you could hear the difference.)

That's how we met, and it was in Vancouver. Outside the window were mountains. They stared at you every day, the North Shore Mountains, Seymour, Grouse, and always the same side, like the moon. The far side was wilderness; I lived there for years and never saw it. While, like a rising tide, a slow flood, houses crept up the familiar face. The mountains, there every day, so painfully, incredibly beautiful: you would think *something* would rub off on the people, *some* feeling for beauty . . .

To her, they just filled up air. She said it was a walled city, emotionally under siege. She wanted the walls to fall down, and all that empty air come rushing in. The city exploding to meet it. The limits broken. Into the outside, limit-less. Air.

—Open the window.

This is just one morning, watching her. Her naked body moves against the light. Her feet upon the floor in a firm stance. Ready for long strides. Her arm flung out across air, to the curtain. Pushing it back, wider, as if there were more space to push it to: a whole prairie. Light spilling around her body, edging its curving lines. No sudden mountains, just a gentle expanse. Her skin eager for wind. Her hair like grain.

She opens the window and a mountain comes in.

I lift the sheets and she spreads over me.

—What is it?

—Nothing.

—No, you're worried. You're moody. It's something.

—O.K. But I don't know. It's not you.

—I love you.

—It's not you, I said that. It's not you.

—It's us?

—Well, it's everything. The city.

—You mean it's the prairie.

—The mountains.

—'In the mountains, there you feel free.'

—Bullshit.

—Eliot.

—I know. It's still bullshit. Anyway, that's one of these fake old women talking. Don't sidetrack me with quotations.

—O.K., it's the mountains. And an absence of prairie. You're homesick.

—God!

—I'm sorry, I didn't mean that lightly.

—O.K. But anyway, I'm not homesick. I don't want to go back. At least, I don't think I want to go back. Hell, I don't know. Do I want to go back?

—You'd feel better? More free?

—You can get trapped there, too.

—You can get trapped anywhere.

—There it's the sky, here it's the mountains. No, I'm not kidding myself. I came away because I was fucking bored to fucking death. I know that. I know that.

—You're not bored here, are you?

—It's not a question of boredom. It's not a question of art galleries and decent movies. It's not even a question of people. I could have met you back there.

—Uh-uh. I'm not prairies. Lived all my life in Vancouver.

—So what?

—So this, you couldn't have met *me* back there. There's no one *like* me back there. You remember what you told me? The first twenty years of your life, you never saw a mountain. Never saw the sea. I mean, Christ, what does that *do* to people? I lived by the sea all my life. Vacations on Vancouver Island. Camped at Long Beach. I mean, what did you think about, when you read about the sea? When you were in school, reading a poem, and the poet was talking about the sea, what did you think of? What kind of image came into your mind?

—Photographs. Movies. Maybe grain moving, in a large field. Things like that.

—Your mind must be so goddamned *horizontal!*

—That's your diagnosis?

—Damn right it is. What's a horizontal mind doing in Vancouver? Every time it turns around it hits against a highrise.

—Like you. You're vertical?

—Hey, parts of me are.

—Highrise?

—Turn out the light, will you? Can you reach it?

—O.K., you can come in now.

I didn't know what to expect. Three weeks we'd been together, this was the first time I'd been to her apartment: an attic, really, in one of the last old houses in Kitsilano. Apartment blocks going up (vertically) all around.

What she'd put on was an artist's smock, once white, smudged with paint in horizontal streaks. (I'd begun to notice, a lot, what was horizontal, what was vertical.) And paintings all around the walls, stacked canvases, one on the easel. I felt uneasily as if I were in a movie set. Archetypal artist's studio, reality copying cliché.

The paintings were, of course, horizontal. Horizon-tall. Most of them absolutely simple: a horizontal line close to the foot of the canvas, one solid block of colour below, another above; but very subtle colours. Very precise colours.

—I abstract them, she explained. There are lots of colours in grain. This one's an early colour, wheat about three weeks before it's ripe. That sky is a sunset green: yes, green, there's sometimes green in the sky, just tiny streaks and suggestions. Only I take that one shade and extend it over the whole sky, the whole block of colour. I've never seen a sky like that, of course, but I'm sure it could happen. Anything could happen to prairie skies.

I saw one painting different. (It looked more vertical.) A Mondrian in shades of gold, entitled 'Streak Mosaic.'

—This is seen from above?

—That's right. You fly over the fields, they look like that. Or at least I guess they would, I've never flown myself.

—I like the title.

—It's a disease.

—What?

—It's a crop disease. Streak mosaic. Look, that colour there—that's it. The whole field's useless, the grain will never ripen, never come to maturity. This field here, next to it, is healthy. There's no reason for it. It just happens sometimes. Next year, the same field could be perfectly O.K.

—And the farmer?

—There's nothing he can do about it. By the time it shows, it's too late. His horse'll know about it before he does.

—Is this a new painting?

—No, it's an old one. Before I met you. Do you like them?

—They're tremendous.

—Crap. They're unoriginal. They're exercises. I'm just beginning, I've a long way to go. I mean, what could be more clichéd? The prairie as horizontal lines. I even drew these lines with a ruler. At least I might have done them freehand, got a few waves and lumps into them. The prairie isn't as flat as that, not really.

—That's what everyone says. But isn't the prairie just what you think it is?

—Uh-uh. No. The prairie's itself. It's a sky magnet. It pulls you upwards, into the air. When I was a kid, I had this tremendous urge to fly. There was so much sky, I kept jumping into it. Icarus was born on the prairies, I bet he was.

—But you never did fly.

—No. I came down on the train.

And then two days later she didn't show up for a date. I went round to her place and confronted the landlady. She'd gone. She'd packed up and left. No messages. No forwarding address.

She'd left only one painting behind.

2

—Where you headed?

—Dry Mud. (Absurd, the name of her town. I'd laughed for ten minutes straight when she told me.)

—Thought so. This road don't go anyplace else.

The hitch-hiker climbed in the front seat beside me. I'd driven over 1200 miles alone, it seemed about time for some company. He was a kid in blue jeans and a checked sports shirt; it looked like he was starting to grow his hair long.

—Do you live in Dry Mud?

—All my life.

—What's it like?

—O.K., I guess. It's a place. Don't figure it's too much different from other places.

He spoke horizontally. I thought, goddamnit, I've got to get this horizontal/vertical thing out of my head! There must be other ways of thinking about life. But he did speak horizontally, that was the only word you could use. Long vowels, long pauses between words. Clipped t's and d's sticking up like telegraph poles, along a flat horizon.

—It's a pretty small place, I guess?

—Depends what you call big.

I thought, in a small town everybody knows everybody else. Should I ask him about her? Whether she's come home?

The car veered suddenly, lurched, bounced, stopped, settled. A flat tire. As if there weren't enough things flat around here.

—Hey, you look tired. Been driving long? Let me fix it. I'm good at fixing things. Go stretch your legs.

So I got out, went over to the side of the road, sat down and looked at the sky. The kid was whistling between his teeth, working slowly but efficiently. There was plenty of time. I looked at the sky.

So the prairie isn't really flat? Maybe. But it sure is flat around Dry Mud. I'd never seen country so flat. I'd never seen so much sky. Nothing to hold you down. It looked like one of her paintings: I could see the shades of blue, resolving obsessively into monochrome, one massive block of colour. It was unreal. I began to feel, this is unreal. This doesn't exist, it's a movie. Who ever heard of a town called Dry Mud anyway? It's all ridiculous. I've fallen inside one of her paintings. I know these colours. (I am these colours.) I know that shade of wheat over there. . . .

—Hey, that field over there. It's diseased, isn't it?

The kid looked up from tightening the bolts. Looked at the field. Narrowed his eyes. Looked back at me.

—You some kind of scientist?

So I guess I was prepared for Dry Mud itself. Another movie set; just like her studio, totally unreal. The archetypal cliché prairie town. Main street with buildings down one side, one big grain elevator on the other. All the stores with false fronts.

I asked the kid if he knew her. Sure he knew her. She left for the coast a year ago. No, she hadn't come back. What would she come back for? Her folks were dead. Nothing for her here. What would she want to come back for?

I dropped him on the main street, spun the car round in the dust in front of the grain elevator, and started quickly back. I didn't want to look at the rears of the buildings. I was afraid they wouldn't be there.

Two hours later I was still driving and I hadn't come to anywhere and that was all wrong. There should have been some small town, a cross-roads, *some*thing. I must have missed a turn-off. But goddamnit, there hadn't *been* any turn-off! Anyway, the fuel gauge said zero, so I pulled over to the side of the road and stopped. Took a look at the map. Wondered where I was. The landscape had no distinguishing features.

O.K., so it wasn't flat. There was a gentle rise to my left. A single, totally improbable tree stuck out of a field to my right. The sun had started down. I looked up into the big sky, and I felt what she called the magnet. The top of my head flipped off. I was being pulled upwards. I wanted to fly.

I laughed at myself and got out of the car. Kicked up the dust in the road. Looked up again. Ribs of cloud were riding, high, high in the sky. I had an acute sensation of its dome shape, but I couldn't pinpoint where the inside surface was. A crazy thought came into my head.

It didn't go away.

I laughed again, and got back into the car. Got out again. Climbed up onto the roof of the car. Surveyed the landscape from that height. Flapped my arms and jumped off.

—Son of a *bitch*! I rolled over in the road, clutching at my ankle. Tried to stand up, and couldn't. Sat there watching it swell.

The kid arrived about half an hour later, in a beat-up panel truck, with a case of beer and a big can of gas.

—Figured you'd end up stuck. Saw you take the wrong turn at the edge of town. Say, what'd you do to your ankle?

—I think it's sprained.

—Too bad. Want a beer?

—Sure.

So we sat together, leaning against my car, and consumed a slow beer. It was getting steadily darker.

—Where does this road go, anyway?

—Nowhere.

—Nowhere at all?

—Used to be a few shacks at the end of it. Ain't nothing now. Used to be a mine for something, but it ran out. Nothing here now but wheat.

—For a road going nowhere, it's in pretty good condition.

—Yeah, well, it's kept up. It's useful. You can bring in the crops, it's easier driving than stubble. A road don't have to go somewhere to be useful.

(A pause, while I appreciated the symbolism.)

—Well, I sure didn't get anywhere.

—Were you trying to?

—I was looking for that girl, I explained. Dropped everything. Walked out on my job, bought a second-hand car, drove through the mountains.

Just like that. Because I thought maybe she came back here. Now look at me.

—How'd you do it?

—What?

—Your ankle. How'd you manage to bust your ankle driving a car?

—Well, I'd stopped and got out. (Another pause.) Well, I . . . This is stupid, you know, I . . . I jumped off the top of the car.

—Looking around?

—Trying to fly.

The kid laughed.

—Doesn't it ever get to you, I asked, sometimes? The prairie, all this sky?

—I live here.

—That makes the difference?

—Hell, it's only fields. What would I do with a mountain anyway? I'd probably shovel it flat.

—O.K. Or climb it. But here there's nothing to *do* with it all. It's just air. Try to fly, you end up like me. Or down like me. You can't climb the sky, there's too much of it.

—There's only what there is.

—Suppose you went away? What would you feel about it then?

—I ain't going away.

—Yes, but suppose.

—No good supposing. What would I want to go away for?

—That girl. She went away.

—Yeah, but you think she came back.

—I don't know. Maybe. Maybe not. Maybe all she wanted was for me to come out here. Maybe she's waiting for me in Vancouver. Or else I won't see her again. How can you tell? Streak mosaic. One field ripens, one field doesn't.

The kid in darkness, barely visible, tilting his head to drink.

—I guess that's for you to figure out, he said.

—I guess so.

—Well, me, I don't figure she'll be coming back out here. Can't really say I knew her. Danced with her a couple of times. She was O.K., but she left. Most people said she would. What's more (he laughed) she took the right turn leaving town.

A chink as he threw his bottle away. Mine was only half-empty. The ankle suddenly started to hurt like hell.

NEESH

Gary Hyland

Neesh the Indian conserved words,
let us puff rollies in his shack
near his creek by the CN line,
dozing in his big rocker
while we struck matches and poses
that could have burned us all—
tough guy pre-adolescents who later
scrubbed brown fingers with snow.

Ten years at least he was there
and was never once outside they say;
there were stories about what he ate
and how he got his tobacco.
In winter by the east window,
in summer by the west, he watched us
playing on the long cinder hills
by the tracks, and on and in his creek.

Often I thought about old Neesh
whether he was wise or mad,
whether a whole tribe slept in him
awaiting a sign of war or peace.
From Sleigh Hill one night I watched
his shadow rocking and smoking
till a winter fog intervened
and I couldn't even see the shack.

Between us, beneath the darkness
and the fog was his creek and
under the ice, Neesh had said, was water
just a bit, refusing to freeze,
keeping the mud moist, and in the mud
were seeds and creatures still alive.
It was Neesh's creek, his observation,
his voice rising through ice and fog.

AND SHE SAID, 'WHISKY?'

One day I was sitting on the stoop of this old shack doing my hair and I see a dot coming across the prairie. By the time my hair had dried and I'd put on a bonnet because of the sun I could see it was a woman. An Indian. She turned off the trail and came up and I called hello and Mother came to the door and said, 'Good Lord, what does she want?' and shut the door. The old woman saw it but didn't let on.

Indians are direct, you know. They see something, they want it, and they ask for it. If they don't get it, well, that is that. Maybe some would come back in the night and take it, but that was their nature. She stopped and said, 'Me thirst.' I went in the house and got a cup of milk from the jar and took it to her. She looked at it and giggled. I might have known Indians don't get that thirsty. She said, 'Me whisky.' Oh no, I said, we don't have whisky. Not in this house. If she'd read English I could have brought out the pledge my father had signed in England saying he'd never allow liquor, spirits, to cross his lips again. It was called The Pledge. They did things like that in those days. Temperance. Rallies. And men would actually go up on the platform and sign, with a pen, pledging that they'd be temperance the rest of their lives. So I went in and got a dipperful of water and she drank that.

She sat down. She wore a skirt and an old sweater. I think they stopped wearing their native clothes as soon as they saw the white man's clothes. On her feet she wore wool socks and moccasins and over the moccasins she had rubbers. It was hot and her feet must have been sweltering.

On the prairie, bones, big ones, and they were buffalo bones. Dad to make things neater had laid these white bones end to end for a few feet out from the door. It made a little path. She touched one and said, 'Him gone.' She meant the buffalo. There had been thousands and thousands, but when they migrated to the States like they did every year the Americans had killed them. It took years, of course. You'd see the rotting skulls out on the prairie if you walked far enough off the trail to where there were no more homesteaders.

The old woman . . . now how old would she be? You could say she was 50, which to me would be old, but maybe she was 70. With those people, some of them, you can't tell. They get old and they just keep the same oldness.

If I'd only had some paper and pencil with me because that old woman told me about the buffalo. She could speak some English but mostly she used gestures. Very good at it. She'd stick her little old wrinkled head out and sniff, nose going like this, squinch, and you could see a bull on guard smelling for a wolf or maybe a white man or maybe an Indian. She would put out her hands so far and stroke the air and do something with her hands and even I could see she was describing a rifle, stroking the butt and working the bolt. She crept through the grass. She'd aim. She'd run forward and cut, cut, cut. That was the women cutting up the buffalo that the men had killed. She'd thrust in. That was cutting the jugular vein of a wounded animal. She would move her arms out wide, from horizon to horizon and say, 'Many.' She'd say that several times.

Indians had horses, of course, and were wonderful riders and she'd give little yips and prance up and down and that was the riders coming in to the camp. She'd rub her tummy and that meant, I'm sure, that they'd have a big feast and she showed me how they dried the meat. We'd call it jerky today. They made pemmican of it, dried meat, ground up, berries and lots of grease. It kept well. She went through all this, a few English words, some muttering in her own tongue, Cree, I guess. And there was the whole story of her life and the sighting of the buffalo down by the river and the young men riding off, yipping, with their rifles. 'Bang, bang, bang,' she'd say. They'd caught up to the herd.

She was simply the most marvelous mimic you've ever seen and not only with her face but with her body. This went on for at least an hour, a whole education for a white child to tell her what the Indian life was like and how it was the Indians' life to hunt and kill the buffalo. She was telling me what it was like for her long before the first settlers came, long before the half-breeds came up the river from Red River. I can see me now, sitting on the stoop fascinated and this old woman putting on this simply marvelous show. A wonderful theater.

Then she sat down in the grass again and I clapped my hands, clapped and clapped, and then you know what that old lady did. Guess what?

She looked at me, grinned. No teeth. Just gums. She grinned at me and held out her hand and she said, 'Whisky?'

As reported to BARRY BROADFOOT

REGIONAL LITERATURE

True regional literature is above all distinctive in that it illustrates the effect of particular, rather than general, physical, economic and racial features upon the lives of ordinary men and women. It should and usually does do many other things besides, but if it does not illustrate the influence of a limited and peculiar environment, it is not true regional literature.

EDWARD McCOURT

SELF-REFRACTING

Ed Upward

i followed the stream to a river
the river had turned into glass
i followed the glass to the ocean
the ocean had turned into grass
i followed the grass to the bottom
the bottom had turned into stone
i followed the stone through the ages
the ages had turned into bone
i followed the bone to the marrow
the marrow had melted away
it fed the stream and the river
and turned all the stone into clay

the clay was all littered with fishes
i fished with a vein and a fang
the fishes i caught were all people
their scales were all notes that i sang
        i freed them
        i freed them
        i freed them
i tossed them away to the sea
their eyes were all mirrors of laughter
reflecting my thoughts into me

THE PRIDE

John Newlove

I

The image/ the pawnees
in their earth-lodge villages,
the clear image
of teton sioux, wild
fickle people the chronicler says,

the crazy dogs, men
tethered with leather dog-thongs
to a stake, fighting until dead,

image: arikaras
with traded spanish sabre blades
mounted on the long
heavy buffalo lances,
riding the sioux
down, the centaurs, the horsemen
scouring the level plains
in war or hunt
until smallpox got them,
4,000 warriors,

image—of a desolate country,
a long way between fires,
unfound lakes, mirages, cold rocks,
and lone men going through it,
cree with good guns
creating terror in athabaska
among the inhabitants, frightened
stone-age people, 'so that
they fled at the mere sight
of a strange smoke miles away.'

II

This western country crammed
with the ghosts of indians,
haunting the coastal stones and shores,
the forested pacific islands,
mountains, hills and plains:

beside the ocean ethlinga,
man in the moon, empties
his bucket, on
a sign from Spirit
of the Wind ethlinga
empties his bucket, refreshing
the earth, and it rains
on the white cities;

that black joker, broken-
jawed raven, most prominent
among haida and tsimshyan tribes,
is in the kwakiutl
dance masks too—
it was he who brought fire,
food and water to man,
the trickster;

and thunderbird hilunga,
little thought of
by haida for lack of thunderstorms
in their district, goes
by many names, exquisite disguises
carved in the painted wood,

he is nootka tootooch, the wings
causing thunder and the tongue
or flashing eyes engendering
rabid white lightning,
whose food was whales,

called kwunusela by the kwakiutl,
it was he who laid down the house-logs
for the people at Place
Where Kwunusela Alighted;

in full force and virtue
and terror of the law, eagle—
he is authority, the sun
assumed his form once,
the sun which used to be
a flicker's eggs, successfully transformed;

and malevolence comes to the land,
the wild woman of the woods;
grinning, she wears
a hummingbird in her hair,
d'sonoqua, the furious one—

they are all ready
to be found, the legends
and the people, or
all their ghosts and memories,
whatever is strong enough
to be remembered.

III
But what image, bewildered
son of all men
under the hot sun,
do you worship,
what completeness
do you hope to have
from these tales,
a half-understood massiveness, mirage,
in men's minds—what
is your purpose;

with what force
will you proceed
along a line
neither straight nor short,
whose future
you cannot know
or result foretell,
whose meaning is still
obscured as the incidents
occur and accumulate?

IV
The country moves on;
there are orchards in the interior,
the mountain passes
are broken, the foothills
covered with cattle and fences,
and the fading hills covered;

but the plains are bare,
not barren, easy
for me to love their people,
for me to love their people
without selection.

V

In 1787, the old cree saukamappee,
aged 75 or thereabout, speaking then
of things that had happened when he was 16,
just a man, told david thompson,
of the raids the shoshonis,
the snakes, had made on the westward-
reaching peigan, of their war-parties
sometimes sent 10 days journey to enemy camps,
the men all afoot in battle array for
the encounter, crouching
behind their giant shields;

the peigan armed with guns
drove these snakes out of the plains,
the plains where their strength had been,
where they had been settled since living
memory (though nothing is remembered
beyond a grandfather's time),
to the west of the rockies;

these people moved without rest,
backward and forward with the wind,
the seasons, the game, great herds,
in hunger and abundance—

in summer and in the bloody fall
they gathered on the killing grounds,
fat and shining with fat, amused
with the luxuries of war and death,

relieved from the steam of knowledge,
consoled by the stream of blood
and steam rising from the fresh hides
and tired horses, wheeling in their pride
on the sweating horses, their pride.

VI
Those are all stories;
the pride, the grand poem
of our land, of the earth itself,
will come, welcome, and
sought for, and found,
in a line of running verse,
sweating, our pride;

we seize on
what has happened before,
one line only
will be enough,

a single line and
then the sunlit brilliant image suddenly floods us
with understanding, shocks our
attentions, and all desire
stops, stands alone;

we stand alone,
we are no longer lonely
but have roots,
and the rooted words
recur in the mind, mirror, so that
we dwell on nothing else, in nothing else,
touched, repeating them,
at home freely
at last, in amazement;

'the unyielding phrase
in tune with the epoch,'
the thing made up
of our desires,
not of its words, not only
of them, but of something else,
as well, that which we desire
so ardently, that which
will not come when
it is summoned alone,
but grows in us
and idles about and hides
until the moment is due—

the knowledge of
our origins, and where
we are in truth,
whose land this is
and is to be.

VII

The unyielding phrase:
when the moment is due, then
it springs upon us
out of our own mouths,
unconsidered, overwhelming
in its knowledge, complete—

not this handful
of fragments, as the indians
are not composed of
the romantic stories
about them, or of the stories
they tell only, but
still ride the soil
in us, dry bones a part
of the dust in our eyes,
needed and troubling
in the glare, in
our breath, in our
ears, in our mouths,
in our bodies entire, in our minds, until at
last we become them

in our desires, our desires,
mirages, mirrors, that are theirs, hard-
riding desires, and they
become our true forbears, moulded
by the same wind or rain,
and in this land we
are their people, come
back to life.

STONE HAMMER POEM

Robert Kroetsch

1
This stone
become a hammer
of stone, this maul

is the colour
of bone (no,
bone is the colour
of this stone maul).

The rawhide loops
are gone, the
hand is gone, the
buffalo's skull
is gone;

the stone is
shaped like the skull
of a child.

2
This paperweight on my desk

where I begin
this poem   was

found in a wheatfield
lost (this hammer,
this poem).

Cut to a function,
this stone was
(the hand is   gone—

3
Grey, two-headed,
the pemmican maul

fell from the travois or
a boy playing   lost it in
the prairie wool or
a squaw   left it in
the brain of a buffalo or

It is a million
years older than
the hand that
chipped stone or
raised slough
water (or blood) or

4
This stone maul
was found

in the field
my grandfather
thought
was his

my father
thought was his

5
It is a stone
old as the last
Ice Age, the
retreating/the
recreating ice,
the retreating
buffalo, the
retreating Indians

(the saskatoons bloom
white (infrequently
the chokecherries the
highbush cranberries the
pincherries bloom
white along the barbed
wire fence (the
pemmican   winter

6
This stone maul
stopped a plow
long enough for one
Gott im Himmel.

The Blackfoot (the
Cree?) not

finding the maul
cursed.

? did he curse
? did he try to
go back
? what happened
I have to/I want
to know (not *know*)
? WHAT HAPPENED

7
The poem
is the stone
chipped and hammered
until it is shaped
like the stone
hammer, the maul.

8
Now the field is
mine because
I gave it
(for a price)

to a young man
(with a growing son)
who did not

notice that the land
did not belong

to the Indian who
gave it to the Queen
(for a price) who
gave it to the CPR

gave it to my grandfather
(for a price) who
gave it to my father
(50 bucks an acre
Gott im Himmel I cut
down all the trees I
picked up all the stones) who
gave it to his son
(who sold it)

9
This won't
surprise you.

My grandfather
lost the stone maul.

10
My father (retired)
grew raspberries.
He dug in his potato patch.
He drank one glass of wine
each morning.
He was lonesome
for death.

He was lonesome for the
hot wind on his face, the smell
of horses, the distant
hum of a threshing machine,
the oilcan he carried, the weight
of a crescent wrench in his hind pocket.

He was lonesome for his absent
son and his daughters,
for his wife, for his own
brothers and sisters and
his own mother and father.
He found the stone maul
on a rockpile in the
northwest corner of what
he thought of
as his wheatfield.

He kept it (the
stone maul) on the railing
of the back porch in
a raspberry basket.

11
I keep it
on my desk
(the stone).
Sometimes I use it
in the (hot) wind
(to hold down paper)

smelling a little of cut
grass or maybe even of
ripening wheat or of
buffalo blood hot
in the dying sun.

Sometimes I write
my poems for that

stone hammer.

Notes on the Contributors

BARBOUR, DOUGLAS (b.1940). Born in Winnipeg, Man., and educated at Acadia, Dalhousie, and Queen's Universities, he teaches Canadian literature at the University of Alberta. His books of poetry include *Land Fall* (1971), *A Poem as Long as the Highway* (1971), *White* (1972), *Songbook* (1973), and *Visions of My Grandfather* (1976). HOUSES, 133.

BOWERING, GEORGE (b.1935) was born in Penticton, B.C. A graduate of the University of British Columbia, he served as an aerial photographer with the RCAF, stationed in Edmonton. Bowering later taught in Calgary, Montreal, and Vancouver, and is currently on the faculty of Simon Fraser University. *Rocky Mountain Foot*, his collection of poems about Alberta, won the Governor General's Award in 1969, along with *The Gangs of Kosmos*. His other books include *Points on the Grid* (1964), *Touch: Selected Poems, 1960-1970* (1971), *In the Flesh* (1974), and *Flycatcher* (1974), a collection of stories. He has also written a novel, *Mirror on the Floor* (1967), and a critical study, *Al Purdy* (1970). GRANDFATHER, 64; THE OIL, 237.

BREWSTER, ELIZABETH (b.1922). Born in Chipman, N.B., she is a graduate of the University of New Brunswick, the University of Toronto Library School, and Indiana University. She has taught and worked in the library at the University of Alberta (Edmonton), and currently teaches at the University of Saskatchewan (Saskatoon). Her volumes of poetry include *East Coast* (1951), *Lillooet* (1954), *Roads* (1957), *Passage of Summer: Selected Poems* (1969), *Sunrise North* (1972), *In Search of Eros* (1974), and *Sometimes I Think of Moving* (1977). She has also written a novel, *The Sisters* (1974). THE FUTURE OF POETRY IN CANADA, 259.

BROADFOOT, BARRY (b.1926). Born in Winnipeg and a graduate of the University of Manitoba, he worked for the *Winnipeg Tribune*, the *Vancouver News-Herald*, and the *Edmonton Bulletin*. He has been a journalist in Vancouver since 1953. His three popular books of oral history, based on taped interviews, include *Ten Lost Years, 1929-1939: Memories of Canadians Who Survived the Depression* (1973), *Six War Years, 1936-1945: Memories of Canadians at Home and Abroad* (1974), and *The Pioneer Years, 1895-1914; Memories of Settlers Who Opened the West* (1976). NOT A PENNY IN THE WORLD, 54; HOW I LEARNED TO MAKE BREAD, 68; THE GREAT LONE LAND, 73; AND SHE SAID, 'WHISKY', 268.

BUTLER, WILLIAM FRANCIS (1838-1910). Born in Tipperary, Ire., he was commissioned in the British Army in 1858 and came to Canada with his regiment in 1867 to combat the Fenian Raids. In 1870 he was sent to Red River as an intelligence officer, in advance of the expedition led by Col. Wolseley. (His description of a meeting with Louis Riel at Fort Garry begins on page 16.) Asked to report on the state of affairs at Hudson Bay Company posts on the Saskatchewan R., he travelled as far as the Rocky Mountains. This winter journey of 2,700 miles is vividly described in *The Great Lone Land* (1872), a classic account of travel in nineteenth-century Canada, which was followed by other books. *Remember Butler* (1967) is a biography by Edward McCourt. THE CREES, 3; THE PRAIRIE OCEAN, 5; HUNDREDS OF THOUSANDS OF SKELETONS . . . ,10; AN ENCOUNTER WITH RIEL, 16. See also THE GREAT LONE LAND, 73.

CLOUTIER, EUGENE (b.1921). Born in Sherbrooke, Que., he was educated at Laval University and the Sorbonne. A writer of novels and travel books in French, he lives in Montreal. The two extracts in this anthology come from *No Passport: A Discovery of Canada* (1967), Joyce Marshall's abridgement and English translation of Cloutier's *Le Canada sans passeport*. IN THE LITERATURE OF SASKATCHEWAN . . . , 83; A CHILD ASKED ME . . . , 257.

CONNOR, RALPH (1860-1937) was the pseudonym of Charles William Gordon, who was born in Glengarry County, C.W. (Ont.), and educated at the University of Toronto and Edinburgh University. Ordained a Presbyterian minister in 1890, he was stationed at Banff, Alta, and later served as senior Protestant chaplain to the Canadian forces during the First World War. He returned to Winnipeg, where he was pastor of St Stephen's until his death. His romantic and melodramatic tales, which often deal with pioneer life, are based on an evangelical religious commitment. Though he wrote over 30 novels, Connor is best remembered for *Black Rock* (1898), a tale of the Selkirks, *The Sky Pilot* (1899), *The Man from Glengarry* (1901), and *Glengarry School Days* (1902). His autobiography, *Postscript to Adventure* (1938), was edited by his son J. King Gordon. THE PILOT'S MEASURE, 65.

DODDS, G. L. One of the many successful and enterprising real-estate dealers during the period of Prairie settlement from 1885 to 1914, he was the editor of, and major contributor to, *The Last West* (1906), which extolled Prairie life and agriculture and also carried advertising for businessmen who, like Dodds, made their fortunes buying and selling large tracts of land, usually with the help of political connections. ACROSTIC, 49.

DUMONT, GABRIEL (1838-1906). Born at Red River (Man.) of Métis parents, he moved to Batoche after the Rebellion in 1870 and became head of the Métis community there. In 1884 he was part of the delegation that went to Montana to invite Louis Riel to return to the Saskatchewan valley and organize a movement for redress of grievances. He joined Riel's provisional government and became his adjutant-general in charge of military operations. In the North West Rebellion of 1885 he led the rebel forces to victory at Duck Lake and Fish Creek, but suffered defeat at Batoche. He fled to the United States, where he lived for several years, travelling with Buffalo Bill's Wild West Show. After the rebels were granted amnesty, Dumont returned to Batoche. THE BATTLE OF DUCK LAKE, 19.

FALCON, PIERRE (1793-1876). Born at Elbow Fort, Rupert's Land, he entered the service of the North West Company in 1808 and later joined the Hudson's Bay Company when the two companies united in 1821. He retired from the fur trade in 1825, settled on a farm near Grantown, and in 1885 was appointed magistrate for the White Horse Plain district. He was present at the Battle of Seven Oaks, which took place in the Red River Settlement in 1816, and later wrote 'Chanson de la Grenouillère', the earliest and most famous of his folk ballads about contemporary events and people, which has been translated by James Reaney (page 6). THE BATTLE OF SEVEN OAKS, 6.

GEDDES, GARY (b.1940) was born in Vancouver, B.C., but spent four of his childhood years on a farm near Yorkton, Sask. Educated at the University of British Columbia and the University of Toronto, he is a freelance writer, editor, and teacher. His volumes of original poetry include *Poems* (1971), *Rivers Inlet* (1972), *Snakeroot* (1973), *Letter of the Master of Horse* (1973), and *War & Other Measures* (1976). He has also edited *20th Century Poetry and Poetics* (1969) and *Skookum Wawa: Writing of the Canadian Northwest* (1975), and co-edited (with Phyllis Bruce) *15 Canadian Poets* (1971). SNAKEROOT, 243.

GRANT, GEORGE MONRO (1835-1902). Born at Albion Mines, N.S., educated at Glasgow University, and ordained in the Church of Scotland in 1860, he became minister of St Matthew's Church, Halifax, and was made moderator of the Presbyterian Church in Canada in 1899. He was also principal of Queen's University from 1877 until his death. During the summer of 1872 Grant acted as secretary to Sir Sandford Fleming for an exploratory journey from the Great Lakes to the Pacific in search of a route for a transcontinental railway. His diary of the trip, which Grant revised and published as *Ocean to Ocean* (1873), has become a travel classic. WESTERN BUMPTIOUSNESS, 13.

GRAY, JAMES (b.1906). Born in Whitemouth, Man., he worked as a journalist and then as a public-relations executive for an oil company in Calgary until his retirement. *The Winter Years* (1966), his first book, is an autobiographical account of the Depression on the Prairie. Subsequent popular social histories include *Men Against the Desert* (1970), *A Boy from Winnipeg* (1970), *Red Lights on the Prairie* (1971), *Booze* (1972), and *The Roar of the Twenties* (1975). LANDLADIES AND A WANT-AD HUSBAND, 116.

GROVE, FREDERICK PHILIP (1879-1948). Born Felix Paul Greve in Radomno on the Polish-Prussian border, he was a writer and translator in Germany before coming to Canada in 1909-10. He began teaching school in Manitoba in 1912 and it was there that he started to write in English. In 1929 he moved to Ottawa, where he was editor of Graphic Press for a year, and spent the rest of his life on a farm near Simcoe, Ont. An important figure among early modern Canadian novelists, he wrote eight ambitiously conceived novels—including *Settlers of the Marsh* (1925) and *The Master of the Mill* (1944)—that explore universal themes and often contain powerful descriptions of nature that illuminate man's struggle against a harsh environment. *Over Prairie Trails* (1922) is a well-known volume of nature essays. Desmond Pacey edited a collection of his previously unpublished short stories, *Tales from the Margin* (1971), and *The Letters* (1976). Many of the fabrications in Grove's autobiography, *In Search of Myself* (1946), were corrected by Douglas Spettigue's revisionist biography, *Frederick Philip Grove: The European Years* (1973). THE SALE, 123. See also F.P. GROVE: THE FINDING, 131.

HAAS, MAARA (b.1920). Born and raised in Winnipeg, Man., she is the daughter of the first pharmacist of Ukrainian origin in Canada. After graduating in journalism from Berkeley University, she began a career teaching creative writing in adult education programs in Winnipeg, where she lives. Her wide range of publications—which often deal with her Ukrainian background—include radio and television scripts; short stories read on CBC's 'This Country in the Morning'; poetry; a novel, *The Street Where I Live* (1976); and occasional journalism. MANITOBA DROUGHT, 111.

HIEBERT, PAUL G. (b.1892). Born at Pilot Mound, Man., he was a professor of chemistry at the University of Manitoba for 28 years. As a writer he is known for *Sarah Binks* (1947), a satire of Prairie life and letters in the 1930s that purported to be a critical study of 'the Sweet Songstress of Saskatchewan' who won the 'Wheat Pool Medal' for such verses as 'Hi, Sooky, Ho, Sooky' and 'The Farmer is King'. With its bluff condescension and footnoted references to Professor Horace B. Marrowfat *et al.*, it is the best parody of literary criticism in Canadian literature. A sequel, *Willows Revisited* (1967), takes the same satiric approach to Sarah's contemporaries. OLE, 244.

HIEMSTRA, MARY (b.1897). Born in England, she was brought to Saskatchewan in 1904 when her parents joined the Barr Colony, which had been founded during the previous year by the Rev. Isaac Barr. In *Gully Farm* (1955), a nostalgic memoir of homesteading, Hiemstra recreates the immigrant experience with great warmth and humanity. PRAIRIE SETTLERS, 50; 'YOU'LL NEVER SEE IT THIS WAY AGAIN', 106.

HIND, HENRY YOULE (1823-1908). Born and educated in England, he immigrated to Canada in 1846 and in 1853 became professor of chemistry and geology at the University of Toronto. He was employed as a geologist by the Province of Canada on the Canadian Exploring Expeditions of 1857 and 1858, which investigated the agricultural possibilities of the Northwest. Among his publications are *Narrative of the Canadian Red River Exploring Expedition of 1857, and of the Assiniboine and Saskatchewan exploring expedition of 1858* (2 vols, 1859, 1860). FORT ELLICE, 11.

HYLAND, GARY (b.1940). Born in Moose Jaw, Sask., where he was raised and educated, he teaches English at Riverview Collegiate, Moose Jaw. His chapbooks include *Poems from a Loft* (1974) and *Home Street* (1976). He has also written poems for CBC programs and published in Canadian literary magazines. NEESH, 267.

KANE, PAUL (1810-71). Born in Ireland, he came to Canada with his family and settled in York (Toronto). After studying portrait painting, he travelled and worked in the United States before moving to Europe to pursue his art studies. He developed an interest in Indian life and in 1846 set out on a tour of Canada that lasted two years and took him as far as the Pacific Ocean. The result of this trip was 100 beautiful canvases of Indian subjects, painted in Toronto from the numerous sketches Kane brought back with him. *Assiniboin Hunting Buffalo* on page 8 is one of such memorable oil paintings. Kane's voluminous notes also provided the basis for his travel book, *Wanderings of an Artist Among the Indians of North America* (1859), which became a Canadian classic. BUFFALO HUNT, 8.

KELSEY, HENRY (c.1667-1724). Born in London, he was apprenticed to the Hudson's Bay Company in 1684 and sent to York Factory on Hudson Bay. In 1690-2 he made a memorable journey with Indians to the Canadian plains, and is thought to be the first white man to view the Prairies and see the buffalo and the grizzly bear. Although chiefly remembered for this trip, he played a major part in most of the significant events in Hudson Bay during his 40 years of service to the Company. In 1718 he was made governor of all the bay settlements and served in this capacity until 1722, when he was recalled to London. His journals, which contain an account of his famous journey and a rhymed prologue, were discovered in 1926. Edited by A. G. Doughty and Chester Martin, they were published in *The Kelsey Papers* (1929). BY ENGLISH YET NOT SEEN, 4.

KREISEL, HENRY (b.1922). Born in Vienna, he escaped from Nazi-occupied Austria in 1938, was interned in England during the Second World War, and came to Canada in 1941. A graduate of the University of Toronto and the University of London, he is professor of English and vice-president of the University of Alberta. His two novels are *The Rich Man* (1948) and *The Betrayal* (1964). He has also written short stories and edited *Aphrodite and other poems* (1958), the lyrics of John Heath. THE PRAIRIE: A STATE OF MIND, 247.

KROETSCH, ROBERT (b.1927). Born at Heisler, Alta, he studied at the University of Alberta, Middlebury College, and the State University of Iowa. Since 1961 he has taught English at the State University of New York (Binghamton). His books include *But We Are Exiles* (1965), a novel set in Alberta that parodies the career of William Aberhart; *Alberta* (1968); *The Studhorse Man* (1969), which received the Governor General's Award for fiction; *Gone Indian* (1973); *Badlands*(1975); and two poetry collections, *The Stone Hammer Poems* (1975) and *The Ledger* (1975). F. P. GROVE: THE FINDING, 131; ELEGY FOR WONG TOY, 202; A CONVERSATION WITH MARGARET LAURENCE, 258; STONE HAMMER POEM, 277.

LAURENCE, MARGARET (b.1926). Born in Neepawa, Man., she was educated at United College, Winnipeg, and lived for several years in Somaliland and Ghana. After dividing her time between England and Canada, she settled near Peterborough, Ont., in 1970. Her early books deal with African themes. *The Stone Angel* (1964), Laurence's first novel set in the Canadian Prairie, marked her emergence as a major novelist. She has also written *A Jest of God* (1966), filmed as 'Rachel, Rachel'; *The Fire-Dwellers* (1969); *A Bird in the House* (1970), a collection of semi-autobiographical short stories set in Manawaka, Man., a fictional community modelled on Neepawa; *The Diviners* (1975); and *Heart of a Stranger* (1976), a collection of essays. THE LOONS, 193.

LIVESAY, DOROTHY (b.1909). Born in Winnipeg, Man., she was raised in Ontario and studied at the University of Toronto and the Sorbonne. A social worker in Montreal, New Jersey, and Vancouver during the Depression, she has since taught in Zambia and at the Universities of British Columbia, Alberta, and Victoria, and has been writer-in-residence at the Universities of New Brunswick and Manitoba, where she now teaches. A journalist, editor, and teacher as well as a poet, she has won numerous awards. Her books include *Green Pitcher* (1928), *Signpost* (1932), *Day and Night* (1944), *Poems for People*, (1947), *New Poems* (1956), *Selected Poems: 1926-1956* (1957), *The Unquiet Bed* (1967), *Plainsongs* (1969), and *Collected Poems: Two Seasons* (1972). She has also written a memoir, *A Winnipeg Childhood* (1973), and edited *Forty Women Poets of Canada* (1972) and *Woman's*

Eye (1974). DAY AND NIGHT, 112.

LUDWIG, JACK (b.1922). Born in Winnipeg and educated at the University of Manitoba and UCLA, he has taught for many years at the State University of New York. His lively and humorous novels about people with cultural and identity problems include *Confusions* (1963), *Above Ground* (1968), and *A Woman of Her Age* (1973). He has also published several works of sports reportage: *Hockey Night in Moscow* (1972), *Games of Fear and Winning: Sports with an Inside View* (1976); and *American Spectaculars* (1976). REQUIEM FOR BIBUL, 216.

McCLUNG, NELLIE (1873-1951). Born in Chatsworth, Ont., and raised and educated in Manitoba, she taught school until 1898, when she married. A popular and fiery lecturer, she took an active part in the work of the Women's Christian Temperance Union and in the struggle for legal and political equality for women. 'The Play' on page 84, published in *Purple Springs* (1921), is a fictional treatment of the Mock Parliament, a successful suffragette meeting held on the evening of 28 Jan. 1914 at the Walker Theatre, in Winnipeg, with Nellie McClung as 'premier'. In 1914 she moved to Alberta and sat in the provincial legislature from 1921 to 1926. As a writer McClung was lively, vivid, and often sentimental. Her first novel, *Sowing Seeds in Danny* (1908), enjoyed a great success and was followed by numerous other novels, collections of short stories, and memoirs. THE PLAY, 84.

McCOURT, EDWARD (1907-72) was born in Ireland. Brought to Alberta by his parents in 1909, he was educated at the University of Alberta and Oxford, and taught at the University of Saskatchewan from 1944 until his retirement. He wrote five novels about the Prairie: *Music at the Close* (1947), *Home is the Stranger* (1950), *The Wooden Sword* (1956), *Walk Through the Valley* (1958), and *Fasting Friar* (1963). His other books were *The Canadian West in Fiction* (1949; rev. 1970); *Remember Butler* (1967), a biography of the author of *The Great Lone Land; The Road Across Canada* (1965); *Saskatchewan* (1968); and *The Yukon and Northwest* (1969). TRUE REGIONAL LITERATURE . . . , 269.

McKINNON, BARRY (b.1944). Born and raised in Calgary, Alta, he lives in Prince George, B.C., where he teaches English at the College of New Caledonia. His six volumes of poetry include *I Wanted to Say Something* (1975), an extract from which begins on page 70; *Death of a Lyric Poet* (1975); and *Songs and Speeches* (1976). I WANTED TO SAY SOMETHING, 70.

MANDEL, ELI (b.1922). Born in Estevan, Sask., he studied at the Universities of Saskatchewan and Toronto. He has taught at the Collège Militaire Royale, the University of Alberta, and York University, where he has been a professor of English and Humanities since 1967. The dense texture of his poetry has been influenced by Northrop Frye's 'mythopoetics'. Mandel's books include *Fuseli Poems* (1960), *Black and Secret Man* (1964), *An Idiot Joy* (1967), *Crusoe: Poems New and Selected* (1973), and *Stony Plain* (1973). He has also edited several anthologies of Canadian literature and criticism, including the influential *Contexts of Canadian Criticism* (1971). THERE IS NO ONE HERE EXCEPT US COMEDIANS, 213.

MARRIOTT, ANNE (b.1913). Born and educated in Victoria, B.C., she lives in North Vancouver, where she teaches creative writing workshops in elementary and secondary schools. Her collections include *The Wind Our Enemy* (1939), drawn from her own experience of living for several months on a farm near Saskatoon during the thirties; *Calling Adventures!* (1941), which won the Governor General's Award; *Salt Marsh and other poems* (1942); *Sandstone and other poems* (1945); and *Countries* (1971). THE WIND OUR ENEMY, 100.

MARTY, SID (b.1944). Born in England, he was brought to Canada in 1945 and raised in Medicine Hat, Alta. After studying at Sir George Williams University and the University of Calgary, he worked as a folk-singer in Montreal before moving west to work as a park warden in Jasper. His poetry collections include *Tumbleweed Harvest* (1973) and

Headwaters (1973). THE PRAIRIE, 74.

MAYNARD, FREDELLE BRUSER (b.1922) grew up in various towns in Saskatchewan and Manitoba. She studied at the Universities of Manitoba and Toronto and at Radcliffe College, where she took her doctorate, before teaching at Radcliffe and Wellesley. She has written *Raisins and Almonds* (1964), a charming memoir of her childhood on the Prairie, and *Guiding Your Child to a More Creative Life* (1973). She lives in Toronto. SATISFACTION GUARANTEED—THE 1928 EATON'S CATALOGUE, 93.

MITCHELL, W. O. (b.1914). Born and raised in Weyburn, Sask., and educated at the Universities of Manitoba and Alberta, he has lived for many years in High River, Alta. A master of the tall tale, Mitchell uses comedy to disguise his sharp social criticism. He created the popular series of 'Jake and the Kid' stories, which appeared in *Maclean's* and were broadcast on CBC Radio in the forties and fifties. A collection of these stories was published as *Jake and the Kid* in 1961 and won a Stephen Leacock Medal for Humour. However, Mitchell's literary reputation rests largely on his first novel, *Who Has Seen the Wind* (1947). 'Saint Sammy', which first appeared in the *Atlantic Monthly* in 1940, was subsequently incorporated into the novel. Mitchell has written two other novels, *The Kite* (1962) and *The Vanishing Point* (1973), in addition to plays for stage, radio, and television, including *Back to Beulah*. SAINT SAMMY, 158.

NEWLOVE, JOHN (b.1938). Born in Regina, Sask., he grew up in several Russian farming communities in eastern Saskatchewan where his mother taught school. After studying at the University of Saskatchewan, he lived in Vancouver, Montreal, and Toronto and has worked as an editor and teacher. His books of verse include *Grave Sirs* (1962), *Elephants, Mothers and Others* (1963), *Moving in Alone* (1965), *What They Say* (1967), *Black Night Window* (1968), *The Cave* (1970), and *Lies* (1972). He edited *Canadian Poetry: The Modern Era* (1977). DOUKHOBOR, 63; THE PRIDE, 271.

RASHLEY, R. E. (1909-75). Born in England, he was brought to Saskatoon, Sask., at the age of two. He studied there at the university and later taught high school. In addition to his critical monograph, *Poetry in Canada: The First Three Steps* (1958), he wrote three volumes of verse: *Voyageur and other poems* (1946), *Portrait and other poems* (1953), and *Paso Por Aqui* (1973). NIGHT JOURNEY AND DEPARTURE, 240.

REANEY, JAMES (b.1926). Born near Stratford, Ont., and educated at the University of Toronto, he taught at the University of Manitoba from 1949 to 1961, when he became a professor of English at the University of Western Ontario. He is one of Canada's best-known poets and playwrights. His verse has been compiled in *Poems* (1972), edited by Germaine Warkentin; *Selected Longer Poems* (1975); and *Selected Shorter Poems* (1976). THE BATTLE OF SEVEN OAKS, 6.

RIEL, LOUIS (1844-85). Born near St Boniface (Man.) in the Red River Settlement, and educated in Montreal, he became leader of a group of Métis who felt threatened by the Province of Canada's plans to acquire the Hudson's Bay Company territories. His resistance (the Red River Rebellion) included the occupation of Fort Garry (Nov. 1869), the declaration of a Provisional Government, and the taking of prisoners, after which he was forced to flee across the border into the United States. Following a period of mental illness (1876-8) and of exile in the United States, he arrived at Batoche in July 1884 to lead the Métis in the abortive North West Rebellion of March 1885. Riel surrendered in May, was tried in July, found guilty of high treason, and hanged on 16 Nov. THE TESTIMONY OF LOUIS RIEL, 25.

RINGWOOD, GWEN PHARIS (b.1910). Born in Magrath, Alta, she was educated at the University of Alberta and studied playwriting at the University of North Carolina. Her plays include *Still Stands the House* (1939), which won the Dominion Drama Festival's first prize for Canadian plays, *Dark Harvest* (1945), a full-length drama, and *The*

Courtship of Marie Jenvrin (1951). STILL STANDS THE HOUSE, 135.

ROSS, SINCLAIR (b.1908). Born at Shellbrook, Sask., he joined the staff of the Royal Bank of Canada and served in many Prairie communities before moving to Montreal. He now lives and works in Spain. His writing is noteworthy for its stark psychological realism and the use of landscape as metaphor. Ross's first book, *As for Me and My House* (1941), is considered to be one of the finest novels by a Canadian; his subsequent novels are *The Well* (1958), *A Whir of Gold* (1970), and *Sawbones Memorial* (1974). Nine of his best stories, including the well-known 'A Field of Wheat' and 'The Painted Door', have been collected in *The Lamp at Noon and Other Stories* (1968). A FIELD OF WHEAT, 151.

ROY, GABRIELLE (b.1909). Born in St Boniface, Man., she was educated there and at the Normal School in Winnipeg. She taught in rural areas of the province, then studied in Europe, and eventually settled in Montreal. Since 1947 she has lived in Quebec City. All her books were written in French and are known to English-speaking readers in translation. They include *The Tin Flute* (1947), a Canadian classic about a family living in a working-class slum in Montreal during the Depression, and three semi-autobiographical books set in Manitoba: *Where Nests the Water Hen* (1951), *Street of Riches* (1957), and *The Road Past Altamont* (1966), an extract from which begins on page 165. Her latest publication is *The Enchanted Summer* (1976), a collection of stories and sketches. THE MOVE, 165.

RYGA, GEORGE (b.1932). Born to Ukrainian parents in Deep Creek, Alta, a farming community, he tried various jobs before becoming a full-time writer for radio, television, and the stage in 1962. His plays include *Indian*, first produced on CBC-TV in 1962; *The Ecstasy of Rita Joe*, premiered by the Vancouver Playhouse in 1967 and turned into a ballet for the Royal Winnipeg Ballet in 1971; *Captives of the Faceless Drummer* (1971); and *Sunrise on Sarah* (1974). He has also written three novels: *Hungry Hills* (1963), an extract from which begins on page 204; *Ballad of a Stone Picker* (1966); and *Night Desk* (1976). AUNT MATILDA, 204.

SCOBIE, STEPHEN (b.1943). Born in Scotland, he has lived in Vancouver and Edmonton, where he teaches at the University of Alberta and writes both fiction and poetry. His books include *Babylondromat* (1966), *In the Silence of the Year* (1973), *The Birken Tree* (1973), *Stone Poems* (1974), and *The Rooms We Are* (1975). STREAK MOSAIC, 260.

SECRETAN, JAMES HENRY EDWARD (1854-1926). A civil engineer in the government service, he made surveys for the Canadian Pacific Railway from 1871 to 1885. His books include *To Klondyke and Back* (1898), an account of the party he led to the Yukon by the Chilkoot Pass during the gold rush of 1898; *Out West* (1910), sketches of western characters; and *Canada's Great Highway: From the First Stake to the Last Spike* (1924). LAYING THE TRACKS, 15.

SIMPSON, KATE B. (1856-1945). Katherine Simpson-Hayes was born in Dalhousie, N.B. She settled in Regina in 1885 and began the city's first Literary and Musical Association three weeks after her arrival. A feminist and journalist, she published *Prairie Pot Pourri* (1895), a collection of verse and prose, under a pseudonym, Mary Markwell. ROUGH BEN, 31.

STEAD, ROBERT (1880-1959). Born in Middleville, Ont., he was raised near Cartwright, Man., by homesteading parents. After working as a newspaper writer, he joined the Department of Immigration and Colonization in 1919, where he superintended publicity for national parks until he retired in 1946. He wrote several novels including *Grain*, a chapter from which begins on page 76. Published in 1926, it has been reissued in the New Canadian Library. THE PRAIRIE AND THE WAR, 76.

STEGNER, WALLACE (b.1909). The well-known American writer lived with his homesteading family in Saskatchewan from 1914 to 1920. He has evoked this land, and his childhood experiences, in *Wolf Willow* (1963). THE QESTION MARK IN THE CIRCLE, 43.

SUKNASKI, ANDREW (b.1942) was born in Wood Mountain, Sask. He studied at the University of Victoria and Simon Fraser University and has worked as an editor specializing in experimental poetry. His volumes of poetry include *The Shadow of Eden Once* (1970), *Suicide Notes, Book One* (1973), *Leaving* (1974), *Leaving Wood Mountain* (1975), and *Wood Mountain Poems* (1976). PHILIP WELL, 72; LANTERNS, 106.

SUMMERS, MERNA grew up on a farm near Mannville, Alta. She lives in Edmonton, where she has worked as a free-lance journalist. *The Skating Party* (1974) is her first collection of short stories. WILLOW SONG, 178.

SZUMIGALSKI, ANNE (b.1926). Born in London, Eng., she came to Canada in 1951 and settled in Saskatoon, Sask. She works in the Saskatchewan 'Poets in the Schools' program, teaches poetry at the Saskatchewan School of the Arts, and is associate editor of *Grain*. Her books of poetry include *BOooOM* (1973), a collection of poetry for children, and *Woman Reading in Bath* (1974). NETTLES, 239.

UHER, LORNA (b.1948). Born in Swift Current, Sask., she was educated at the University of Saskatchewan (Saskatoon) and teaches high school in Swift Current. She has also taught writing at the Saskatchewan Summer School of the Arts. Her poems have appeared in many literary magazines. Her first collection, *Inside Is the Sky*, was published in 1976. IMMIGRANT, 47; I AM A LAKE, 242.

UPWARD, EDWARD (b.1948). Born in Portage la Prairie, Man., where he lives, he has written both poems and short stories that have been published in Canadian literary magazines. SELF-REFRACTING, 270.

VALGARDSON, W. D. (b.1939). Born near Gimli, Man., where he was raised, he studied at the Universities of Manitoba and Iowa. He teaches in the Creative Writing Department at the University of Victoria. Though he has written poetry, he is best known for his collections of short stories, including *Bloodflowers* (1973) and *God Is Not a Fish Inspector* (1975). HUNTING, 226.

WADDINGTON, MIRIAM (b.1917). Born in Winnipeg, Man., she studied at the University of Toronto and the Pennsylvania School of Social Work. A well-known lyric poet, she was one of the Montreal poets whose writings were a significant part of the literary climate in the 1940s. She is now professor of English at York University, Toronto. Her books of verse include *Call Them Canadians* (1968), *Driving Home: Poems New and Collected* (1972), and *The Price of Gold* (1976). She has also written a critical study, *A. M. Klein* (1970). THE NINETEEN THIRTIES ARE OVER, 176; UKRAINIAN CHURCH, 214.

WIEBE, RUDY (b.1934). Born near Fairholme, Sask., he was educated at the Mennonite High School in Coaldale, Alta., and at the Universities of Alberta and Tuebingen, West Germany. He teaches English at the University of Alberta. His books include two novels about the Mennonite immigration to western Canada, *Peace Shall Destroy Many* (1962) and *The Blue Mountains of China* (1970); *First and Vital Candle* (1966) and *The Temptations of Big Bear* (1973), novels dealing with Indian life; and *Where Is the Voice Coming From?* (1974), a collection of short stories. He has also edited several anthologies, including *The Story-Makers* (1970), *Stories from Western Canada* (1972), and *Double Vision* (1976). WHERE IS THE VOICE COMING FROM?, 35.

WRIGHT, JAMES F. C. (1904-70) was a journalist and editor of *The Union Farmer*. He received the Governor General's Award for his readable and sensitive account of Doukhobor views and attitudes, *Slava Bohu* (1940). His other books include *All Clear Canada* (1944) and *Saskatchewan: The History of a Province* (1955). 'KODAM', 56.

ZIEROTH, DALE (b.1946). Born in Neepawa, Man., he lived on the Prairie before moving to Toronto to teach school. He now works as a park naturalist in Kootenay National Park. His poetry collection *Clearing: Poems From a Journey* was published in 1973. FATHER, 225.

Contributors